MW01195767

TAKING CHARGE

Your Education, Your Career, Your Life

Third Edition

KAREN MITCHELL SMITH &
KATHARINE O'MOORE-KLOPF

Texas State
Technical College

© 2013 Texas State Technical College Waco

ISBN 978-1-936603-18-3 (softback)

All rights reserved, including the right to reproduce this book
or any portion thereof in any form. Requests for such permissions
should be addressed to:

IDEAS Center - Publications
Texas State Technical College Waco
3801 Campus Drive
Waco, Texas 76705

https://www.waco.tstc.edu/ideas

Publishing editor: Ana Wraight
Art director: Stacie Buterbaugh
Editorial intern: Brian Tucker
Graphics interns: Jessica Hollingsworth and Adriana Calderon

Manufactured in the United States of America

Third edition

Publisher's Cataloging-in-Publication
(Provided by Quality Books, Inc.)

Smith, Karen Mitchell.
    Taking charge : your education, your career, your
life / Karen Mitchell Smith & Katharine O'Moore-Klopf.
-- 3rd ed.
    p. cm.
    Includes index.
    ISBN 978-1-936603-18-3 (softback)
    1. Academic achievement. 2. Success. 3. Education,
Higher. 4. Employees--Training of.   I. O'Moore-Klopf,
Katherine. II. Title.

LB1062.6.S65 2012   153.1'5
                          QBI12-600045

Table of Contents

Preface

It is my pleasure to introduce you to Texas State Technical College Waco. For more than forty years, TSTC Waco has been providing top-quality technical education for Texas and Texans. The college is nationally recognized for the number and quality of our technology graduates. With more than 40,000 TSTC graduates employed throughout the state and nation, our tradition of excellence is strong.

TSTC Waco is committed to providing you with a highly specialized and advanced technical education that can lead to great career opportunities. TSTC offers technical associate degrees, certificate programs, and workforce mastery skills that give our students a competitive edge in the job market. Our students gain extensive hands-on experience in laboratories, spending nearly 60 percent of their time working with the tools, technology, and equipment they will use in their future careers.

TSTC offers career training for the future by providing solid basics and advanced technology applications and processes. Our faculty members are experts in their fields, bringing real-world industry experience into the classroom and labs. In addition to our faculty, our strong partnerships with business and industry put TSTC graduates at the top of employers' hiring lists. TSTC has more than 900 industry advisory committee members, ensuring our students always receive the latest available training. These industry partners help design our curriculum, matching our instruction to industry needs and helping ensure our graduates will be work-ready from their first day on the job.

Upon successful completion of the curriculum, you can look forward to outstanding career opportunities. Experts indicate that technical positions are the largest and fastest-growing employment groups for the 21st century. New and exciting jobs are being created in a variety of industries, including solar, wind technology, fuel cell, aviation, and robotics. That means more employment opportunities for those individuals with technical training and skills, so TSTC students are especially in demand!

I can assure you that dedication to your education at TSTC will be an investment with generous returns.

Dr. Elton E. Stuckly, Jr.
TSTC Waco President

CHAPTER 1

Planning Your Future

STUDENT DISORIENTATION

Carlos needed a change, something he could do to spice up his life. His job was fine and he had earned a good living, but he just felt passionless about it now. Going back to college to study something new had been on his mind, but he thought he couldn't afford it and that it was a waste of time.

In the end he decided to go for it and apply to college. He had gotten great scholarships, which made college very afford-able. He wasn't going to use the horrible motto he overused last time through, "Just graduate." He understood that college had so much more to offer than a piece of paper saying "I did it!"

"Carlos!" Misha bounced in on his thoughts as he ate at the food court. "How are your classes going so far?"

"Pretty good," he responded. "Better than they are going for Aaron, apparently. He was passed out in class, and it's only the second week."

"It's not my fault! I should have never chosen an 8 a.m. class." Aaron walked in, as if on cue.

"You had all summer to sleep," said Misha, laughing.

College was going to be good. Carlos had good friends and a new pace of life. He was glad he finally decided to do something new and exciting with his life. He had no idea what he was going to study, but it was already week two. No going back now.

CHAPTER OBJECTIVES:

- Establishing SMART goals

- Forming realistic expectations for college

- Researching your dream career

As you work through this book, you will keep a success journal so you can watch your progress. Feel free to use whatever medium you like best for your journal, whether you use an online service or purchase a journal from your local bookstore. Make sure it is something you can access easily and keep near you as you read this book.

Throughout the chapter you will find several exercises, some to be kept privately in your journal and some to be shared with others. You are encouraged to review your journal as you progress through the semester, checking periodically to see whether you are on track to meet your goals and dreams.

Personal Goals – Success Starts with You

If someone asked you how much money you hope to be making ten years from now, would you have an answer? Do you know what type of home you'd like to live in? Which make of car you want to drive?

A good rule of thumb to remember is "if you can't see it, you can't achieve it." In other words, you need to be able to visualize success if you want to achieve success. Coaches have athletes practice all week for the big game, but they don't tell them to imagine sitting on the bench, their heads hanging down after a devastating loss to come. Instead, they have their athletes visualize what the win will feel like and what the crowd will sound like at the final buzzer.

The beginning of your first semester is a good time to put a specific name to your goals. Many students say things such as "I want to be happy," or "I want to make good money." When asked, those same students can't say what being happy means or how much money is good money. Stating a goal in a specific manner, such as "I want to make $40,000 a year by the second year I'm out of school," puts a tangible measurement on your goal so you will know when you have achieved it.

> **" A goal is a dream with a deadline. "**
>
> —Napoleon Hill

▶ **EXERCISE 1.1**

Set up the vision section of your journal. Using photographs or magazine pictures, put representations of the things you want to own, the places you want to go, and the things you want to achieve on the pages.

SMART

Creating goals that follow the SMART technique - specific, measurable, attainable, realistic, and timed – increase your chances of success.

Specific: Instead of saying, "I want to live in a big house someday with a nice family," try saying, "I want to live in a two-story, four-bedroom house with my life partner and two children by the time I'm thirty-five." You can visualize this goal, and when you visualize a specific goal on a regular basis, it becomes a part of who you are. Professional life and career coaches call this technique vision casting. There will be times when school is difficult, and you may question your decision to attend. When that time comes, pull out your journal and remind yourself of where you want to go and what you want to accomplish.

Measurable: Making your goals measurable means you have certain steps associated with achieving your goal. An example of a measurable personal goal might be losing weight. If you have a total of twenty-five pounds to lose, you should mark milestones at every five pounds, allowing yourself to celebrate with a new purchase or a night out with each accomplishment. Breaking the goal into measurable units will build your confidence as you achieve each level. The more steps you conquer, the more likely it is you will tackle other difficult projects with confidence.

Attainable and Realistic: Making personal goals attainable and realistic will also add to your self-confidence. Planning to lose twenty-five pounds might be attainable, but expecting to do it in a month is not realistic. Always evaluate your goals to make sure they are realistic for you.

SMART technique

A technique that helps you increase the chances of reaching your goals; stands for specific, measurable, attainable, realistic, and timed

To participate in the online poll, scan the QR code or visit: *http://bit.ly/TC1Poll*

It's your first semester. What are your primary goals?

○ Being social and making as many friends as possible

○ Attaining a degree and getting out in the workplace as soon as possible

○ Finding a new career path that I can be passionate about

○ Balancing home, work, and a social life

43Things

Scan the code for additional information or visit: *http://bit.ly/TC1Things*

Need help keeping track of your progress towards your goals? Try 43Things. Prioritize your life goals and resolutions. Write journal entries associated with each goal and look back on completed goals for motivation.

GOALS CHECKLIST

- ☐ Can I visualize my goal?
- ☐ Is my goal specific?
- ☐ Do I have specific steps to accomplish my goal?
- ☐ Is my goal attainable?
- ☐ Is the time frame I have established for my goal realistic?
- ☐ Have I set a timeline to achieve this goal, keeping in mind the steps?
- ☐ Have I written the steps to achieve my goal in my journal or on my calendar?

Timed: Creating a specific timeline keeps you focused as you move toward your desired results. One of the biggest reasons New Year's resolutions seldom succeed is the lack of a time-specific boundary. If say you want to kick a bad habit but don't put a time limit on accomplishing it, your goal lacks accountability.

To make sure your goals meet all of the SMART criteria, write them down and check each against the acronym. If all of the pieces aren't there, restate the goal. Once you have outlined your personal goals, you are ready to move on to the education ones.

▶ WORKSHEET

Use the following document to make sure your goals meet all of the SMART criteria.

For the sample template, scan the QR code or visit: *http://bit.ly/TC1smart*

My goal is:

S	
M	
A	
R	
T	

Review details of the acronym SMART in the personal goals section of this chapter. Think about where your personal life is now compared with where you want it to be.

a.) What things do you need to change or refocus? Be honest with yourself.

b.) After a thorough self-evaluation, write out three to five personal goals in your journal. Be sure each one fits every part of the acronym SMART.

c.) Choose one personal goal you can share aloud in class.

Education Goals – The Path to Your Future

If you recently finished high school, you'll find that you – not your teachers or your parents – are now the one in charge of your education. When you were in high school, school administrators made most of the decisions about what classes you took, and state laws both mandated your regular attendance in those classes and regulated class sizes. Teachers gave you your textbooks at no charge to you, paid for through local taxes.

Now that you are in college, you choose which classes to take based on the degree you wish to pursue. State laws do not require your attendance, although your instructors expect you to adhere to their attendance policies and may even take points off your final grade if you miss too many classes. You may find that some of your classes have 100 or more students. In addition, you will be paying for all of your textbooks and other class materials, including instruments or tools.

Now is the time to determine what your academic goals will be. A statement of purpose, written at the beginning of your freshman year, will give you something tangible to look at and think about when you feel tempted to give up. Make your statement specific and be sure to include the result you are working toward.

❝The secret of achievement is to hold a picture of a successful outcome in the mind.❞

—Henry David Thoreau

THE REALITIES OF COLLEGE LIFE

You may have unrealistic expectations about how things will work in college. Popular culture spins college as one party after another, often highlighting drunken soirees over the time spent in the classroom and studying. Based on these impressions, you may develop false expectations as to what you will experience in college. The following chart compares some common expectations of new college students with the realities they'll face:

Expectations	Realities
College will be as easy as high school.	The level of course material you will encounter is more advanced than in high school and will require more work to learn.
If you have roommates, you'll automatically be friends.	People are different; you won't get along with everyone you meet.
If you live on campus, you won't miss your family at home at all.	Most people experience at least a little homesickness.
You won't have any responsibilities.	You have to take care of yourself by ensuring you have enough to eat, managing your money, arranging for transportation, obtaining health care, and scheduling time for your studies.
You won't have to attend every single class.	Most instructors have attendance policies that affect your grades, so you will have to attend classes regularly.
You can go to parties every weekend and go out with friends every weeknight and still get good grades.	Too much time playing means too little time studying, which means poor grades.

associate degree

A type of degree awarded to students at a U.S. community college, usually after two years of a full-time load of classes

For example, "I will complete an **associate degree** in aviation maintenance technology within twenty-four months because I want to get a job as a tech working at the DFW Airport" makes a much stronger statement than "I want an education so I can get a good job."

For education goals, the SMART acronym still applies, but because education involves more difficult challenges, you may find you need help

In your journal, write out a statement of purpose for your college plan.

a.) What you are majoring in and why?

b.) What obstacles do you expect to encounter? How you will overcome them?

c.) What do you want to achieve with your education?

in planning. Education is a marathon, not a sprint. Although each semester lasts only a few months, the entire process can take several years, depending on the degree you seek. Students who look at each class individually without checking the big picture may waste time and money on unnecessary classes. Check your college catalog to identify which courses you need, and then discuss the order in which you should take them with your academic adviser.

Once you have formed the basis for your coursework in the upcoming semesters, look at your personal life to see how it fits. Take into consideration time challenges such as jobs, family obligations, social life, and study time. (Plan for two hours of studying per one hour in class.) If you already have family obligations, such as to a life partner and/or children that require your full-time attention, you may need to consider taking fewer semester hours. Keep your academic adviser in the loop; it's the adviser's job to help you adjust to college life and help you make decisions that set you up for success.

adviser

School official, usually assigned by your college or university, who can help you choose your classes and make sure you are taking the right courses to graduate

Free Time

Scan the code for additional information or visit: *http://bit.ly/TC1Free*

Free Time helps you organize your academic, family, and social life. It syncs with your calendar and shows you where you have free blocks of time, for example, to have lunch with a friend, go catch a film, or see one of your favorite bands.

The best time to review your notes and study is as soon as possible after class, while the information is still fresh in your mind. You will find you remember more and are able to apply what you have learned in class to what you are studying more readily.

Even after you've made a plan for your education, you will find that many distractions arise during your college years. You must prioritize your time effectively in order to succeed. Everyone wants to have a great time at college, and you should enjoy these years. Finding a balance between study

Some careers have professional organizations for those in the field. Many invite people who are interested in the career to join or are more than happy to talk with students about the field.

time and your social life, though, is imperative to success. If you have the willpower to choose studying for a test or completing a project by its due date over the concert you want to attend, then you are well on your way to college success.

Perseverance is the key to your success. It is easy to talk big and make exciting plans, but when the days turn into weeks and the weeks turn into months of studying, doing homework, and going to class daily, you will have to determine if you are truly ready to make the kind of commitment it takes to graduate from college. With dropout rates at more than 50 percent and rising, now is the time to make a commitment to complete your studies – no matter the odds. You've probably heard the old sayings "Winning is 90 percent mental" and "Whether you think you can or think you can't, you're right." Your mindset must be established at the outset. If you've already won the battle in your mind, persevering when the road is long and rough won't be an issue.

Professional Goals – Achieving Your Dreams

With two or more years of education ahead of you, it may seem early to discuss professional goals, but it's actually the perfect time. Perhaps you have dreams of a management position someday. Setting professional goals now can help ensure you don't end up stagnated, unable to move any higher on the pay scale. If you haven't already done so, start by thoroughly researching the career you are interested in. Find out how much money you can expect to make starting out, as well as farther down the road when you have more experience.

> **My philosophy of life is that if we make up our minds what we are going to make of our lives, then work hard toward that goal, we never lose.**
>
> **— Former President Ronald Reagan**

Next, discover whether your career offers opportunities for advancement. Will you need advanced degrees to attain the position you eventually desire? Are renewed certificates or continuing-education classes required? The *Occupational Outlook Handbook*, published online by the U.S. Bureau of Labor Statistics, can provide you with information about your career. The handbook includes information like job description, salary ranges, and the career's growth outlook over the next few years.

You can also contact the companies you might enjoy working for. Ask to shadow someone on the job who is in the position you desire. **Job shadowing** is an excellent way to discover what a career is really like, and most companies are happy to show potential employees around.

Maybe you did much of this research before you started college. If so, congratulations on your wise planning. Unfortunately, the truth is many students randomly choose a career field because it sounds prestigious or because they think people in that field make good money. Choosing a career should not be like throwing darts at a globe to find a random vacation spot you'd like to visit someday. You want to make certain the path you have chosen leads to the results you desire.

job shadowing

A technique for learning more about the job you would like to pursue by spending one or more days following a person as he or she works

ETHICAL DILEMMA

About halfway through your degree, a company approaches you and offers you a job. It's not necessarily in the field you have been studying, but the pay is better than what you receive now. What do you do?

Scan the code for additional information or visit: *http://bit.ly/TC1ED*

a.) Thank the company for their offer and say you would consider taking the position once you have completed your degree.

b.) It's not the career you're working toward, so you decline graciously.

c.) Say yes. After all, the point of the degree was to find a job to make more money. If you find one before you finish your degree, it's a plus.

d.) Ask the company what kind of policy they have about continuing education and see if your particular degree program fits.

Once you have verified the potential of your career, it's time to set goals. As you do, refer to the SMART acronym. Visualize yourself working in your chosen field and set your goals in measurable units. Remember it takes time to work your way up in a career or company. Make sure your professional goals are both attainable and realistic. Reaching for higher standards will challenge and stimulate you.

ON THE WEB

To find out how much people in your career earn in various cities visit:

http://bit.ly/TC1Salary

Still, take a moment for a reality check so you do not waste time working toward something that isn't possible for your particular career. Changing course does not indicate failure. Goals should be flexible and transient so you can control them, not the other way around. Consider whether the career you are choosing offers opportunities for advancement. If so, set a tentative timeline for reaching the various levels you would like to achieve. Having a promotion timeline in mind from the outset will keep your forward momentum going.

▶ EXERCISE 1.4

Call a company in the professional field you are interested in pursuing. Ask to shadow a person who works in your specific area. Keep notes throughout your job-shadow day, paying special attention to duties you like and don't like. Ask the employee about advancement opportunities, typical pay scale, and education requirements. Write a summary of your experience in your journal. Share this with the instructor or the class.

Conclusion

The wonderful thing about your future is that it is yours. No matter how much your friends and family love you, they cannot plan your future. You have been given the wonderful gift of opportunity as you stand at the threshold of a new career. What you make of it, or don't make of it, will be entirely up to you. If you make up your mind now that you will succeed, and if you set the goals to get you there, the career you have desired will be waiting at the end of this short education journey. If you continue with the goal-setting discipline in your career, the life you desire can be yours, too.

Keep your journal close at hand and refer to it when school becomes more challenging than you had expected or if you feel the temptation to quit. Look at the pictures of the life you want to have and remind yourself that the temporary sacrifices you make now are steppingstones to your future.

COACH'S CORNER

Daring to reach for your dreams is a key element to success. In Coach's Corner, Coach discusses the importance of reaching high.

http://bit.ly/TC1CCorner

Further Reading

The 7 Habits of Highly Effective People. Stephen R. Covey. 15th edition.
Free Press: 2004.

Write It Down, Make It Happen: Knowing What You Want and Getting It.
Henriette Anne Klauser. Fireside Books: 2001.

REVIEW QUESTIONS | What did you LEARN?

1. Why should you visualize your goals?

2. What does SMART stand for?

3. Why is it important for you to set up specific goals?

4. How can dividing your goal into smaller steps help you succeed?

5. Why should your goals have time frames, or deadlines?

6. What is job shadowing?

7. How is job shadowing helpful in your career research?

8. Why is perseverance important?

9. Why is it important for you to research your future career ahead of time?

10. How can SMART be applied to your professional goals?

▶▶ Are you puzzled?

Scan this code to access the puzzle online or visit: *http://bit.ly/TC1Crword*

Across

1. Goals should be flexible and ____ so that you can control them, not the other way around.

3. Type of academic term, generally fall and spring

7. If you can't see it, you can't ____ it.

8. Who said, "The secret of achievement is to hold a picture of a successful outcome in mind"?

10. What does the T in SMART stand for?

12. A technique for following a professional to learn more about the job you would like to have after you graduate (2 words)

15. What does the M in SMART stand for?

16. The wonderful thing about your future is that it is ____.

18. Who said, "Our plans miscarry because they have no aim. When a man does not know what harbor he is making for, no wind is the right wind"?

19. What app helps you keep track of your progress towards your goals?

20. A technique that helps you increase the chances of reaching your goals

Down

2. A type of degree awarded to students at a U.S. community college, usually after two years of a full-time load of classes (2 words)

4. Winning is 90 percent ____.

5. Once you have set your personal goals, you are ready to move on to the ____ ones.

6. What app helps you keep track of your progress towards your goals?

9. Always evaluate your goals to make sure they are ____ for you.

11. What app helps you organize your academic, family, and social life?

13. A school official, usually assigned by your college or university, who can help you choose your classes and make sure you are taking the right courses to graduate

14. The beginning of the semester is a good time to name your what?

17. The best time to review your notes and study is right after what?

ROB WOLAVER
College Executive Vice President

Scan this code for additional info
or visit: *http://bit.ly/TC1Wolaver*

Do Not be Afraid to Take Risks

Goals are important when it comes to succeeding in life. "Finding balance between creating realistic, achievable goals and creating goals from your dreams is important," says Executive Vice President Rob Wolaver.

In recent semesters, he taught a cabinet-building class and loved the chance it gave him to teach students as well as build relationships with them. While he does not have much time, he hopes to teach a class like that again, so that he can increase his interactions with students to a daily basis.

When he became the executive vice president, the interaction he had with students decreased. "The only students I deal with regularly are those who are having some kind of trouble, and I wish I were able to interact with more students in a positive way," says Wolaver.

Wolaver always encourages students to take risks in order to be extraordinary people and reach their dreams. Taking risks is important, especially when it comes to setting goals. "While it is important to set realistic goals, it is also important to set goals that are challenging and might lead to failure," claims Wolaver. He constantly tells those who seek his advice, "Do not be afraid to take risks. Do not be afraid if you're wrong or fail. Failure is part of success."

Over the years, Wolaver has helped many students, whether they were in trouble or simply needed advice or encouragement. More often than not, he does not get to see the outcome of the students he helps. That's why his biggest reward is receiving cards or visits from past students who thanked him for his help.

"I get to see the actual impact I had on someone, and when it's positive, it really lifts up my day," says Wolaver. He also believes it is important to remember "true value is not our worth, job, or title, but the impact we have on others."

Expenses
Dépenses
Kosten
Spese
Gastos
Expenses
Dépenses
Kosten
Spese
Gastos
COMMUNICATION

STUDENT DISORIENTATION

Two weeks ago, Aaron had plenty of time to do his documentary video project. One week ago, Aaron thought he should probably start working on the video soon. The day before it was due, Aaron knew he was done for. He had rushed together an awkward video clip for some pointless project, but he knew he should have started weeks ago. There was no way he was getting any sleep tonight, and even if he did sleep, he knew his project was going to be, at best, a D.

The next evening he sent out this message to everyone: "All right, guys, scheduling-the-rest-of-the-semesters'-projects party at my place in thirty minutes. I can't procrastinate like that again."

Everyone sat on the floor with calendars, to-do lists, and syllabi from every class. Aaron wasn't the only one falling into the procrastination rut. Misha hadn't even started studying for her midterm because of how much time she had spent on her creative projects. Kristen just wanted more free time and wanted less of her time consumed by homework. Carlos was so overloaded he didn't know where to start. Beth and Brad were scrolling through pictures and videos on the Internet and succeeding far too well at distracting everyone.

"There is just too much. My calendar looks like it's bleeding with all this red ink all over it." Aaron fell back from his scribbling, defeated.

"Just focus and put the most important things on top of your lists and go down as quickly as possible." Carlos tried to calm his friend.

"All he really needs to do is close Facebook and stop watching TV until homework is done," said Misha.

"No Facebook and no TV? What is the point of life?" Aaron replied, distraught.

CHAPTER OBJECTIVES:

- Creating a master schedule

- Overcoming lack of motivation at school

- Focusing at the workplace

"If only I had more time for the things I need to do!" How often do you find yourself saying these words? "Time management" has been a popular concept for several decades now, yet can time really be managed? Self-help guru David Allen, author of *Getting Things Done: The Art of Stress-Free Productivity*, says no. "You can't manage time; it just is. So 'time management' is a mislabeled problem, which has little chance of being an effective approach. What you really manage is your activity during time."

During your college years, you will feel time obligations pulling at you from all directions. You may even feel like the circus performer who rides a unicycle on a high wire while spinning plates on long, thin poles. The objective, of course, is to maintain balance while keeping all the plates in the air and spinning at the same time. If even one plate crashes, they all come down. Managing activity, not time, is your goal.

Knowing how to manage productivity effectively during the time you have each day is the key, but before you can do that, think about how you want to spend your time. What is truly important to you at this particular time in your life? Refer to the goals you set in Chapter 1 if you need a reminder.

Next, consider the three main areas of your life: personal, education, and professional. In order to keep all the plates spinning, you must attend to each plate – each area of your life. In this chapter, you will learn some coping strategies to help you meet the needs in each of these areas and help you feel not only satisfied but also balanced.

Personal Time Management

Being in college doesn't mean you don't have personal obligations and objectives. In fact, the time required to be successful in college has just added a few more plates to those you already had spinning before you registered for your first courses. Your personal time is most likely filled with financial obligations, such as bill paying; family obligations, such as spending time with a life partner, children, or other relatives; housekeeping duties, such as doing laundry, cleaning, and cooking; and leisure time. These requirements in themselves could take up a whole day.

❝ I recommend you to take care of the minutes, for hours will take care of themselves. **❞**

—Philip Stanhope, 4th Earl of Chesterfield

Lists

David Allen of the "Getting Things Done" personal management model says while our minds are incredible, complex marvels, much like computers, no one can remember everything they must do at all times. At the end of each day, make a list of everything you must do the next day. Assign a letter to indicate the importance of each of these items. *A* means most important, *B* means medium importance, and *C* means least important.

Keep in mind, the idea is to manage the list, not let it manage you. Flexibility is important. As certain situations arise, you may find the need to modify your list, either by deleting an activity or adding a new one. When you prioritize your items by importance, it will be easy to see which items can be deleted or postponed when necessary.

During the day, keep a running list of the personal to-do items for the following day. Before you go to bed, look at the list and add any last-minute items. This way, you go to sleep relieved of anxiety about remembering important things and wake up refreshed with a focused purpose.

Quick TIP

Keep a pen and a pad of paper on your bedside table or use an app like TeuxDeux on your cellphone to keep track of the items you need to do the next day. This way, you won't worry about whether you remember them and can sleep at ease.

Cozi

Scan the code for additional information or visit: *http://bit.ly/TC2Cozi*

Trying to juggle family life, academics, and work can feel overwhelming at times. Cozi offers a great solution. You can organize your personal calendar, keep a to-do list for each day, record your shopping lists, and plan your weekly meals. It also syncs with your iPhone, iPad, iPod Touch, Android, or Blackberry.

▶ EXERCISE 2.1

Purchase or download and print a planning calendar with enough space to write several items each day. Fill in your calendar with your everyday chores/duties, work schedule, class schedule, family time, study time, and free time. In your journal, write about the areas of your life that take up the most time and where you would rather your time be spent. Try to come up with a plan that realistically allows you to spend more time doing what you want.

The following document is a master schedule template for you to fill out to keep track of your assignments and to-do lists for each day. Feel free to modify it to fit your personal schedule.

For the sample template, scan the QR code or visit:
http://bit.ly/TC2msched

	Sunday	Monday	Tuesday	Wednesday	Thursday	Friday	Saturday
7:00 a.m.							
8:00 a.m.							
9:00 a.m.							
10:00 a.m.							
11:00 a.m.							
12:00 p.m.							
1:00 p.m.							
2:00 p.m.							
3:00 p.m.							
4:00 p.m.							
5:00 p.m.							

TO DO : _____

_____

_____

_____

Master Schedule

Purchase a calendar or planner with spaces large enough to write several items in time slots for each day. On Sunday evening, take out your calendar and create a master schedule for the week. Don't forget to take into account holidays, long weekends, and school breaks. This master schedule is in addition to your daily list.

Fill in your week's schedule to the best of your ability, including all appointments, special events, or planned outings. As the week progresses, continue filling in time slots when appointments or other occasions arise. Remember to include each of these on your daily list. Now you have a big picture for each week's activities, as well as a focused agenda for the day. Pay careful attention to which activities receive the majority of your time. Do those activities line up with your personal goals? If not, you may need to readjust your priorities.

The activities that fill up your master schedule and/or daily list will fall into several categories:

- **Academic needs:** classes, laboratories, assignments, tests, research projects, meetings with instructors, and internships

- **Relationship needs:** time spent with your family, life partner, boyfriend or girlfriend, children, friends, and yourself

- **Personal needs:** food and clothing shopping, clothing maintenance (laundry or repairs), housekeeping, exercise, and sleep

- **Social needs:** outings with friends and parties

- **Volunteer efforts:** participating in student government, tutoring, and volunteering for a local charity

Because some of these categories of needs will be more important than others, you will have to prioritize. You are a student now, so your academic needs will take precedence over your social needs. You need plenty of sleep and enough exercise to function well as a student, both mentally and physically, so don't skimp when scheduling in these areas. If you have to save time somewhere, cut back on how much time you spend meeting the less-important needs rather than cutting them out entirely.

The POSEC Method

In time-management principles, POSEC stands for prioritize, organize, streamline, economize, and contribute. The POSEC method is a concept loosely developed around psychologist Abraham Maslow's hierarchy of needs. The idea of the POSEC method is when your personal life is in order, you are better able to shoulder outside responsibilities.

POSEC method

A time-management method that helps you control your personal time in order to better handle outside responsibilities; stands for prioritize, organize, streamline, economize, and contribute

hierarchy of needs

A categorization of the levels of human need

MASLOW'S HIERARCHY OF NEEDS

Maslow noted in his research that, for monkeys at least, some needs came before others. For example, monkeys will attend to their need for water before they will focus on their need for food. He theorized that humans operate in the same way: They take care of essential needs before less urgent needs.

The first level of Maslow's hierarchy of needs is made up of physiological needs. These are the needs you have for oxygen, nutrients, water, physical activity, and sleep. If you're too hungry or sleepy, for example, you're not going to be able to focus on studying – or on any other areas of life.

The second level is made up of safety and security needs. Once you've met your body's needs, you are interested in finding and maintaining a safe living space, seeking stability in your life, and protecting yourself against danger and unwanted surprises. You may crave and then set up structure and order in your life. You seek job security and want to plan ahead for retirement and for financial emergencies. You may begin saving money and purchasing insurance.

▶ EXERCISE 2.2

For each level in the hierarchy, write down examples of when that level has taken precedence for you over tasks that you were supposed to be accomplishing, such as studying. Then describe how you could have changed your actions before the need arose to avoid its getting in the way of important tasks. Be prepared to discuss your insights in class.

By **prioritizing** your time according to your life's goals, you will be able to see the measurable parts of your goals come into focus. You will accomplish the most important items when they need to be done, and you will be able to filter out distractions.

Organize the things in your life that must be accomplished on a regular basis, such as financial and family obligations. The organizational idea from Merlin Mann, editor of the 43 Folders blog, may be helpful to you. You use twelve folders for the twelve months of the year and thirty-one folders for the maximum number of days in any one month. Put event tickets, bills, assignments, and similar items into the appropriate folder

The third level is made up of love and belonging needs. You feel a need to make friends, find a love relationship, have children, and feel a sense of community. You work to maintain friendships, seek a life partner, try to become a parent, and get involved in your community through religious organizations, clubs, teams, and civic organizations.

The fourth is made up of esteem needs. You're looking to boost your self-esteem. Maslow postulated two levels of needs for esteem. At this level, you may try to make the honor roll in college, seek to move up the ladder at your job, or lead others in a community project.

The fifth is made up of self-actualization needs. At this level, you seek to reach your full potential. The activities you get involved in have such motivations as truth, justice, wisdom, and meaning. You may join a campaign to change laws or regulations you perceive to be unfair or volunteer your services for a cause that you believe can change society. Maslow believed few people reach this level, but those who do often have feelings of profound happiness and interconnection with the world.

for the day on which it is due in the current month. At the end of the month, you move any remaining items into the appropriate folder for the due date of the next month, and so on.

We all have tasks that we dread but know must be done. By **streamlining** your time on these tasks, you can limit your time. One way to accomplish this is to group your tasks by like items. If you are doing the dishes, see what else needs to be done in the kitchen. Sweep the floor, wash the table, and make your shopping list, all while you are right there in the area. When you finish these items, turn out the light and leave the room. Go to the next task on your list.

Another way to streamline is to set a timer. If you're performing a task you don't enjoy, you are likely to take longer because you let your mind wander or you become distracted. Decide how much time you can spend on that one task, set the timer for that amount of time, and stick to the task until the timer rings. If the task is not finished and can wait until tomorrow, add it to tomorrow's list. If the task absolutely must be accomplished, give yourself a little more time and set the timer again. This will help you stay focused and give you the mental awareness that this chore has a specific ending time.

ON THE WEB

For more information about the 43 Folders method, visit:

http://bit.ly/TC2Folders

TIME MANAGEMENT CHECKLIST

- ☐ My class schedule
- ☐ Study time
- ☐ Homework assignment due dates and exam dates
- ☐ Other important school dates
- ☐ Important family events
- ☐ Internship, externship, or work hours
- ☐ Relaxation time or social time

Economizing your time helps you balance the things you have to do with the things you want to do. It's easy to spend more time on things we want to do in our free time, and we definitely should reward ourselves by doing these things. However, controlling the amount of time spent here means better management of necessary activities, which in turn often pays off with more free time. Include a block of time every day, or several small blocks, that let you enjoy downtime. Without this, stress and anxiety can build up, unbalancing your life and leading to illness or burnout.

A large part of personal fulfillment comes from making positive **contributions** to society. Some people volunteer for charities, while other people are active in religious or civic organizations. Whatever your choice, setting aside time to give back to your community is a great way to relieve stress and remember that you are an integral part of society.

At first glance, all of these strategies may seem like another time hog. Remember, you control how much time you spend on any one activity, including making, organizing, and reading lists. Although making these lists, schedules, and folders may seem cumbersome at first, the freedom you gain by having greater control over how you spend your time will be worth it in the long run. Once you have created your activity-management strategies, it's time to incorporate education.

> " You will never 'find' time for anything. If you want time, you must make it. "
>
> —Charles Bruxton

Education Time Management

While you alone have control over how and when you spend your personal time, many time requirements related to college will be out of your control. Class schedules, for example, are predetermined by instructors, who also control due dates and test dates. While you have the option of when to study, the discipline still must be worked into your day, every day. Most instructors recommend the philosophy of "two hours of studying for each hour in class" for academic success, but some classes will require even more time outside of class. Add in internships, externships, or part-time (and for some, full-time) jobs, and you have a completely new set of plates to keep spinning.

No doubt college life sometimes brings enormous pressures and stresses, but a positive mind-set is a priceless asset. College is temporary. Keep your eyes focused on the goals you set in Chapter 1. Why are you attending college? Where will it take you? If you can see the route ahead, you know where you are going and how to manage any obstacles or detours. Once you have reaffirmed your goals and your destination, implement positive activity-management strategies to keep you from feeling overwhelmed and off balance.

externship

Supervised professional work done with a company outside of the classroom as a part of a course or class

ETHICAL DILEMMA

Your best friend has just scored tickets to your favorite singer's gig for next week. You have a test the day after the gig, and you know you will be out late. The test is 40 percent of your final grade. What do you do?

a.) Study as much as possible before the gig so that you feel comfortable with the material ahead of time.

b.) Go to the gig and then cram once you get back. With enough caffeine in your system, you won't need to worry about sleep.

c.) Skip the gig. You love the singer, but you know need to keep up your grades in order to graduate from college.

d.) Talk to your professor/instructor about rescheduling the test. Maybe you can take it early.

Scan the code for additional information or visit: *http://bit.ly/TC2ED*

Master Schedule

Most professors begin the semester by handing out a syllabus. This document lists daily reading assignments, homework/project assignments and due dates, and test dates. Take out your master schedule and fill in all the important dates for each class for the whole semester. Block off the time you will be in class so you don't accidentally overbook yourself.

syllabus

A description of a course that also lists the dates of major exams, assignments, and projects

As your instructors add or delete assignment dates, keep your calendar updated. Keeping in mind the rule about two hours of studying per one hour of class, block out time each day to study and work on the assigned projects.

Lists

Before you go to bed each evening, add the next day's school obligations to your to-do list. If you have a project-group meeting in the library, write it on the list. If you need to locate the lecture notes you took last week, write a reminder to look for them tomorrow. Remember, clearing your mind of the things you must do tomorrow will make for a better night's sleep tonight.

Motivating and focusing yourself to take care of personal business is much easier and – admit it – more fun than motivating yourself to write a term paper. All the time-management strategies in the world will do you no good if you don't stay focused and get things done. There are some tips and tricks you can use to help you stay motivated and keep from becoming overwhelmed by your responsibilities.

▶ **EXERCISE 2.3**

Practice making a to-do list every night before you go to bed for one full week. Check off the items you completed and star the items you never got to. At the end of the week, bring your lists to class. Be prepared to discuss with your classmates and instructors the following:

a.) How did writing down important things the night before make you feel?

b.) What percentage, overall, of your to-do list was completed?

c.) How likely are you to continue this discipline?

Reward yourself. Go to a movie and dinner with a friend when you've turned in a big project. What motivates you may not be the same thing that motivates your roommate, so make your rewards personal. You'll have something to look forward to when you complete difficult tasks.

How do you eat an elephant? Break large projects into manageable chunks. If each portion is equally important, start with the easiest first. Your feeling of accomplishment will motivate you to finish the project.

X marks the spot. David Burns, author of *Feeling Good: The New Mood Therapy*, says giving yourself permission to cross some things off your list, even if not accomplished, will make you feel less overwhelmed and more excited about completing other tasks. Evaluate your daily list for things that can be postponed until tomorrow and cross a couple of things off.

Shut yourself away from distractions. Put your email alert on mute, silence your cellphone, and don't answer the door. The information age we live in often overloads us with incoming stimulation. Carve out a quiet place and time to tackle your projects, or you'll never even get started.

Professional Time Management

Most people need the same activity-management skills at work that they used in their college days. In fact, you may need those strategies even more, depending on your job. Distractions are constant, and motivation can be just as much of an issue as it was when you had a term paper to write.

A few coping strategies to help you stay focused at work will make climbing the promotion ladder easier and more enjoyable. You'll also be more likely to leave your stress at the office, something your family will be very glad about.

Don't be a jack of all trades. The old saying is "jack of all trades, master of none." When you are at work, your employer is paying you to do your job to the best of your ability. You may feel pressed for time and tempted to take shortcuts or to multitask, but resist the urge. Focus on the task at hand, complete it, and move on. The rewards you reap from the satisfaction of completing the tasks will far outweigh the minutes you could have saved.

Do first things first. Gina Trapani, editor of the popular Lifehacker blog (lifehacker.com), recommends what she calls "the morning dash." Before she checks emails or voicemails in the morning, the first thing she does is spend an hour on the most pressing piece of her to-do list. Even if you can't complete your project in an hour, you're much more likely to come back to it later, once you've gotten it started. In fact, simply starting a project can be the most daunting task of all.

> **"** But where no plan is laid, where the disposal of time is surrendered merely to the chance of incidence, chaos will soon reign. **"**
>
> —Victor Hugo

To participate in the online poll, scan the QR code or visit: *http://bit.ly/TC2Poll*

What is your top distraction at work?

○ Email and phone communication

○ Social media websites

○ News and blogs

○ Noise in the work environment

Do something – anything. Staring at a blank computer screen for an hour won't help you get started on a difficult project. Instead, make yourself begin. If you have a report to write, start writing. You may come back later to edit and revise, but just getting started will help the creative juices flow.

Don't confuse activity with results. Don't confuse activity with results. You can spend an enormous amount of time organizing a desk, deleting old emails, checking voicemails, and refilling your stapler, all while you're at work, but that doesn't mean you have actually worked. To achieve results, you must focus on the task at hand and stick to it until it's completed.

 **APT APPS!**

Hit Me Later

Scan the code for additional information or visit: *http://bit.ly/TC2hml*

Sometimes you just can't deal with an email right away, but you don't want it to get lost in the sea of daily personal, work, and spam emails. Hit Me Later allows you to hit the "snooze" button on your emails. If you need a couple of hours before you can deal with the email, forward it to 2@hitmelater.com (the number determines how many hours), and the email will be resent to you in two hours.

Work smarter, not harder. The Pareto Principle, developed by Joseph Juran and named after Vilfredo Pareto, can be applied in many ways and in many contexts. When it comes to time management, one of the Pareto Principle's applications says unfocused effort generates only 20 percent of results. The remaining 80 percent of results can be achieved with only 20 percent of the effort. The idea is to optimize your time so you spend as much of it and your energy as possible on the high-payoff tasks.

Avoid the tyranny of the urgent. Just because someone leaves you a voicemail or sends an email doesn't mean you have to respond immediately. If the matter isn't urgent, let it wait until you have a few free moments.

▶ EXERCISE 2.4

Make a list in your journal about all of the major distractions you have at work or that you anticipate having once you enter the workforce. Prioritize that list according to which distractions reduce your productivity the most. Write down some possible solutions that will help you manage these distractions.

Throughout your day at work, situations will come up that demand your attention. Look at them wisely. Urgent doesn't necessarily mean important. Prioritize your day by importance, not urgency.

Be firm yet flexible. Your manager or direct supervisor at work will also be closely involved with helping you to decide what is important and what is urgent. Many companies hold weekly, some even daily, planning meetings where goals and time constraints are set, assessed, and reorganized. Don't be surprised if some of the items on your top priority list get moved to the bottom of the pile by your manager. Flexibility goes hand in hand with job stability.

COACH'S CORNER

Balancing school and life is difficult. In Coach's Corner, Coach emphasizes the importance of prioritizing your responsibilities.

http://bit.ly/TC2CCorner

Conclusion

You stand at the threshold of an exciting journey that, if handled properly, will lead you to the career you desire. The strategies laid out in this chapter are meant to help you not only achieve the goals you set in the previous chapter, but also achieve them with peace of mind and balance in your life. There is no magic pill to keep you from feeling like that man on the high wire, poles in hand, plates spinning wildly, unicycle tipping precariously. However, implementing effective time-management strategies and using them daily can turn that little high wire into a wooden plank.

Quick TIP

Rough drafts are just that, rough. Use rough drafts as jumping off points for your creativity. Whether writing a paper for school or a report for work, start writing without worrying about formality and format to get your ideas flowing. You can go back later to clean things up.

Further Reading

Feeling Good: The New Mood Therapy. David Burns. Harper: 1999.

Time Management for Dummies. Jeffrey J. Mayer. 2nd edition. For Dummies: 1999.

What did you LEARN?

1. In the "Getting Things Done" personal management model, how do you prioritize each task on your list?

2. What are the five categories of activities you should include when filling in your master schedule?

3. What does POSEC stand for? How is it applied?

4. What are the levels of Maslow's hierarchy of needs?

5. How is the 43 folders organizational idea applied?

6. What are some of the methods discussed in the chapter to help reduce lack of motivation and focus?

7. What are externships?

8. What is a syllabus? Why is it important for your master schedule?

9. What is "the morning dash"? How is it helpful when starting your day at work?

10. What is the Pareto Principle?

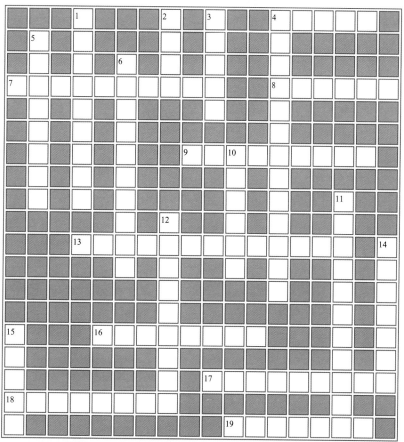

Scan this code to access the puzzle online or visit:
http://bit.ly/TC2Crword

Across

4. What method was loosely developed around psychologist Abraham Maslow's hierarchy of needs?

7. Because some of the categories of needs will be more important than others, you will have to ____.

8. What day should you create a master schedule for the week?

9. To achieve results, you must focus on the task at hand and stick to it until it is ____.

13. According to the Pareto Principle, how much of a result do you get with unfocused effort? (2 words)

16. A description of a course that also lists the dates of major exams, assignments, and projects

17. Once you have created your activity-management strategies, it's time to incorporate ____.

18. Managing ____, not time, is your goal.

19. If each portion is equally important, start with the ____ first.

Down

1. The third level of Maslow's hierarchy of needs deals with love and what other need?

2. What app helps you organize your personal calendar?

3. Who said, "You can't manage time; it just is"?

4. The first level of Maslow's hierarchy of needs is made up of what kind of needs?

5. What type of needs deal with shopping, food preparation, clothing maintenance, housekeeping, exercise, and sleep?

6. What is the name of Gina Trapani's blog?

10. The old saying is "jack of all trades, ____ of none."

11. Supervised professional work done with a company outside of the classroom as a part of a course or class

12. Flexibility goes hand in hand with job ____.

14. Who said, "You will never 'find' time for anything. If you want time, you must make it"?

15. Who developed the Pareto Principle?

GUADALUPE CHAVEZ
Director for High School Programs

Scan this code for additional info
or visit: *http://bit.ly/TC2Chavez*

Managing Your Time

As a director for high school programs, Guadalupe Chavez is extremely talented with multi-tasking. "I provide leadership, planning, coordination, and evaluation of all components of dual enrollment programs," Chavez says. "I also work closely with the Office of Accountability to leverage grants, community and professional partnership opportunities for model projects, and the overall sustainability of the programs under high school programs and services."

Chavez received certificates in data entry and in bookkeeping from Texas State Technical Institute, now Texas State Technical College Harlingen, in 1990. In 2003, he received a bachelor's in applied technology from the University of Texas at Pan American. As busy as he is, he is pursuing a master's degree in adult education from Texas A&M Kingsville.

"As a first-generation college student coming from a migrant family, helping students become successful in college is a great privilege for me," Chavez says.

For more than twenty-two years, Chavez has worked in higher education in areas of student support and student academic services, including six years of teaching "College Success" as an adjunct faculty member. Now as a director for high school programs, Chavez oversees the administration, fiscal, and programmatic daily operations of numerous programs designed to help students adjust to college and provide them with the best learning experience.

A typical day for Chavez begins by updating his to-do list from the day before. Aside from checking emails, making phone calls to high school principals and counselors, and attending meetings, Chavez also spends time writing grants and visiting with students currently going through their programs.

"I'm always looking for ways to enhance our programs and conversing with staff on how I may help them perform their job more efficiently and effectively," Chavez says.

Chavez attributes his everyday success in running multiple programs to time-management, a task he says many students find difficult to deal with. Knowing how to prioritize and delegating work is both important and crucial to success.

"Time management, prioritizing your work in order of importance, and knowing how to work on multiple projects will give students a sense of accomplishment at the end of the day. College requires excellent time management and planning skills, so the best advice I can give is to make sure you acquire these skills immediately," Chavez says. "Having these skills will allow you to plan accordingly and complete all college work in a timely manner and not at the last minute."

Chavez has spent years perfecting the skills necessary to both run and direct programs to prepare students for higher education. He takes great pride in the work he does and clearly sees the benefit of his job.

"My favorite part of the job is seeing students take advantage of our many high school programs available at the college. Knowing we have all the student support and academic resources they need to be successful and seeing them succeed by completing their programs is rewarding."

CHAPTER 3

Handling Your Money Wisely

STUDENT DISORIENTATION

Carlos had found a part-time job, was passing all his classes, and had made plenty of friends. He thought everything was going fine, until one day, his debit card was declined. He hadn't really thought about his money since he had gotten so many scholarships. He didn't imagine he was spending so much money on just eating out and hanging with friends. It was kind of terrifying how much money could go out without him even realizing it.

He never had failed to pay a bill before, and only because Aaron let him borrow $100 could he continue to say that.

"I guess it's ramen for the next few years then, huh?" Carlos mumbled, embarrassed as he took the money from Aaron.

"Join the club with the rest of us college kids."

"You just have to be more careful with money," said Beth. "Books, materials, transportation, and rent add up pretty quickly."

Carlos said, "What is the point of going back to college to get some excitement and a new direction for my life if I have to basically live paycheck to paycheck?"

CHAPTER OBJECTIVES:

- Creating a monthly budget

- Paying for college

- Managing expenses in your career

33

If someone asked you, "What is the one thing you never have enough of?" what would your answer be? Money? If so, you're not alone. Young Money, a website designed to educate students about financial management, discovered in a 2007 poll that 57 percent of students worried about the rising costs of tuition and other costs, and 21 percent expressed concern over insufficient financial aid. For most students, it is a given that college is a time of making do with what you have and getting by on as little as possible.

This chapter will help you manage your finances. You may be thinking, "What finances? I'm practically broke!" If so, then this is the perfect time for you to learn how to handle money wisely, so when you do have plenty of it, you can keep it and maybe even grow it.

Financing Your Life

Knowing how you currently spend your money can help you plan better ways to spend it in the future. Financial planners recommend tracking all of your expenses for a full month before you set a budget. Keep a small notebook with you and write down each expense immediately, even fees for using bank automated teller machines. The little things can add up quickly. That five-dollar-a-day gourmet coffee habit can add up to $150 a month.

Then, jot down a few financial goals. Remember the SMART acronym from Chapter 1 and keep your goals specific, measurable, attainable, realistic, and timed. Maybe you'd like a pay increase by the end of the year. Perhaps you would like to save money toward a down payment for a car. Choose a specific amount to save and decide how much you'll need to save out of each check to get there. Once you know where your money goes (current expenditures) and where you want it to go (your financial goals), you're ready to design a budget that suits your lifestyle. If even the word *budget* brings a groan to your lips, remember this: Having a budget doesn't mean you have to do without. It means you hold the reins, deciding where and when to spend your money. Control is a powerful thing, and once you're accustomed to living within your budget, you'll realize you are controlling your money, not the other way around.

> **"**If you know how to spend less than you get, you have the philosopher's stone. **"**
>
> —Benjamin Franklin

Budgeting Basics

Building a budget is as simple as making a list of fixed expenses (what items you must spend money on, including your bills and debts), variable expenses (what you need to spend money on, including household goods, groceries, and toiletries), and discretionary expenses (what you want to spend money on, including movies, music, and eating out). Start with your net income, or how much money you bring home monthly and your financial aid awards. Then, start subtracting as your expenses.

COACH'S CORNER

The dreaded "b" word – Budget – strikes fear into the hearts of many. In Coach's Corner, Coach helps you overcome your fear of budgeting.

http://bit.ly/TC3CoachC

▶ WORKSHEET

The following budget worksheet provides an excellent resource for you. Feel free to change, expand, or remove elements to best suit your budgeting needs.

For the sample template, scan the QR code or visit: *http://bit.ly/TC3WSheet*

	August	September	October	November	December
Income					
Rent/mortgage					
Utilities					
Cellphone bill					
Groceries					
Child care					
Gas/fuel					
Car insurance					

BUDGET CHECKLIST

I have included:

- [ ] Net income
- [ ] Credit card bills
- [ ] Student loan bills
- [ ] Car insurance
- [ ] Cellphone bill
- [ ] Utility bills

- [ ] Rent
- [ ] Transportation expenses
- [ ] Average grocery expenses
- [ ] Entertainment
- [ ] Savings plan
- [ ] Emergency fund

Personal Monthly Budget

As you fill out your budget, you will find that not everything fits into your available resources. In fact, you will have to determine which items aren't that important after all. Budgeting helps you make choices based on your needs first, then your desires. You make the call on which expenditures receive your hard-earned dollars.

Finally, remember to leave some space in your budget for fun, but make it within your means. No one wants to feel deprived. If you have to give up everything you enjoy doing, you can be sure your budget plan will fail after just a month or two.

▶ EXERCISE 3.1

Use the budget worksheet to set out a semester budget for yourself. Place the sheet in your journal. Answer the following questions and bring your answers to class for discussion:

a.) How did you feel when you were making your budget? Why did you feel this way?

b.) What items did you decide you would have to cut back on to live within your budget?

c.) How likely are you to stick to your budget?

Saving for a Rainy Day

Saving money may be the furthest thing from your mind when it takes nearly every penny you make to live, but it is important to develop a savings habit now. Many financial experts recommend saving at least 10 percent of your income, but during college, when finances are at their tightest, this may prove difficult.

Take another look at your budget to see if there is anything you could cut out so you can put some money away. If not, don't despair. Bankrate (Bankrate.com) suggests you save all of your loose change in a jar for thirty days. If you break a dollar, save the change from it and put it in the jar. If you find money under your car seat or couch cushions, put it in the jar. At the end of thirty days, take it to a change counter at your bank or grocery store, then use the money to open a no-fee savings account (most banks offer them for students), one that earns interest if possible. Yes, it's a small start, but it *is* a start. Continue the habit monthly, and by the end of the year, you'll be surprised at what you've saved. If you have the discipline to save even higher amounts, that is all the better.

Quick TIP

College students often thrive on coffee to make it through the early mornings. Rather than going to a coffee shop, make your own coffee at home with a French press or coffee machine. If you drink coffee every day, you could save nearly $900 a year.

APT APPS!

You Need a Budget

Scan the code for additional information or visit: *http://bit.ly/TC3ynab*

The You Need a Budget (YNAB) app helps you establish a budget, break budget items up according to category, and see monthly charts on what you've spent where. The app's website also offers free daily classes to help you get the most out of your finances.

Stretching Your Dollar

There are many ways to make the most of the dollars in your wallet. Be creative. Plenty of fun activities are free or low-cost. Theaters and restaurants offer student discounts. Invite a few friends over for a movie rental night and ask everyone to bring a snack to share. If you are creative and look for alternative ways to enjoy yourself, you can have a great time without breaking the bank.

Clip coupons. Many grocery stores offer triple coupons up to $1 in value, some even more. Watch your local paper for "buy one, get one free" sales at your favorite restaurants. Go online to search for coupons or visit your favorite brands' websites to look for deals. Some stores like Michaels and Jo-Ann Fabric & Craft Stores even have an app for your phone that lets you access coupons.

Buy used books. When it's time to go to the campus bookstore, look for used books or find a student who just finished the class you've registered for. Also, check online bookstores; they may be more competitive in pricing, and many sell used books, too.

Watch the physical and online bulletin boards at school. Students sell everything from iPods to cellphones to computers when they need cash. Keep an eye on the bulletin boards in your commons area for great deals from other students.

Handling Credit

As a college student, chances are you receive a large number of credit card offers every semester. MSNBC, the financial news network, says 75 percent of college students have at least one credit card. Credit, when handled well, can help you achieve your financial goals, but if you let it get out of hand by missing payments or paying late, it can take years to reestablish credit.

Using a credit card wisely can build your credit score so that when you leave college you will have a better opportunity to secure the loans you need for cars and homes. Keep in mind, your student loans can build or break your credit as well. Every creditor or lender you have reports to the three main credit bureaus: Equifax, Experian, and TransUnion. These reports show how much debt you have, whether you make payments on time, and how long you've had the debt. Each of the bureaus gives you a score based on this information – the higher your score, the better your reputation as a debtor. Having too much credit (too many available credit cards or too much money on loan) can damage your score just as badly as making late payments.

Before you make a decision whether to apply for a credit card, conduct an honest evaluation of yourself. Are you the kind of person who has trouble taking care of responsibilities? Do you have a habit of paying your bills late? Are you an impulse shopper, buying things spontaneously and regretting it later? If you answered yes, you might do better to stay away from credit cards.

Protecting Your Identity

KXAN, the NBC news affiliate in Austin, Texas, reported that identity theft is the fastest-growing crime in the United States. During 2007, more than 162 million records were reported lost or stolen, three times the number reported in 2006.

Whether you currently have credit cards doesn't matter – you most likely will seek credit in the near future. Taking certain precautionary steps to make sure your credit and assets are protected now can make that process much smoother and prevent heartache and loss down the road.

Never keep your Social Security card in your wallet. Keep it in a secure location, where you can find it easily when needed. Consider the information someone would obtain if your wallet were stolen: your driver's license (which lists your home address), your credit cards (including the three-digit security code on the back), and your Social Security card. That's hitting the jackpot if you're an identity thief.

ETHICAL DILEMMA

Your parents have given you a credit card for emergencies only. So far, you haven't had to use it. Then, your friends organize a trip to Colorado for spring break and invite you to come along. You don't have the funds in your bank account, but there is enough credit on the card. What do you do?

Scan the code for
additional information or visit:
http://bit.ly/TC3EthD

- a.) Tell your friends you will have to go on the next trip. You can't afford this one.

- b.) Talk to your parents about using the credit card or borrowing money for your trip with the intention of paying them back.

- c.) Use the credit card and tell your parents about it later.

- d.) See how much money you can save up before spring break. There may be expenses you can cut back on long enough to fund the trip.

Shred all mail or unwanted documents containing any personal information, even if just your address on the front. College students typically receive an avalanche of junk mail with offers for credit cards and financial assistance loans. If you throw these offers away without shredding them, anyone going through your trash could pick them up and open bogus accounts in your name. Even though you did not authorize the accounts, and they might not even have your Social Security number attached, you could be held liable for any charges. At the very least, your credit would be ruined.

Don't leave your checkbook, credit cards, or mail containing personal information lying around your dorm or apartment. Not everyone you meet will be trustworthy. College apartments tend to be beehives of activity – parties and study groups may bring people you don't know into your home. Keep your personal financial information out of sight and put away.

Be aware when putting personal information on social networking sites. Sites such as Facebook allow users to have personal pages and post to blogs and bulletin boards. These sites are virtual playgrounds for identity thieves. Internet search engines are filled with page after page of articles warning of identity theft dangers associated with social networking sites.

A credit card is not free money. Whatever you buy on credit must be paid for later. Pay in full each month to avoid finance charges. A credit card is nothing more than a high-interest loan. The card company is allowing you to use their money to pay for your purchases, but they will extract interest from you unless you pay the bill in full every month by the due date. To make sure you can do this, put only a small amount on the card monthly and be sure you have set the payment aside in your bank account so you have it ready at the end of your billing cycle.

Pay attention to interest rates and annual fees. Many companies offer free credit cards with low or zero percent interest rates for short time periods – such as up to six months. Evaluate the card offers before making a decision so you can be sure you are getting the best deal.

Limit the number of cards you have. Remember, the more cards you have, the lower your credit score will be. Have one card, guard it carefully, use it sparingly, and make your payments on time.

In fact, your birthday and name on a social networking site may be enough information for an identity thief to target you. Recently an eighteen-year-old student at the University of Tennessee at Martin was able to hack into a co-ed's iTunes account with just her birthday, which he found on her MySpace page. He then changed her password and charged hundreds of dollars' worth of iPods and other goods to the young woman's account. To protect yourself when using a social networking site, be sure you do not post any personal information and set your viewing restrictions to friends only.

> **Invest in yourself, in your education. There's nothing better.**
>
> —Sylvia Porter

Financing Your Education

While the U.S. Department of Education currently distributes about $83 million of student assistance per year, making up 60 percent of all financial aid, the idea of monetary assistance for college, in some form or other, has been around for centuries. The first recorded scholarship for Harvard University was awarded in 1643. After the Russians beat the United States in the Space Race, launching Sputnik in 1957, the United

States began to consider government financial assistance to encourage more students to attend college, and in the early 1960s, the first federally funded education assistance program was born.

Today, paying for a college education has become an increasing cause of concern among students and parents alike. Costs for completing a two-year degree easily can exceed $20,000, but remember college is an investment in your future. The return on investment you reap down the road will prove that the sacrifices you are making now are worth it.

Getting Professional Assistance

If you are still having problems paying for college and living expenses, look first to your school. Colleges have financial aid departments, and many have money-management counselors. Financial aid officers help you investigate sources of financial aid and help you go through, apply for, and track funds from these sources. Money-management counselors will go beyond helping you get financial aid. They help you create a budget, through which you can determine your income from all sources. Then they help you determine necessary expenses, find ways to decrease your expenses, and find ways to increase your income, if necessary.

Types of Financial Aid

Mention the words "financial aid" and most students will immediately think of the FAFSA form. FAFSA stands for Free Application for Federal Student Aid, and although government assistance does make up the majority of student financing, there are other kinds as well. Financial assistance for education may include private grants, scholarships, government grants and loans, work-study programs, tuition reimbursement, and tax credits. If you've only used the primary form of assistance – federal financial aid – you may have overlooked other available money.

ON THE WEB

For more information and to apply online for FAFSA, visit:

http://bit.ly/TC3fafsa

Government Financial Assistance

Available government assistance includes the Pell Grant, student loans, and parent loans. Students and parents apply for these by filling out the FAFSA form, which is free. Awarded assistance is spread out over two semesters, and students must reapply annually. To apply as an independent student, meaning your parents' income and assets will not be used in making award decisions, you must fit one of these requirements:

- You are twenty-four years old by December 31 of the year when you will receive financial aid.

grant

A form of financial aid from a nonprofit organization (such as the government) that you do not have to repay

- You are a veteran of the U.S. Armed Forces.

- You are married.

- You support a child on your own.

- You are a ward of the court.

- You are a graduate or professional student.

If you don't fit at least one of these criteria, you will need your parents to assist you with obtaining financial aid. For exceptional situations, visit with your school's financial aid officer to discuss alternatives.

When you fill out the FAFSA form, you are applying for all available government assistance. The Pell Grant is awarded on a need basis, meaning you must demonstrate financial need to receive it. The federal student loans consist of an unsubsidized loan (meaning the government does not defer interest until after graduation), which all students can qualify for, and a subsidized loan (no interest accrues on this loan until after graduation), which only students with financial need can qualify for. Neither of these loans requires repayment until six months after graduation. Typically, the loans are awarded through a government-lending agency and are low-interest loans with a ten-year repayment schedule.

Parents can apply for the federal PLUS Loan (Parent Loan for Undergraduate Students) to offset their student's education expenses. Your parents must be credit-worthy to qualify. The repayment period begins within sixty days after the final disbursement of the loan.

You should research the latest government regulations for federal student aid before you apply for assistance because they sometimes change. For example, income-based repayment (IBR) has been available since July 2009. This program means that when you are repaying any federal student loans, your payments will be based on your income so they are more affordable. IBR payments are calculated to be less than 10 percent of your income. In 2010, legislation was passed to increase access to federal student aid and make loan repayment easier. Your campus financial aid officers should have information on the latest federal aid regulations.

In addition to these grants and loans, some states offer assistance, such as the Texas B-On-Time Loan. With this state-specific loan, students who graduate in the allotted amount of time do not have to repay the loan.

Private or Specialty Grants

Nonprofit organizations and various foundations often offer grants to students who seek areas of study that can further the organization's goals. While private grants exist, they can be difficult to find, and students

ON THE WEB

To search for private grants, visit:

http://bit.ly/TC3Grant

need to be aware this is one area where parents and students often fall prey to scams. Never pay anyone to find financial assistance for you. Financial aid information is free.

Scholarships

Two types of scholarships exist. Public scholarships provided by companies or organizations do not require any affiliation with them in order to compete for the awards. Private scholarships are offered by entities that do require affiliation as a qualification for the awards. An example would be Walmart's Higher REACH scholarship, offered only to company employees.

▶ **EXERCISE 3.2**

On the Internet, go to the following scholarship sites and list five scholarships you can apply for this year. Write the essay required for one of the scholarships.

a.) www.fastweb.com

b.) www.brokescholar.com

c.) www.wiredscholar.com

According to Daniel J. Cassidy's *The Scholarship Book: The Complete Guide to Private-Sector Scholarships, Fellowships, Grants, and Loans for the Undergraduate*, more than $2 billion will be awarded this year to students in the United States. Many students have the mistaken belief that scholarships require a 4.0 grade point average (GPA), but the truth is that a large number require no more than a 2.0 GPA. Granting committees base their decisions on factors such as community service, personal qualities, or ethnic background. Apply for many scholarships and apply every year you are eligible. One thing is certain: If you don't apply, you won't win.

Work-Study and Tuition Reimbursement Programs

The work-study program is another federally funded form of assistance. With this program, colleges use government funds to pay students to work at on-campus jobs. Students may work at campus bookstores, cafeterias, or offices, and these jobs are arranged through the college's financial aid department.

ON THE WEB

For information about the Hope Scholarship Tax Credit and Lifetime Learning Tax Credit, visit:

http://bit.ly/TC3hltax

Some students work for off-campus companies that provide tuition reimbursement plans. Several major companies, including Blockbuster, AT&T, and UPS, reimburse a portion of an employee's tuition based on the number of class hours taken and the grade achieved in the course. If you already have a job, check with your company's benefits department to see if this program is available. If you are looking for a job, try to find one that offers this benefit and take advantage of it.

Tax Advantages

There are two tax benefits available for independent students or for the parents of dependent students. The Hope Scholarship Tax Credit is an income tax deduction for students in their first through fourth years of college, up to a maximum of $1,800 per year. Formerly, the credit was available only in the first and second years of college. For at least tax years 2009 and 2010, the credit limit was raised to $2,500, under a modification of the credit called the American Opportunity Credit. The Hope Scholarship Tax Credit is based on income, so be sure to read current IRS rules carefully.

The Lifetime Learning Tax Credit is for students not eligible for the Hope Scholarship Tax Credit and may be used during all the years a student is in college. The maximum benefit per year is $2,000.

Paying for college doesn't have to be a major stress. Once you understand the various forms of financial aid and the requirements for eligibility, you can apply with confidence. Your campus financial aid officers will be able to help you with financial aid questions.

> **Money is only a tool. It will take you wherever you wish, but it will not replace you as the driver.**
> —Ayn Rand

Professional Financial Management

According to YoungMoney, the average college student earns around $8 an hour. The average college graduate makes between $15 and $30 an hour. While you will most likely have to scrimp and save to get by during your college years, your career will most likely bring you stronger monetary rewards. That is the reason, after all, for the sacrifices you make now.

With greater cash flow comes greater financial responsibilities. Once you are working in your chosen career, you may have the opportunity to contribute to a corporate-sponsored retirement savings plan. You may be offered an opportunity to participate in stock-sharing programs or other profit-sharing incentives. Career professionals need to be able to manage their personal day-to-day finances, their short-term savings accounts, and their retirement funds.

Lemon
Scan the code for additional information or visit: *http://bit.ly/TC3Lemon*

Never lose a receipt again. Keep track of work and personal receipts with Lemon. Lemon collects all of your receipts in one place, allowing you to email digital copies to your account, or you can snap a photo and let Lemon digitize the information.

Back to Basics

The budgeting principles you used to get you through college will be the same principles that carry you into and through your career. Going from an $8-an-hour job to a $43,000-a-year salary is a heady feeling for a recent college graduate. Many graduates fall into the trap of immediately spending more because they have more. Avoid the temptation to buy, buy, buy just because you can. Instead, reevaluate your budget. Adjust your income levels to your new salary, and then take some time to consider thoroughly your monthly obligations.

Reevaluate your goals. Take another look at the goals you set back in Chapter 1. Do they still fit your lifestyle? Perhaps by the time you graduate from college you will have experienced major life changes, such as marriage or the birth of a child. You may need to reset your goals based on your new circumstances.

Form a big picture of how you want your life to be. Do you want to travel? Would you like to retire at age fifty? Keep your goals SMART (specific, measurable, attainable, realistic, and timed), and write them down. Refer to them as you form your budget and savings plan. You can't get where you want to be in the future if you don't chart the course now.

Don't spend money just because you make it. If you spend all of your cash as you earn it, then how will you make ends meet during lean times? Financial experts recommend you establish an emergency savings fund that will tide you over during times of job loss. Try to set aside 10 to 20 percent of your monthly income to go toward this fund. Keep the money in an interest-bearing account that is easily accessible, and then pretend you don't have it. If you never need the money, it will grow into a nice retirement nest egg, but if you lose your job, the kids are hungry, and the bills are due, you will be glad you were so wise.

Form a slush fund and contribute to it monthly. A slush fund refers to a savings account from which money flows in and out. This is a savings account to handle minor emergencies, such as a new fuel pump on the

Remember when filling out your budget that your student loan payments will start about six months after you graduate (the time frame may vary depending on where you got your loan).

car or repairs on your home's air-conditioner. You may want to use this savings account to pay for something special for your family, such as a trip or a flat screen television. Having this account will help you feel more comfortable when a situation arises that requires you to spend more than you had anticipated.

Take advantage of company-sponsored savings plans. Many companies offer a corporation-sponsored retirement account – a 401k in most instances or a 403b if your employer is a civil government, nonprofit organization, or public school. These retirement accounts allow you to contribute pretax dollars from each paycheck. The company will then match a portion of that money. This essentially gives you a raise.

If you contribute $300 per month, and your company matches 25 percent, you are earning an extra $75 per month, or an extra $900 per year. Because this money comes to your retirement fund tax-deferred (meaning you do not pay taxes on it until you use it), it is actually the equivalent of earning $1,125 extra per year, if you are in the 20 percent tax bracket. Additionally, the money you contribute to your account is also tax-deferred, and that is the equivalent of keeping an extra $720 per year, assuming that you are in the 20 percent tax bracket. With all of this taken into account, you are earning an extra $1,845 per year just by contributing to a tax-advantaged savings plan.

Know your options. You will be able to direct how you want your 401k invested. Some plans offer a money market savings, or stable-value option, which grows at a slower but steady rate. You may be allowed to invest in company stock, which can cause the value of your retirement savings to fluctuate with the stock market. A third option will usually be to invest in mutual funds, or a group of stocks, selected and maintained by a fund manager. This option will also fluctuate with the market, but the swings will be more stable than with company stock. Any growth on your account is tax-deferred until your retirement.

► EXERCISE 3.3

Contact the human resources department of one of the companies you are interested in working for. Explain that you are a college student doing research on benefits. Ask what benefits are typically offered to their employees. Make a list of the benefits and include it in your journal. Explain what each benefit is and how it works.

Don't get penalized. Because the idea of the 401k is to help employees prepare for retirement, you can be penalized if you withdraw any of the funds before turning fifty-nine to sixty years old. Certain exceptions, such

as withdrawing for education purposes or for the down payment on your first house, do apply. You will also be allowed to borrow against your fund after a certain time, and if you take this option, you'll make payments, with interest, back to yourself. If you leave your job at any time before retirement, you can always take your own contributions with you by rolling them over into another tax-advantaged plan, such as an individual retirement account (IRA) or annuity, or even a 401k at your new employer. Any contributions your employer made will be given to you on a prorated basis, depending on how many years you worked for the company. This is called vesting. Typically, most employees are vested only a portion per year up to five years, then enjoy full vesting, meaning that 100 percent of your 401k is yours. Your benefits administrator will have detailed information and assistance for you.

Don't forget insurance. Any solid plan for financial well-being must include insurance. One major illness or accident and everything you've worked for could go to hospital bills and doctors. Typically, employers offer employees the opportunity to participate in corporate health insurance benefits. (If you work for a very small company, this may not be the case.) Very few companies pay 100 percent of an employee's health insurance costs anymore. Mostly likely, your company will pay a portion and you will pay a portion, but as is the case with your 401k, employers take pretax dollars out of your check to pay for your health insurance.

Additionally, your company may provide life insurance or disability insurance on their employees, and if not, they may offer these plans to you at a reduced rate. Take advantage of extra insurance when you can afford to do so and always take the health insurance on yourself and your family. If your company does not provide insurance, check the Internet for health insurance. Additionally, some states, including Texas, offer insurance benefits for children, provided their families meet certain income restrictions and no other insurance covers them.

Conclusion

Making the transition from college to your career will bring exciting opportunities, both financially and personally. Making sure you've already laid the groundwork for a solid plan of how and when to spend, where to save, and how to invest wisely will prevent much of the financial stress that plagues many adults. A recent CNN report states that nearly a quarter of Americans have no spare cash left to save at the end of the month, and 42 percent of Americans see debt repayment as their biggest financial concern.

To participate in the online poll, scan the QR code or visit: *http://bit.ly/TC3Poll*

What is your biggest expense?

○ Cellphone bill

○ Rent

○ Entertainment

○ Transportation (gas/insurance/repairs)

Further Reading

The Scholarship Book: The Complete Guide to Private-Sector Scholarships, Fellowships, Grants, and Loans for the Undergraduate by Daniel J. Cassidy. Prentice Hall Press: 2008.

Zombie Economics: A Guide to Personal Finance by Lisa Desjardins and Rick Emerson. Avery Trade: 2011.

REVIEW QUESTIONS | What did you LEARN?

1. How can SMART be applied to your finances?

2. What are the three general kinds of expenses you should include in your budget?

3. Why should you save for a rainy day?

4. What are some techniques to stretch your dollar?

5. What is a benefit of having a credit card?

6. What are some techniques to keep in charge of your credit card?

7. What are some ways to protect your identity?

8. What is the FAFSA?

9. Why is having a slush fund important?

10. What are examples of work benefits that may affect your finances?

Scan this code to access
the puzzle online or visit:
http://bit.ly/TC3Crword

Across

4. The Pell Grant is awarded on a _____ basis.

5. What app helps you establish a budget, break budget items up according to category, and see monthly charts of what you've spent where?

9. Where should you never keep your Social Security card?

11. A credit card is nothing more than a high-interest _____.

12. Having a _____ doesn't mean you have to do without?

14. A five-dollar-a-day gourmet _____ habit can add up to $150 a month.

16. A form of financial aid from a nonprofit organization (such as the government) that you do not have to repay

18. Colleges have financial aid departments, and many have money-management _____.

19. Money you receive for your tuition or other college expenses that you may or may not have to pay back (2 words)

20. What app helps you keep track of work and personal receipts?

Down

1. What should you do with all mail or unwanted documents containing any personal information?

2. Who said, "Money is only a tool. It will take you wherever you wish, but it will not replace you as the driver"?

3. What form comes to most students' minds when the words "financial aid" are said?

6. Bankrate.com suggests you save all of your loose _____ in a jar for thirty days.

7. A form of financial aid you must repay (2 words)

8. Remember to leave some space in your budget for what?

10. Who said, "Invest in yourself, in your education. There's nothing better"?

13. Don't spend money just because you _____ it.

15. Who said, "If you know how to spend less than you get, you have the philosopher's stone"?

17. When is it important to develop a saving habit?

STEPHANIE SUTTON
Dean of Enrollment and Financial Services

Scan this code for additional info
or visit: *http://bit.ly/TC3Sutton*

Practicing Good Budgeting Skills Today for Tomorrow

According to Stephanie Sutton, dean of enrollment and financial services, financial issues are some of the most important issues students deal with, and she would know. Sutton worked as a student worker in 1979, and six months later, she was hired at an office of financial aid and placement. After taking a "break" to raise her two daughters from 1985 to 1992, Sutton returned to work. Since 1995, she has had the responsibility for a financial aid office, and there are few places she would rather be.

"I have the best job in the world," says Sutton. "I assist students in enrolling in college and finding a way to help pay for their education! I truly believe a college education is the gateway to a productive and positive future."

Sutton cares deeply about her job and making sure students are well-educated about their financial decision, especially the repercussions of those decisions. Sutton stresses that students need to learn to look to the future instead of merely living for the present. It is this way of thinking that has caused so many financial issues for students.

"Students need to realize the financial decisions they make today will impact their tomorrows. Unnecessary credit card and student loan debt can be a detriment to future jobs, finding a car, or even buying a house."

One of the primary skills Sutton says is necessary to combat poor financial decisions is to plan and maintain a monthly budget. Sutton credits her and her husband's ability to own their own home, provide for their children, and plan for retirement to the fact that they both have managed to keep and maintain a monthly budget.

"It is important for college students to learn how to develop a monthly budget and to live within their means," says Sutton. "A budget will force them to be cognizant about what their expenses are and the income necessary to pay their expenses. It is also very important for students to begin saving for their future, even if it means only saving a few dollars a week. This will add up and will provide good habits for the future."

Notes

_____

_____

_____

_____

_____

_____

_____

_____

_____

_____

_____

_____

_____

_____

_____

_____

_____

_____

_____

_____

_____

_____

_____

_____

_____

_____

_____

_____

_____

_____

_____

_____

Keeping Yourself Healthy and Safe

STUDENT DISORIENTATION

"Can I get a medium French fries with some ketchup?" Misha asked the lady behind the counter.

"Sweetie, seriously…" Aaron said. "You can't eat just fries every day."

"I'm fine!" Misha responded sharply as they sat to eat with the rest of the group.

"At least she is consistent." Carlos sighed.

"You can't be serious," Beth said. "You need to eat real food. French fries for a whole meal are not going to be enough to get you through all the studying you do."

"Buying a full meal is a waste of money. I'm not that hungry, so I'm not going to eat it anyway." Misha tried to end the conversation.

"You eat terribly, you don't exercise, and you study your brains out for entertainment," Kristen said. "You're lucky you look great now, but your health is going to catch up with you before you know it."

"I'm sure there is a way for you to eat your small portions and maintain a reasonable diet without wasting money." Beth suggested.

"Cooking is too much work and buying healthy food especially when eating out is too expensive. Fries are the only option left!" Misha smiled and ate another fry to add to the note of finality she wanted on the conversation.

CHAPTER OBJECTIVES:

- Taking care of your body and mind

- Staying safe at college

- Maintaining a safe work environment

Ramen noodles. Pizza. Fast-food 99-cent menu. Sound familiar? Most college students consider these the staples of the college diet. For many, the focus on grades, homework, tests, and projects becomes so intense that personal concerns such as eating well, making time for exercise, and getting enough sleep fade into obscurity.

Teachers and students joke about first-year students putting on the "freshman 15." Unfortunately, it's no joke. A recent study by Cornell University found that on average, college freshmen gain about 0.3 pounds a week – almost eleven times more than the average weight gain among seventeen- and eighteen-year-olds and twenty times more than the average weight gain among American adults.

Worse yet, putting on a little weight pales in comparison to some of the other problems college students face. The high academic stress levels, coupled with the freedom from parental control that comes with college life, may tempt students into developing risky behavior as a pressure release. College campuses throughout the United States document increasing incidences of alcohol bingeing, unprotected sex (often with multiple partners), and narcotic experimentation. Additionally, a report in 2000 by the National Mental Health Association says 30 percent of freshmen admit to feeling overwhelmed or depressed.

With so much bad news reported almost daily, is there any good news at all about college? Yes! The good news is that you don't have to fall prey to any of these pitfalls. Personal health and safety is mostly a matter of personal choice. Developing healthy habits and making wise decisions now can benefit you throughout your life and help you transition smoothly from college life into your career and beyond.

Guarding Your Health

> "Happiness lies, first of all, in health."
>
> —George William Curtis

When you are young and full of optimism, it's hard to think about osteoarthritis, heart disease, diabetes, or high cholesterol. However, if you don't take care of your body now, it won't take care of you later. Those all-night study sessions with double-meat cheeseburgers to keep you going may not affect you at age twenty, but by age forty, your cholesterol levels, which are raised by a high-fat diet and lack of exercise, may be putting you at risk for a heart attack.

Brain Food

College students are on the go most of the time. It's tempting to grab something out of a machine or swing into a fast-food drive-through as you run between school and work. However, plenty of healthy choices exist. With a little planning and forethought, you can make food choices that will

help you feel more energetic, stave off the freshman 15, and still fit within your busy lifestyle.

To avoid energy dips and keep your brain functioning at an optimum level throughout your busy day, choose fruits and vegetables. The natural sugars in these foods feed your craving for sweets, while the fiber increases your feeling of fullness and works to keep your blood sugar even. Drop an apple into your backpack as you go out the door in the morning. Go for a banana instead of a candy bar when you want something sweet. Keep baby carrots, raisins, nuts, and fruits in your pantry for quick snacks that energize your brain and body.

Whole grains are another excellent food choice that keeps you feeling full and energized. Fit whole grains into your diet by choosing whole-wheat waffles and bagels, wheat bread, whole-grain cereals, and long-grain rice. White grains are high in sugar and contribute to blood-sugar swings that can cause you to lose focus in your day.

Get together with friends or roommates and make a large, healthy meal. Put the leftovers into individual serving containers and freeze them. You'll save money, and you'll have enough for a couple of future meals.

TRACKING NUTRITION CHECKLIST

Just as it is important to track calories in and calories out, it is important to keep track of the types of foods you are consuming. Use the following checklist to mark off each type of food. This is a helpful tool, but it should not replace any advice or recommendations from your nutritionist or doctor.

- [ ] **Whole Grains and Legumes** (6 servings)
  Like pasta, bread, and black beans

- [ ] **Calcium** (4 servings)
  Like milk, cheese, yogurt, and sesame seeds

- [ ] **Veggies and Fruits** (3-4 servings)
  Like squash, spinach, cantaloupe, and papaya

- [ ] **Vitamin C** (3 servings)
  Like oranges, grapefruits, and strawberry

- [ ] **Protein** (3 servings)
  Like poultry, beef, lamb, fish and seafood, tofu, and edamame

- [ ] **Iron** (3 servings)
  Like beef, spinach, soy products, and oat bran

- [ ] **Fats** (roughly 4 servings)
  Like peanut butter, avocado, oil, butter, and mayonnaise

- [ ] **Water** (at least 8 servings of 8 ounces)

APT APPS!

MyFitnessPal

Scan the code for additional information or visit: *http://bit.ly/TC4mfitpal*

MyFitnessPal is an ideal way to keep track of your nutrition and exercise each day. This app allows you to keep a food journal, and has thousands of brands of food already programmed in. The app also lets you keep track of how much of each nutrient you have consumed. In addition, you can keep track of your exercise and see an estimate of how many calories you burned.

Quick **TIP**

Avoid napping. Nappers sleep less than non-nappers. If you do nap, rest early in the day and keep it short.

leptin

The hormone that tells your body either that you're full or that you need to eat more

Sleep Tight

Physicians and researchers agree that adults should get an average of eight hours of sleep a night. College students, on average, get less than seven. All-night cram sessions and parties contribute to sleep deprivation. The occasional midnight-oil session is inevitable and won't harm you, but making a habit of getting by on as little sleep as possible can lead to a host of problems. The University of Michigan Health Service reports that sleeping less than six and a half hours a night (or more than nine on a regular basis) can lead to:

- Decreased academic performance

- Automobile accidents

- Increased illnesses such as colds and flu

- Depression

In fact, college students are twice as likely as the general population to experience depression, and researchers believe that one of the main causes is lack of sleep.

In addition, more and more scientific studies are finding that sleep deprivation can also lead to obesity. The level of **leptin** – the hormone in your body that tells your body either that you're full or that you need to eat more – builds up in your body as you sleep, because you don't need to eat while you're sleeping. If you don't get enough sleep, your leptin level doesn't increase enough, leaving your body to believe you are hungry. If a cycle of sleep deprivation and decreasing leptin level goes on long enough, it slows down your metabolism and thus results in more weight gain.

In your journal, keep a personal health diary for five days. Document what you eat during each day, how much exercise you do, and how many hours of sleep you get. Answer these questions about your choices:

a.) Did you make healthy food choices most of the time?

b.) What were the healthiest foods you ate?

c.) What time of the day did you tend to eat the most junk food?

d.) How many hours of sleep per night did you average?

e.) How did you feel during the day when you slept the least?

f.) How can you better organize your day to help you get more sleep if you need it?

g.) What kinds of exercise did you participate in?

h.) How much time exercising did you average over the five days?

i.) How can you change your daily routine to improve your personal health? What areas need the most improvement?

These tips, published by the University of Michigan Health Service, can help you get the sleep you need for better academic performance and increased physical and mental health:

- Maintain regular bedtimes (and morning rising times) every night, including weekends.

- Take a hot bath (for about fifteen minutes) an hour and a half before bedtime.

To participate in the online poll, scan the QR code or visit: *http://bit.ly/TC4Poll*

Which segment of your health do you need to work on most?

○ Creating and maintaining a healthy sleep habit

○ Eating healthier foods

○ Becoming more active

○ Drinking more water

- Turn down the thermostat and avoid electric blankets at bedtime.

- Restrict caffeine to one to two cups before 10 a.m. and avoid nicotine (smoking tobacco) in the evening. These stimulants make it more difficult to relax enough to sleep.

- Don't eat food within two hours of bedtime. Large meals take time to digest and make sleep difficult.

- Limit or avoid alcohol because it disrupts sleep. Also, be aware that alcohol can magnify the effects of sleep deprivation.

- Avoid routine use of sleeping pills or other sleep aids that reduce sleep quality.

- Create your own sleep rituals – listen to calming music, brush your teeth, read a book, write in a journal – to signal your body and mind that it is time to sleep.

Germ Wars

Take the pressure of a killer midterm, add to it a couple of all-nighters, throw in a little flu, and you have a recipe for a stress meltdown. To a college student, little is worse than becoming seriously ill in the middle of exam time, yet it is a very real possibility. Factors such as stress, lack of sleep, and an unhealthy diet all break down the immune system, making students vulnerable to illnesses such as colds and flu.

Because college students live in close proximity and tend to share food and drinks, germs spread easily and quickly. Bacterial meningitis, which can cause debilitating brain damage, has emerged as a serious threat on college campuses around the country, and many schools require students to be vaccinated against it. Mononucleosis – mono for short – can knock a student's health down for at least six weeks, sometimes more.

Fortunately, a few common sense steps can help you enjoy a healthy semester. Wash your hands with antibacterial soap often, especially after shaking hands with others, being in public places, or using shared items such as phones or computers. Use a paper towel to turn off faucets in public bathrooms or to open the door as you leave. Never eat or drink after anyone. Get plenty of sleep, drink water, and make healthy food choices. Keep your vaccinations up-to-date, including:

- Tetanus-diphtheria-pertussis (TDAP vaccine, good for ten years)

- HPV (series of three vaccines currently for girls and women only)

- Meningococcal (MCV4 vaccine, to prevent bacterial meningitis)

- Chicken pox (varicella vaccine, for students who've never had chicken pox)

- Influenza (every year)

- Hepatitis B

Hit the Gym

Students who exercise regularly report feeling happier and having more energy. The U.S. Department of Health and Human Services recommends an hour of moderate to vigorous activity most days of the week. The thought of doing jumping jacks doesn't excite you? That's okay. Look for activities you enjoy, and you will be more likely to stick with exercising. A brisk game of basketball, a power walk, or a session of Zumba are all excellent for getting your heart rate up and burning calories. Besides being fun, regular exercise will help you rest better at night.

 WORKSHEET

Sometimes the hardest part about setting up a workout routine is your schedule. Some of us don't have time to hit the gym for an hour, but we can find four or five shorter segments of time to do some form of exercise. Use this calendar to map out a few short workouts you can do throughout your day.

For the sample template, scan the QR code or visit: *http://bit.ly/TC4Wkout*

	Sunday	Monday	Tuesday	Wednesday	Thursday	Friday	Saturday
Workout 1							
Workout 2							
Workout 3							
Workout 4							
Workout 5							

APT APPS!

Skimble

Scan the code for additional information or visit: *http://bit.ly/TC4Skimble*

The Workout Trainer from Skimble provides you with many different workout plans and ideas. Focus on one particular part of your body or set up a full workout program. The app provides plenty of photos and videos to guide you through each routine.

If you don't have an extra sixty minutes to devote to exercise, look for quick alternatives. Ride your bike to class, taking the long way there and back. Park your car farther from the grocery store door. Take the stairs instead of the elevator. Recent studies show that short segments of intense activity, spread throughout the day, can provide similar benefits to long exercise sessions.

However you choose to exercise, the important thing to remember is that you must move. College students spend long hours engaged in sedentary activity. Make finding time to enjoy physical activity a priority.

Play It Safe at School

> *He is most free from danger, who, even when safe, is on his guard.*
>
> —**Publilius Syrus**

College is a time of fun, exploration, and adventure. Students make new, lifelong friends; embrace new concepts; and experience situations they never dreamed of while in high school. College can also be a dangerous place if students do not use common sense to make wise decisions.

"Moderation in all things." These words of Greek philosopher Aristotle hold as true today as they did in the third century BC. Many students experiment with alcohol once they move away to college. You've heard it before: If you drink, don't drive. It's that simple. Alcohol and vehicles make a deadly mix. Designate a driver who drinks absolutely no alcohol during the evening. Take a cab or a call a friend to come get you, but don't get behind the wheel. Because alcohol severely impairs judgment, you may have had more to drink than you remember or realize. Most drunk drivers think they can handle themselves. They are wrong.

Additionally, alcohol takes away people's normal inhibitions and internal warning systems. If you drink at a party, keep the alcohol to a minimum so that you are in control of your faculties.

The optimism and health of youth tend to make college students feel invincible. In the absence of parental authority, students may feel it's time to experience life the way they want to live it. In part, these years are exactly for that – growing up, discovering yourself. However, these years also pose certain dangers and risks for students who do not use common sense to protect themselves. A 2004 article in the *Michigan Daily*, the University of Michigan's official newspaper, said that one in five college students has a sexually transmitted disease. In December 2007, Dr. Susan Blumenthal reported on Huffington Post that the percentage is actually much higher. She said that up to 25 percent of college students report having a sexually transmitted disease and nearly one-half of all newly reported sexually transmitted infections occur in people who are fifteen to twenty-four years old.

Practice classroom/laboratory safety. As you move through your major courses, you will have many classes that offer laboratory experience. Laboratory work will be invaluable to your education but can be hazardous when not handled correctly. It is very important to treat the laboratory and all equipment with great respect, following your instructor's rules and the general safety rules recommended for your specific laboratory. Some safety precautions, such as the ones that follow, are universal:

- Don't wear loose, floppy clothing in the laboratory.

- Wear closed-toe shoes.

- If you are handling chemicals, remember your personal protective equipment (PPE) – safety glasses and vinyl or nitrile gloves.

- In laboratories that involve heavy equipment, power tools, rotating equipment, or construction materials, you may need a hardhat, ear protection, and steel-toe boots, in addition to safety glasses. Additionally, if certain hazardous chemicals are present, you may need a respirator.

- Don't eat or drink in a chemical laboratory.

- Familiarize yourself with the location and use of fire extinguishers, eyewash stations, and first-aid kits.

- When using electrical equipment, follow proper safety procedures, including keeping live current away from water, wearing electrically insulated lineman gloves, and using electrically insulated tools.

Even though your instructors control the laboratory and have the responsibility of seeing that everyone follows the rules, your personal safety is ultimately in your hands. Follow established safety guidelines and don't take shortcuts, even if an instructor says you can. Lastly, if you don't feel comfortable with certain procedures or if you feel sufficient safety measures are not in place, speak up immediately.

Pay attention to campus safety suggestions and use common sense. As with many of the dangers mentioned in this chapter, common sense can make the difference between being a victim and being safe. Because of the Jeanne Clery Act of 1990 – named for a young woman who was brutally tortured, raped, and murdered on the Lehigh University campus – all colleges are required to make their crime statistics public. Following these simple suggestions can help you protect yourself:

- Keep your doors locked at all times. Don't open them to people you don't know.

- Don't leave valuables or personal information lying around.

- Don't accept rides from people you don't know.

- Be aware of your surroundings – criminals look for targets who are distracted and vulnerable.

- Keep your car doors locked when driving. Lock your car when you leave it and take any valuables with you.

- Try to avoid being out at night alone. If you must be out, carry pepper spray in your hand. Another idea is to make your hand into a fist, with a key poking out between your fingers. You could use this as a defensive weapon if necessary.

- Avoid drunkenness, as you are more vulnerable when inebriated.

Many students will someday look back on their college years and describe them as the best in their life. Staying safe, healthy, and in control can make sure you have an opportunity to do the same.

> **" Precaution is better than cure. "**
> —Edward Coke

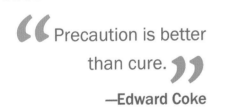

On-the-Job Safety

As you make the transition from college life to the workplace, personal safety concerns move beyond ordinary health and home safety. The **Occupational Safety and Health Administration (OSHA)** reported in 2002 that every year approximately 6,000 American employees die from workplace-related injuries and another 50,000 die from illnesses caused by exposure to workplace hazards. Additionally, 6 million workers sustain nonfatal workplace injuries, at an annual cost to U.S. businesses of more than $125 billion.

Employers must create controls to prevent injuries to their employees through employee training on hazards and instituting controls, such as guarding and the use of PPE. While many safety standards have now been in place for thirty years or more, others must evolve continually as emerging technologies bring new potential hazards. For example, the use and production of genetically modified organisms and nanotechnology present new safety challenges as well as growing concerns over worker exposure to various toxins in the disassembly of electronic waste.

Occupational Safety and Health Administration (OSHA)

The main federal agency charged with the enforcement of safety and health legislation

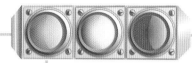

THE BIRTH OF OSHA

During the Industrial Revolution of the late 1800s, workers handled hazardous materials (such as dynamite and nitroglycerin for mine blasting); worked in unsafe, unstable mines; and worked with heavy moving equipment without protective equipment. Very few, if any, workplace safety precautions existed, and there were certainly no national safety standards. Though some injured workers and families of deceased workers sued employers over unsafe conditions, the judges usually ruled in favor of the employers. A number of surveys taken around 1900 showed that only about half of the families of all fatally injured workers recovered anything, and their average compensation equaled approximately half a year's pay.

As labor unions gained more power, the demand for better workplace conditions gained momentum. By 1910, the state of New York had enacted one of the first workers' compensation laws. Other states followed suit over the years. Finally, in 1971, OSHA was formed to establish a federal standard of workplace safety that encompasses most employers in the United States. These standards provide requirements for employers to evaluate job-site hazards, whether chemical, mechanical, environmental, or physical.

Watching Out for Number One – You

When you begin your career, your employer will have certain workplace safety guidelines and controls in place, according to OSHA's rules and specific to the type of career you have chosen. You can expect to find regulations and training pertaining to material handling, construction safety, electrical safety, and hazardous materials, among other concerns. Issues such as slip/trip hazards, noise and vibration concerns, and avoidance of musculoskeletal disorders through the employment of ergonomic design fall under the OSHA's jurisdiction. You may be required to attend extra hours of training on how to avoid certain hazards and injuries or on how to deal

ON THE WEB

For information about the Occupational Safety and Health Administration, visit:

http://bit.ly/TC4osha

with such issues as anonymously reporting safety violations by coworkers. Many companies offer bonuses and awards as safety training and compliance incentives, because any incidents of on-the-job injuries could trigger an OSHA investigation and the resulting punitive measures.

One of the most important things you can do to protect yourself and your coworkers is to partner with the safety director or risk manager at your workplace in implementing and following all safety guidelines. At times, employees, and even supervisors, are tempted to take shortcuts to make work move faster. However, taking shortcuts can lead to serious injury, permanent disability, or even fatalities.

Certified safety professional Gregory Smith reports investigating hundreds of these traumatic employee injuries. Two of the accidents he has investigated stand out as prime examples of the life-altering hazards present in many industrial settings. In both cases, employee decisions to take shortcuts and ignore safety protocol brought severe consequences.

ETHICAL DILEMMA

You work in a commercial construction company. Your boss is encouraging employees to cut corners to speed up the work, even if it means not following safety protocol. Some workers are not wearing harnesses. Others have stopped wearing safety glasses because they say it's harder to see with them on. You noticed an electrician not taking time to put on insulated gloves or check for live wires before working. What should you do?

Scan the code for additional information or visit:
http://bit.ly/TC4EthD

a.) Make sure you follow all the safety guidelines. If anyone gets in trouble, it'll be his or her own fault.

b.) Approach your employer with your concerns. Make him know that you see danger and are worried. Make suggestions for how the problems could be remedied.

c.) Follow the safety guidelines and talk with your coworkers about the guidelines Everyone is at risk when even one person isn't following them.

d.) Use your company's complaint policy or file with OSHA without speaking to your boss or coworkers.

The first accident resulted in permanent disability when a 2,000-pound counterweight crushed a man's foot to a thickness of approximately 3/4 of an inch. This young man had disregarded safety guidelines to save time, climbing a barrier fence and a counterweight mast to dislodge a jam in an automated material lift. Once the jam was cleared, the counterweight traveled down the mast, crushing his foot between the mast frame and counterweight. The man was trapped in the device for over twenty minutes before being discovered.

In another case, a man was killed when a bridge-column cage assembly toppled and fell on him. The man's death could have been prevented if his coworkers had followed established rigging guidelines, which detail how supporting cables should be rigged to the column assembly. As with the overwhelming majority of employee injuries, the accident and resulting injury or fatality in both of these incidents could have been prevented if only proper procedures and safety protocol had been followed.

What Is PPE?

Depending on your job, you may be required to wear personal protective equipment (PPE). At times, this equipment can be cumbersome, but your life could be at stake if you don't follow company policies. The PPE you might use includes the following:

- Hardhats

- Safety eyewear

- Ear protection

- Gloves

- Protective footwear

- Fall protection

- Respiratory protection

COACH'S CORNER

Eating healthy is sometimes easier said than done, especially when processed food often tastes "better." In Coach's Corner, Coach talks about "retraining" your taste buds to enjoy the diverse flavors of healthy food.

http://bit.ly/TC4CCorner

▶ EXERCISE 4.2

Thinking of the career you plan to pursue, what safety problems do you foresee? What type of PPE do you expect you'll need? What type of safety rules do you expect to encounter? List these in your journal.

What If My Boss Doesn't Follow the Rules?

The safety precautions your employer puts in place are for your benefit as an employee. If at any time you feel your employer is not following safety standards, it is your responsibility to yourself and your coworkers to speak out. Here are a few of the rights employees have under OSHA guidelines:

- Review employer-provided OSHA standards, regulations, and requirements

- Request information from your employer on emergency procedures

- Ask the OSHA area director to investigate hazardous conditions or violations of standards in your workplace

- File anonymous complaints with OSHA

- Be advised of OSHA actions regarding your complaint and have an informal review of any decision not to inspect or to issue a citation

- Have your employee representative accompany the OSHA compliance officer on inspection

- Seek safe and healthy working conditions without your employer retaliating against you

- Observe any monitoring or measuring of toxic substances or harmful physical agents and review any related monitoring or medical records

Conclusion

"Know safety, no injuries." "Success is no accident." "Watch out for number one." You'll probably see slogans and signs with these or similar messages posted throughout your college or workplace as a reminder that safety doesn't just happen. It's a matter of making wise decisions and following protocol. You work hard to get where you want to be in your career. Making sure you're aware of the safety standards and regulations and sticking to them can make the difference between a long, successful career and a disability that makes you unable to work.

Further Reading

The Healthy College Cookbook by Alexandra Nimetz, Jason Stanley, Emeline Starr, and Rachel Holcomb. Storey Publishing: 2009.

College Safety 101 by Kathleen Baty. Chronicle Books: 2011.

REVIEW QUESTIONS | What did you LEARN?

1. What are examples of brain foods?

2. What are the effects caused by getting less than six and a half hours of sleep a night?

3. What is leptin?

4. What are some of the vaccinations you should keep up-to-date?

5. List safety precautions that should be followed in a laboratory.

6. What does OSHA stand for?

7. In your own words, explain the history of workplace safety standards in the United States.

8. What happened in one of the safety cases Gregory Smith investigated?

9. What is PPE? What are some examples of PPE?

10. What are a few of the rights employees have under OSHA guidelines?

Scan this code to access
the puzzle online or visit:
http://bit.ly/TC4Crword

Across

2. Depending on your job, you may be required to wear what?

5. If you don't have an extra sixty minutes to devote to exercise, look for _____ alternatives.

9. What app helps you keep track of your nutrition and exercise each day?

10. College students spend long hours engaged in _____ activity.

13. If you don't feel comfortable with certain procedures, when should you speak up?

16. A report by the National Mental Health Association says what percentage of students admit to feeling overwhelmed or depressed?

18. Students who _____ regularly report feeling happier and having more energy.

20. What app helps you with many different workout plans and ideas?

Down

1. What disease can knock a student's health down for at least six weeks, sometimes more?

3. How many hours should you sleep on average each night?

4. If you drink, don't _____.

6. Who said, "Happiness lies, first of all, in health"?

7. As with many of the dangers mentioned in this chapter, _____ can make the difference between being a victim and being safe. (2 words)

8. Many students will someday look back on their college years and describe them as the _____ in their life.

11. Who said, "Moderation in all things"?

12. One in _____ college students has an sexually transmitted disease.

14. How much more likely are college students to get depression than the general population?

15. The hormone in your body that tells your body either that you're full or that you need to eat more

17. Don't eat food within _____ hours of bedtime.

19. The main federal agency charged with the enforcement of safety and health legislation

CINDY VOLNEY
Human and Organization Development Associate

Scan this code for additional info
or visit: *http://bit.ly/TC4CVolney*

Better Safe Than Sorry

Human and Organization Development Associate Cindy Volney understands there is safety in numbers. Since 1997, she's been involved with safety, retirement, and insurance for employees, and she says solving issues in these areas is a group effort.

"We are very proactive when it comes to our employees' safety, and we work very closely with the State of Texas, the fire marshals, Texas Department of Insurance, and the State Office of Risk Management," Volney says. "There's not really a hazard we couldn't take care of or reduce the risk of."

What kinds of risks or safety issues exist on college campuses? Volney lists health issues resulting from alcohol and drug usage and accidents caused by lack of knowledge and training as some possibilities. She thinks, though, students may have an advantage because of the particular safety courses offered in high-risk programs.

"I think these students are more attuned to what the risks are," says Volney. Yet she warns students against complacency because safety will be an important issue after college as well. "In most of the fields students are going into, those risks are things they need to worry about," she explains.

Students and employees often are instructed on safety guidelines during student orientation and new-hire orientation, and Volney says these guidelines are important in risky situations. In new-hire orientation, employees learn about their rights, the causes of accidents, how to report accidents, unsafe working conditions, and the care of an injured person.

Volney says the most important issue in campus safety is communication. "We would like people to report things they see as unsafe," she says. "I can't correct something unless someone reports it." Volney also says it's important for students and employees to know which "direction" to go according to each safety or health issue – whether it's the health-services nurse, the police station, or the hospital.

Volney's advice for students and employees is to be aware of their surroundings and unsafe work areas. "It should be total awareness all the time," she says.

CHAPTER 5 Using Critical Thinking

STUDENT DISORIENTATION

"Oh, my professor is going to regret messing with me." Aaron vented to Brad, Kristen, Misha, and Carlos.

"What did she do this time?" Brad asked.

"She gave me another project on top of the one I already have to still do, and it is due right before midterms!" Aaron said.

"Why would she just now assign two projects right before a midterm?" Kristen asked.

Aaron shuffled awkwardly. "Well, she didn't assign two just now, but she made them both due at the same time."

"Can you talk to her and get her to give you an extension on the second project or something?" Kristen suggested.

"She is crazy. She won't listen. She's just overloading us with information and expecting us to be able to work like mad people!" Ethan said. "No real teacher would assign this much stuff right before midterms. She is clearly trying to prove herself as this is only her second time teaching this class."

"She's a new teacher?"

"Well, no, just this class, but I overheard one of the other kids saying that ever since her boyfriend left her, she has gotten a lot crazier with homework." Aaron smirked.

"Wait, first you say she is trying to prove herself, now you say she is taking her vengeance out on you because of a bad breakup? Are you sure that's the real reason?" Brad shook his head.

"I don't know or care," Aaron said. "She clearly hates us for some reason and wants us to all die of homework overload."

CHAPTER OBJECTIVES:

- Learning to problem solve

- Applying critical thinking at school

- Overcoming bias to make smart decisions

Every day brings new choices. It begins with what to wear, what to eat for breakfast, and which route to take on the way to school or work. You probably don't waste much energy thinking about these choices; you just make a quick decision and go with it.

Unfortunately, not every decision you'll make will be as easy. In fact, the majority of the decisions you make will need to be thought out carefully. Being able to make a decision based fully on logic is called critical thinking.

Thinking Critically in Your Personal Life

You might not have thought about the decisions you make as critical thinking, but when you make an informed and logical choice, you have used evaluative reasoning skills. As you progress in your college studies and into your chosen career, you will come across various situations that require you to think more critically. The three areas in your personal life where you're most likely to use critical thinking are in solving problems, making judgments, and making decisions.

> **Thinking is skilled work. It is not true that we are naturally endowed with the ability to think clearly and logically – without learning how, or without practicing.**
>
> —Benjamin Franklin

Problem Solving

The truth is everyone has problems; some are more difficult to solve than others. How you handle your problems can make a big difference in how effectively you solve them. In *Cut to the Chase: and 99 Other Rules to Liberate Yourself and Gain Back the Gift of Time*, former Dale Carnegie CEO Stuart Levine writes, "If you're making a lot of different mistakes, you're learning. If you're making the same mistake more than once, you're wasting time. Successful people learn from their mistakes right away and don't repeat them."

If you look at your problem as a growth opportunity rather than as a problem, you are well on your way to achieving a successful solution. While some people handle problem solving better than others, everyone can learn to use critical thinking to bring their issues to a successful resolution.

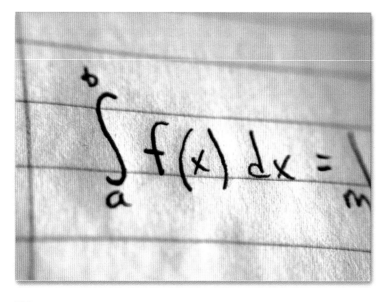

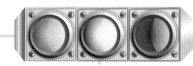

ETHICAL DILEMMA

After review time, you did not get a raise. You evaluate the situation and realize you're never on time, which could have been a factor. You have to take your son to school before you go to work, and he can't be dropped off before 8 a.m. You're supposed to be at work at 8 a.m., but it's actually closer to 8:15 a.m. by the time you get there every day. You ask your boss for flexible hours and communicate your problem completely, making sure she understands you tried other solutions first. She says no and is not willing to negotiate. What do you do?

Scan the code for additional information or visit: *http://bit.ly/TC5ED*

a.) Quit. Your son comes first, and if your boss is not willing to be flexible about a few minutes, then the job just isn't worth it.

b.) Ask the boss in a non-confrontational way what she would do in this situation. Maybe she has some alternative ideas you haven't thought of before.

c.) Go to your boss's superior, if she has one. Explain the situation there.

d.) Continue being late anyway. The worst she can do is fire you.

Perform a root cause analysis. Here's a simple example: Not getting a pay raise at review time may seem like a problem to you. However, it's actually only a symptom of the problem. Trace the symptom back to the root. Do you habitually come to work late? If so, you've found your root cause. Perhaps you have a boss who makes promises he never keeps. Then the problem may be out of your control. Either way, you must take the next step.

Evaluate the available information. Let's say you didn't get the pay raise you wanted because you are habitually late. Why? Look at what you already know – the reasons behind your tardiness. Perhaps you have to take your son to school before you go to work, and he can't be dropped

🔍 **ON THE WEB**

For more information about problem solving, visit:

http://bit.ly/TC5otw

off before 8 a.m. You're supposed to be at work at 8 a.m., but it's actually closer to 8:15 a.m. by the time you get there every day. Analyze your information and look at possible solutions. Do you have a neighbor you could ask about carpooling? Could your son ride the bus? Could you talk to your employer, explain the situation, and offer to make up those fifteen minutes during lunch or after work?

Critical thinking engages us in looking at the information in the context of the system in which it exists and then in knowing how to distinguish facts from inferences, assumptions, and guesses. You must actively analyze your problems and possible solutions for facts that relate directly to the issue at hand, without allowing assumptions to cloud your view.

Effectively communicate your information to those connected to your problem. You have now identified the problem (I'm always late to work) as opposed to the symptom (I didn't get a raise). You've evaluated your information and looked for solutions. Now you must communicate your problem and prospective solution to those involved. If you plan to ask the neighbor for carpooling help, you will need to explain the situation thoroughly and include the information that you will not be able to take turns driving. Perhaps you can offer to help with gas instead. If you have to ask your boss for flexible hours, communicate your problem completely, making sure your manager understands you tried other solutions first. No matter what happens next, as far as your boss's reaction to the situation, you must make a decision.

Make an informed decision and act on it. If you have taken all the crucial steps to active problem solving, you have now arrived at decision time. If your manager is not willing to allow you to work flexible hours, you must make a decision. Many people struggle with decision making, procrastinating, and avoiding the issues. If you want your situation to change, you must act accordingly, because as the popular saying goes, "For things to change, you must change." Now you are faced with the decision to let things remain the same and accept the status quo or to make a change that is based on your needs.

Information Overload

Hundreds of times a day, our world bombards us with information. Television, radio, the Internet, newsprint, and billboards are all designed to get our attention and cause us to make judgments based on what we see, hear, or read. This product is better. This candidate is more believable and trustworthy. With so much information, how can we draw sound conclusions? Organizational consultant and author Warren Bennis stated, "There is a profound difference between information and meaning." The fact that information can be instantly at your fingertips doesn't mean the information is accurate or that you will use it well, even if it is correct. The key to making accurate judgments is analyzing information, arguments, or positions for logical facts.

Logical Fallacies

Wrong, or fallacious, ways of thinking have also been categorized by philosophers over the years. At times, invalid arguments can appear completely logical, creating a facade of truth that might lead you astray. When you are making judgments, it's very important to understand the difference between valid thinking and fallacious thinking. It's easy to be swayed by a wrong argument unless you are able to think critically and make judgments based on the facts you have analyzed, evaluated, and developed inferences from. The danger of a logical fallacy is that it uses deductive reasoning to arrive at a seemingly logical conclusion. Understanding a few of the logical fallacies will help develop your ability to evaluate and use information.

fallacious

Incorrect or logically unsound

No True Scotsman: The fallacy of presumption is one of the most common. You may hear it referred to on business or news channels such as MSNBC or CNN. The "No True Scotsman" fallacy plays out this way:

- Angus McFadden, a Scotsman from Glasgow, puts sugar on his porridge.

- No true Scotsman puts sugar on his porridge.

- Therefore, Angus cannot be a true Scotsman.

This type of reasoning is called a circular argument, in which you assume an existing belief is true and therefore think anything that does not line up with that belief must be wrong. Rather than looking at the existing belief to see whether it should be adjusted, you accept it to be wholly true and do not allow for differences.

circular argument

An existing belief is true and therefore anything that does not align with the belief must be wrong

▶ EXERCISE 5.1

Read the following paragraph and write out the areas of flawed reasoning in your journal:

The Internet provides a world of information at our fingertips. Previous generations depended solely on print media such as books, newspapers, and magazines for their information. Today, accurate information on practically any subject can be had at the click of a mouse. Because of this, information is better, faster to find, and more up-to-date than ever before. People who still prefer not to use computers are usually operating on faulty information and may not be reliable sources in important discussion.

The Bandwagon Fallacy: This fallacy also could be known as the "everybody's doing it" fallacy. This argument is based on the idea that a theory, fad, or action is correct because most people are attracted to it. However, popularity doesn't make the idea true or morally right. You will have to use your critical thinking, values, and ethics to make wise decisions and avoid this fallacy.

The Genetics Fallacy: This common fallacy occurs when an argument or proposition is rejected or accepted simply on the basis of source. In its most basic form, the fallacy looks like this:

- Mommy says the Tooth Fairy is real.

- The Tooth Fairy is real.

Do not necessarily believe everything from a particular source will be completely true or even untrue just because of who or what the source is.

The Appeal to Tradition: This fallacy appeals to the "we've always done it this way" idea. Tradition does not necessarily provide a sound reason for continuing on a particular course and, in fact, can be a hindrance to progress.

EXERCISE 5.2

Use the Internet to research the topic of logical fallacies. Identify three logical fallacies that are not included in this book. Give an example for each of the three that you identify. Write your answers in your journal; be prepared for class discussion.

All of these fallacies have one thing in common — they make sweeping generalizations. Critical thinkers are able to look at the individual points of any argument or idea and make judgments based on true logic.

Decision Making

What criteria do you typically use to make decisions? Do you have a method? Some decisions just don't need much thought or discussion. A decision such as what to eat for dinner comes easily and usually doesn't carry much consequence, no matter which choice you make, unless you have health issues.

What if your decision is between going into debt for a new car or continuing to spend money on repairs for your old one? Perhaps you have to decide whether to cut back on school hours to work more so you can earn more money, knowing too that the sooner you graduate, the sooner you can get started on your career and potentially make higher wages.

The ability to look forward and see the consequences that will come with the decisions you make is the hallmark of a critical thinker.

Have a strategy. A strategy can help you feel more relaxed when you're faced with a serious choice that brings important, and possibly negative, consequences. Benjamin Franklin, one of the greatest critical thinkers in American history, used a method we now call the "Pro/Con List" to make his decision. He would draw a giant *T* in the middle of a piece of paper. On the left side of the *T*, he would write "pros," and on the right side, he would write "cons." Then he would list the positive points of the matter on the pros side and the negative points on the cons side. When he had thought of every possible reason for and against a particular matter, he would evaluate the list, adding up the pros and the cons. If the pros outweighed the cons, then he would decide for the matter, but if the cons side was longer, then he would not.

Think before you act. This may seem like a no-brainer, but unfortunately, many people fall into the trap of making spur-of-the-moment decisions based on emotion rather than logic. If possible, take yourself

COACH'S CORNER

Decision making is difficult, even for the small things. In Coach's Corner, Coach presents a new decision-making tool: Plus/Minus/Interesting.

http://bit.ly/TC5CCorner

▶ WORKSHEET

Use the following document when making a decision. In the "Pro" section, write all the reasons why you should make the decision. In the "Con" section, write all the reasons why you should not. When you've filled it out as much as you can, take a look at your list. Which side is longer?

For the sample template, scan the QR code or visit: *http://bit.ly/TC5procon*

PRO	CON

away from the situation, especially if the decision involves making a spontaneous buy that will bust your budget. They don't call it buyer's remorse for nothing. Advertising is geared to stir your emotions – cause you to think you "need" something when, most likely, you really don't. If you put the purchase decision on hold for twenty-four hours, you may find the craving you had for those fantastic $100 shoes goes away.

PRO vs. CON
Scan the code for additional information or visit: *http://bit.ly/TC5provcon*

The Pro vs. Con app allows you to make your Pro/Con lists right on your smartphone. You type in arguments for both sides and add values to each argument. At the end, the app reviews the values and lets you know which decision to go for based on your input.

Conduct your due diligence. Making a serious decision, whether it is for a purchase or a life change, would be foolish unless you first conduct thorough research. Websites such as nextag.com and bizrate.com compare prices on merchandise and offer consumer-written reviews. You can read movie reviews at rottentomatoes.com or at fandango.com. Consumersearch.com and consumerreports.org provide professional consumer reports about everything from cars to technology to appliances.

Movies by Flixster
Scan the code for additional information or visit: *http://bit.ly/TC5Movies*

Sometimes you need help even making small decisions like which movie to see this weekend. The Movies app by Flixster with Rotten Tomatoes allows you to watch trailers, read movie reviews from Rotten Tomatoes, and look up showtimes.

Lifehacker (lifehacker.com) offers particularly helpful information on technology, including open-source (meaning free and legal) downloads. You can often download open-source software as an alternative to similar but expensive proprietary versions that you would have to purchase at a tech store. For example, if you don't have money to spend on Microsoft Office but need the word-processing capabilities of Word, try Open Office (available from Openoffice.org), a free word-processing software that includes the same components as Microsoft Office.

A word to the wise: Just because information is on the Internet, that doesn't make it true! Be sure you get your information from reputable sites. If you visit a manufacturer's website, remember the advertising there is biased. Although you may be reading actual testimonials, you can be sure the manufacturer left out any negative comments. The same is true for print advertorials. They may look like full-page articles in a newspaper or magazine, but advertorials are simply paid advertising. While there's nothing wrong with including them in your product research, don't make a buying decision on the basis of the manufacturer's claims alone.

advertorial

An advertisement in a magazine or newspaper that resembles an editorial article

Even if you need to make a decision that doesn't involve a purchase, you still must do your research. When you're trying to choose where to live, research property values and taxes, crime rates, school locations and qualities, distance to your job or classes, and accessibility to shopping areas. If you're interviewing for a job, conduct due diligence on the company. If it is publicly traded, look at its profit and loss statements. How long has the company been in business? How many employees does it have? What opportunities for advancement exist?

No matter what kind of decision you need to make, conducting thorough research and using critical-thinking skills to analyze and evaluate the data you find will help you. The ability to think critically is one of the most important aspects you can develop in your personal life. It will help you save money, choose wisely, avoid most negative consequences, be more satisfied with what you have, and recognize new opportunities when they come along.

Critical Thinking in Education

At one time, educated people believed the Earth was the center of the universe. Any other idea, including that the sun was the actual center of the universe, was considered heretical by the Roman Catholic Church, which was then all-powerful. In the eighteenth century, people thought to be witches were burned at the stake or drowned. At the turn of the nineteenth century, scientists taught that the human body would disintegrate at speeds over twenty-five mph. How did human knowledge ever move past such thinking? The answer, of course, is critical thinking. Discovery of new purposes for proven ideas or correction of wrong ideas comes with investigation – asking the questions "Why?" and "What if?"

" It is the mark of an educated mind to be able to entertain a thought without accepting it. "

—Aristotle

During your studies, you will apply critical-thinking processes in a variety of areas, and you will have to adjust your thought processes to fit the particular subject at any given time. Thinking critically for science is different from thinking critically in literature. You don't apply the same thought processes for creating art that you do for creating music. Any technical field will

require you to learn certain principles and techniques, but knowing how to apply them in different situations and on a variety of equipment will come from the ability to think analytically. The ability to think critically has its basis in intellectual criteria that go beyond subject-matter divisions and that include clarity, credibility, accuracy, precision, relevance, depth, breadth, logic, significance, and fairness.

USE IT OR LOSE IT

As a college student, you will need to develop critical-thinking skills quickly to survive the requirements of your major. Knowing facts and knowing how to apply them are two very different things. The purpose of education should be to teach students to think well and apply the knowledge they've acquired, but unfortunately, at the elementary through high school levels, teachers are required to present so many facts that students have little time to practice critical-thinking skills.

Advances in math, science, and technology, especially in the latter half of the twentieth century, have paved the way in the discovery of new ideas. Yet unless students take time to question the processes and ideas they are learning by delving deeper and going below the surface for more applications, the facts they learn are just that, facts. How much of what you learned in high school history do you think you retained? How many facts do you remember?

Education is a two-part process. When you learn a fact, you internalize it. Unless you use the facts you learn, however, you eventually forget them. When you reflect on a fact, question it, and use it, you have applied the fact. Now you have taken ownership of it.

Socratic Method

Socrates used a given set of questions to engage his students in critical thinking. Whether you're in a science class or a biomedical equipment technology class, the Socratic Method can lead you to further applications of the concepts you will learn. Here are some sample Socratic questions:

- What do you mean by ...? (Fill in the blank with your answer to any given question posed by your teacher or your text.)

- How did you come to that conclusion?

- What was said in the text?

- What is the source of your information?

- What is the source of the information in the report?

- What assumption led you to this conclusion?

- Suppose you are wrong. What are the implications?

- Why did you make that inference? Is another one more consistent with the data?

- Why is this issue significant?

- How do I know what you are saying is true?

- What is an alternative explanation for this phenomenon, process, or result?

Answering the questions of the Socratic Method can help you move beyond the most obvious implication or application of data you learn in the classroom to finding other uses for it.

SOCRATIC METHOD CHECKLIST

When reviewing your research, answer the following questions from the Socratic Method:

- ☐ What was said in the text?
- ☐ What is the source of the information in the report?
- ☐ What assumption led you to this conclusion?
- ☐ Suppose you are wrong. What are the implications?
- ☐ Why did you make that inference? Is another one more consistent with the data?
- ☐ Why is this issue significant?
- ☐ How do I know what you are saying is true?
- ☐ What is an alternative explanation for this phenomenon, process, or result?

▶ EXERCISE 5.3

Write a brief essay on how critical thinking is important to your specific major. Include how you will use it in your classes, and then how you will employ the analytical skills you develop during school in your career.

To participate in the online poll, scan the QR code or visit: *http://bit.ly/TC5Poll*

In what area of your academic life do you find yourself using critical thinking the most?

- ○ Labs
- ○ Homework
- ○ Term papers
- ○ Exams
- ○ Lectures

When determining if a source is credible, look at the author's credentials. Has this person studied the topic or worked in the field for many years? What do other people have to say about him/her, and what he/she has written?

Academic Areas for Critical Thinking

Lectures: To get the most out of your instructor's lectures, you must be an active listener. It's impossible to think analytically if you've let your mind wander during a lecture. Take notes as your instructor talks. Engage in class discussion and ask questions about other applications. Review your lecture notes later to be sure you remember everything you went over in class that day. Take time to reflect on the notes as you review them.

Laboratories: Laboratories are a great place for critical thinking because you will see various scenarios play out before your eyes. It is important you understand not only what the instructor asks you to do, such as combining certain chemicals in chemistry, but also what will happen when you do and why it happens.

Homework: When you do homework assignments, go beyond the most simple answer. Determine why something occurred, and give supporting details when appropriate, using your textbook material or other sources. Evaluate whether the sources you used to answer the question are credible.

Term Papers: Writing a term paper may not be your favorite project, but the experience you gain from it is invaluable. You'll learn how to categorize and document research material, analyze data, evaluate theories, distinguish between primary and secondary resources, and record and expound on the information you gather.

Exams: Exams that ask for more than a simple multiple-choice answer require critical thinking. You'll need to think out an answer before you begin writing, making sure you can support your position with material you've covered without rambling.

Developing the discipline of critical thinking takes continual practice. You must habitually look beyond the obvious to extrapolate deeper meaning before you can fully understand a concept and apply it correctly to various situations you will come across in your career. By the time you leave college, your instructors will have invested themselves in you, teaching you everything they could to prepare you for the career ahead. What you do with the information you've learned – how you use it or don't use it, how you take ownership of it – is all up to you.

Critical Thinking for Your Career

It's the middle of the night. As a biomedical equipment technician, you've been called on an emergency repair to All Saints Hospital for a malfunctioning ultrasound machine. An unborn baby's life depends on you. You look at the equipment. It's a model you've never seen. You open it up and very little looks familiar. What do you do?

Roger Bowles, department chair of the Biomedical Equipment Technology Department at Texas State Technical College Waco, remembers a similar situation early in his career. "I was called out on a Saturday to repair an ATL (now Philips) ultrasound machine that I was not too familiar with," he said. "I had been trained on Toshiba ultrasound machines but not ATL. It turned out that a probe needed replacing. The symptoms are similar for different kinds of ultrasound machines. Once a technician understands the basics of how a particular type of machine works, he or she can apply this knowledge to the same type of machine, no matter who makes it."

You will find the same rule applies to most technical disciplines. Use what you already know to take you through a clear progression of questions and answers, making educated inferences based on your evaluation to arrive at a logical conclusion.

Intuition Versus Critical Thinking

As you gain experience in your career, you may be tempted to rely more on intuition. Be aware that while intuition has its place, it does not replace critical thinking. Intuition relies on what you feel, what you've experienced in the past, or what you expect will happen. Critical thinking deals with facts gained through rationalization, examination, evaluation, and experience. It adheres to relevance, logic, and reliability.

Intuition comes into play more often in people situations than in technological situations. In other words, intuition is important in understanding how to manage your workforce or how to approach various customer-service situations. However, in technological situations, rely on critical thinking to solve your problem.

Check Your Ego at the Door, Please

Critical thinking must take place in the absence of personal wants and desires. Biases, preformed opinions, stereotypes, and prejudices have no place in critical thinking and certainly do not belong in the workplace. In his article "The Path to Critical Thinking," Steven Robbins of the Harvard Business School writes, "When insecurity, ego, and panic drive decisions, companies become toxic and may even die. Just look at all the corporate meltdowns over the last five years to quickly understand where emotional decision making can lead."

Managers are not immune to the pitfalls of emotional decision making and must be aware that personal biases can cloud judgment, leading to unfair treatment, discontent, and low morale. Stereotyping – whether of ethnic groups, genders, religions, or anything else – creates a hostile work environment. If you are a manager, or ever plan to rise to that position in your career, make a practice of setting aside bias. For a company to move forward, managers must employ critical thinking to stay on track and focus on long-term goals.

Biases, of course, are not all related to other people. A person's own cognitive bias (or skewed thinking) can keep him or her from interpret-

> " Too often we hold fast to the clichés of our forebears. ... We enjoy the comfort of opinion without the discomfort of thought. "
>
> — Former President John F. Kennedy

When making a decision based on critical thinking rather than intuition, try taking yourself out of the mix. Imagine someone else is faced with the decision and come up with possible solutions he or she might come up with.

ing data correctly, hearing other viewpoints, or making wise decisions. The following cognitive biases are a few of the areas where employees and managers need to be on guard:

- **Inertia:** unwillingness to change thought patterns we've used in the past, even in the face of new data

- **Experiential limitations:** unwillingness to look beyond our past experiences, hurts, or rejections

- **Wishful thinking:** choosing always to see things in a positive light, which can skew perception of facts

- **Groupthink:** peer pressure to conform to the opinions of the majority

- **Premature termination of evidence search:** accepting the first likely explanation or first alternative

- **Selective evidence search:** gathering evidence that supports a bias, leaving out the evidence that would support an opposite position

▶ EXERCISE 5.4

Refer to the long-term goals you set in Chapter 1. How will critical-thinking skills help you meet your goals? What if you don't apply critical-thinking skills? What kinds of pitfalls could keep you from accomplishing your goals? Use your journal to log your answers.

Conclusion

Critical-thinking skills can make or break a career. It's that simple. People who develop and practice the discipline of analytical thinking advance in their careers, while those who think mostly in survival mode normally do not advance. It's tempting to take the intellectually lazy way out – look for the quickest solution, the most obvious answer, the easiest repair. Critical thinking requires going to the root cause.

Critical thinking cannot simply be taught; it must be learned by a willing student. Remembering the skills used in critical thinking will help you learn the right techniques so you can develop the discipline of analytical thinking in all areas of your life: personal, education, and professional.

Further Reading

The Little Blue Reasoning Book: 50 Powerful Principles for Clear and Effective Thinking by Brandon Royal. Maven Publishing: 2010.

Problem Solving 101: A Simple Book for Smart People by Ken Watanabe. Portfolio Hardcover: 2009.

REVIEW QUESTIONS | What did you LEARN?

1. What is an advertorial?

2. What is a circular argument?

3. What are some examples of logical fallacies? Define them in your own words.

4. What do all fallacies have in common?

5. How is a pro/con list helpful?

6. What are the questions you should ask in the Socratic Method?

7. What are some areas in your academics that you can apply critical thinking?

8. Why should you try to make decisions based on critical thinking rather than intuition?

9. How can a bias affect making a decision?

10. What are some kinds of cognitive biases?

Scan this code to access the puzzle online or visit: *http://bit.ly/TC5Crword*

Across

1. If you have taken all the crucial steps to active problem solving, you have now arrived at _____ time.

3. Knowing facts and knowing how to _____ them are two very different things.

6. What app has Rotten Tomatoes and allows you to watch trailers, read movie reviews, and look up showtimes?

7. Who said, "It is the mark of an educated mind to be able to entertain a thought without accepting it "?

9. What creates a hostile work environment?

13. Being able to make a decision based fully on logic is called what? (2 words)

14. If something is "open-source," that means it is free and what else?

17. An advertisement in a magazine or newspaper that resembles an editorial article

18. The danger of a logical fallacy is that it uses _____ reasoning to arrive at a logical conclusion.

19. Unless you _____ the facts you learn, you eventually forget them.

20. Who said, "Too often we hold fast to the clichés of our forebears. ... We enjoy the comfort of opinion without the discomfort of thought"?

Down

2. An existing belief is true and therefore anything that does not align with that belief must be wrong (2 words)

4. To get the most out of your instructor's lectures, you must be an active _____.

5. The key to making accurate judgments is analyzing _____.

8. All of the fallacies mentioned in the book make sweeping _____.

10. At the turn of the nineteenth century, scientists taught that the human body would disintegrate at speeds over _____ mph.

11. The ability to think _____ is one of the most important aspects you can develop in your personal life.

12. Incorrect or logically unsound

15. _____ does not necessarily provide a sound reason for continuing on a particular course and, in fact, can be a hindrance to progress.

16. Just because information is on the _____, that doesn't make it true!

JUDY CARR
Department Chair for Psychology and Sociology

Scan this code for additional info
or visit: *http://bit.ly/TC5JCarr*

Thinking Critically:
The Ultimate Tool for Success

"The potential is limitless." This is how Judy Carr, department chair for psychology and sociology, views her students. She practices critical thinking on a daily basis and encourages her students to do the same.

Carr received her bachelor's degree in psychology and sociology at Southwest Baptist University in 1982, and her master's degree in sociology at Arkansas State University in 1984. While working on her doctoral degree (2000-2003) at Forest Institute in Springfield, Missouri, she became the division chair.

In addition to teaching twelve hours a semester, Carr holds the position of division chair, acting as a communication liaison between full-time faculty members and the office of academic affairs. On top of that, Carr advises more than fifty students. "The students are the reason I exist here, and my core job is to ensure they receive a top quality education. Sometimes when I am stressed about the administrative side to this job, I have to step back and remember why I decided to teach: the students. They give my life great challenge and great meaning. I love what I do."

Critical thinking plays an important role not only in Carr's life, but also in her way of teaching as well. "I want my students to think from multiple perspectives and see life in more than two dimensions. Critical thinking is a tool I use in classes to help students see the applications of psychology and sociology in their daily lives."

Her role as an educator gives her the perfect opportunity to pass on her understanding of critical thinking and the important role it plays in everyday life. "I believe all students benefit from education. Education is the great equalizer. It cannot be taken away, once received. Critical thought has a chance to flower and bloom within educational opportunities."

Carr is in touch with the core value of teaching – giving students the opportunity to figure things out for themselves. "When you can engage a student in a conversation that leads them to the answer to a problem they are trying to solve, they feel like they have the tools necessary to do this again and again. Question everything! Do not take things for their face value. Look at things around you in a different light. If they practice critical thinking, the potential is limitless."

CHAPTER 6

Doing the Research

STUDENT DISORIENTATION

"How could he give you a D, Misha?" Aaron asked, puzzled.

"I don't know!" Misha said, nearly sobbing. "I've never gotten anything but an A before!"

Misha couldn't believe how horrible this teacher was. He had written "Where are your sources?" on her paper in big red letters right below the circled D. He gave her a D on her paper all because she didn't write where she got her information from? It was just ridiculous. She got all the information perfect; she knew she did. Everything was beautifully written and factually spot-on. Why did her teacher care where she got her information? If it was right, it was right.

"You want sources? I'll give you sources!" Misha said as she sat down to her computer.

She typed in her project topic into a search engine and started copying and pasting links that looked even remotely related to her topic without thoroughly checking them or formatting them.

"Ha!" Misha smiled in triumph. "There, plenty of sources, and the information is just fine. I'll turn it in now."

Misha attached her now certainly perfect paper to an email and sent it off, eagerly anticipating her new grade of an A.

CHAPTER OBJECTIVES:

- Researching before big purchases

- Conducting academic research

- Joining professional associations

Suppose you want to buy a used car. How will you know you're getting the best deal? How can you be sure you're not being charged too much? What if the car came from an area devastated by a hurricane and has flood damage? Knowing how to think critically can help you evaluate information, but if you don't know where to go to gather your information, you might as well be throwing darts in the dark.

Because of the Internet, information can be had easily, but you must know where to look. Whether you're planning a personal purchase, researching a topic for a school term paper, or looking for information to help you do your job better, knowing how to research a topic effectively will empower you to make decisions from a place of knowledge, rather than speculation.

Research in Your Personal Life

Consumer research is nothing new. Arthur Nielsen pioneered the field of consumer research as a statistical science when he founded the ACNielsen Company in 1923, then later the A. C. Nielsen Center for Marketing Research. Consumers want assurances that they are buying a great product, and salespeople have always relied on advertisements to help convince the public to buy. From snake oil salespeople who planted "repeat customers" in the crowd to the highly sophisticated television infomercials of today, advertising drives sales.

Fortunately, today's consumer doesn't have to rely solely on what a given company says about its product. With the enormous amount of information available on the Internet, along with print advertisements and consumer reviews, more people than ever have access to databases, reports, reviews, and product comparisons.

❝ Research is formalized curiosity. It is poking and prying with a purpose. ❞

—Zora Neale Hurston

The Pew Internet and American Life Project, a producer of "reports that explore the impact of the Internet on families, communities, work and home, daily life, education, health care, and civic and political life," found that 66 percent of Internet users have purchased something online at least once. Additionally, the "Customer Focus: Decade of Data" study found that "in 2004, 31 percent of adults indicated they entered a store without any prior research; this number is down to 17 percent in 2008. Before entering a store in 2008, the study indicates approximately 57 percent of adults will look through advertising circulars, 50 percent will conduct research on the Internet, and 38 percent will utilize catalogs to retrieve additional information."

ShopScanner

Scan the code for additional information or visit: *http://bit.ly/TC6SScanner*

Shop smarter using scanner apps like ShopScanner. The ShopScanner app lets you compare millions of products for local deals.

A wise consumer will take advantage of the material available before committing to a big expenditure. It's important to understand, however, that the value of research is not limited only to helping you decide where to spend your dollars. Personal research should be conducted before choosing a professional to do work for hire, before deciding where to live, and even before making a choice on vacation spots. Having an organized system in mind for conducting your research will help you stay focused and keep you from feeling overwhelmed by the amount of information available.

COACH'S CORNER

It's important to do research before making any large purchase. In Coach's Corner, Coach gives you tips on how to avoid buyer's remorse with big purchases and get all the information you need.

http://bit.ly/TC6CC

CONDUCTING YOUR RESEARCH

Let's imagine you want to buy a home surround-sound system. Many brands exist, all with different specifications (specs), limitations, and prices.

Before researching a topic, break the topic into manageable pieces. Make a spreadsheet. Across the top of the spreadsheet, write down the surround-sound brands you are considering. To the left, begin listing the various details that will help you decide. Start with price, then go through the remaining specs, such as wattage, warranty, and recommended room size. Now you have a clearly organized way of managing the information as you gather it.

Use a concentric circle method for conducting your research. Begin in the center by going directly to the website of the manufacturers of the various surround-sound systems you want to consider. Read all the specs and fill in your spreadsheet as you go, making notes to the side (still on your spreadsheet, so you don't have to look for your notes later) of which models most impress you. Remember any reviews you find on the manufacturer's site will be slanted, or biased, toward the manufacturer.

Now widen your circle. Look for product reviews on the brands you liked. The most effective way to do this, of course, is

▶ EXERCISE 6.1

Imagine that you plan to make a big purchase, perhaps an appliance or some type of technology. Decide what your purchase will be, and then make a spreadsheet as described in the "Conducting Your Research" section of this chapter. You can do the spreadsheet on the computer or by hand, but put a copy of it in your journal.

Beyond Buying

As you practice organized, efficient research methods, you will find the skills come more easily to you, and you'll find other uses for personal research. In fact, you will most likely get to the point where you're uncomfortable making any decision you have not thoroughly researched. Emotion-based decisions frequently bring regret and negative consequences,

on the Internet. If you don't have access at home, go to a public or campus library. Read through the reviews, making notes as various comments impress you, either positively or negatively. Even if you already had a product picked out, keep an open mind. You want to be sure you're getting the most for your money.

Now, widen your circle even more. If you know someone who has purchased the system you are leaning toward buying, ask to see and hear the system in that person's home. Remember, however, the sound quality of any system can vary widely according to how the user has it set up and how big the room is. Go to the electronics store that sells the product you want. If they have it set up, ask a salesperson to walk you through all the various settings and elements.

Once you've narrowed down your favorite choices, check pricing. Many online stores offer sales or rebates that their big-box counterparts do not. Nextag and Bizrate both offer price comparisons that are helpful. Once you've compared the reviews and pricing, you're ready to make a decision on which product will best fit your budget. Knowing how to research a product effectively before you make a decision will give you peace of mind and help you avoid buyer's remorse.

while well-researched, deeply analyzed decisions build confidence and are more likely to bring lasting satisfaction.

Efficient research practices will help you in many areas of your personal life. If you need to hire a professional, such as a lawyer, personal research will help ensure you find someone who meets your needs. Even though lawyers can solicit business, the best way to find a lawyer is through a referral. Your state bar offers lawyer referral services and answers general legal questions.

For help finding the right medical professionals to suit your needs or to get medical questions answered, ask friends and family who they visit or research reviews people leave online about their experiences. Thinking about relocating after you graduate from college? Research the cost of living, crime rates, and quality of life in various cities. Perhaps you'd like to find the best savings rate for your money market account, or maybe you'd like some investment advice. Try Bank of America, Bankrate.com, or Fool.com.

Of course, some people still prefer to use traditional research, such as books, newsprint, and advertorials. If you choose this route, keep in mind you may not be getting access to the most up-to-date or reliable sources, as information can change in real time on the Internet.

As you review the item you're looking to buy, also review the companies selling it. Sometimes it's better to spend a little bit more money on a company you trust than to go for the best deal with a company you've never heard of.

Research in Your Education Career

Your level of success in college will be greatly affected by your ability to research and use information well. Many of your classes will include homework that requires research. Just as in your personal life, knowing where to find the most accurate information for your project will make your task easier.

As a college or university student, you have access to your campus library, which has access to many other libraries and thus can share resources. Databases your campus library can access offer everything from literature to archival information to technical journals. Many of the articles and books in these databases can be read in their entirety online, but you will need your library card number to access the databases.

When you have a research assignment, you will most likely need books as well as online resources. This means you must be able to use your library and the Internet equally well. If you are not familiar with how your library is set up, now is a good time to check things out. Generally, here's what you can expect to find:

- Libraries are usually divided into fiction and nonfiction categories.

- Some nonfiction books are categorized as reference and cannot be checked out. You will need to make copies of any material you want from a reference.

- You can use the library's computerized catalog to find books by subject, title, or author.

When you go to the library to conduct research, be sure to take a notebook for jotting down information, change for the copy machine, and your library card. The reference librarian will be able to help you locate books or use the online catalog.

When you begin your research, start broad. Gather general information from a source such as an encyclopedia. A general source such as an encyclopedia is called a **tertiary source** because it is a compilation of information from various sources.

Search for books on your topic. Using the library's online catalog, enter keywords related to your topic. Next, go into the records and find the actual subject headings. Redo your search using a subject search with the subject heading to refine your search and locate things you may have missed before. Books that quote experts in a given field are called **secondary sources**. Once you've located the book, review the index to

> " Research is creating new knowledge. "
>
> —Neil Armstrong

tertiary source

A collection of primary and secondary sources, such as in encyclopedias, almanacs, and directories

secondary source

An evaluation, discussion, and/or interpretation of a primary source, such as biographies, history books, and journal articles see if it has the information you are looking for. Don't forget to also pick up other books that might be related to your topic, even if not directly related.

Look for newspaper, *professional journal*, and magazine articles. Your library will have both online and print articles you can search and make copies of. These sources are called primary sources because they are at the time under study (such as historical events) by someone who experienced, was involved, or witnessed the event; it's an inside view into an event.

professional journal

A periodical or magazine published by a professional organization, society, or group

To participate in the online poll, scan the QR code or visit: *http://bit.ly/TC6RPoll*

How do you organize your research?

○ Index/note cards

○ Microsoft Excel or similar software

○ Word document or notebook

○ Sticky notes

APT APPS! AccessMyLibrary

Scan the code for additional information or visit: *http://bit.ly/TC6Mylib*

Access your school library on the go with the AccessMyLibrary School Edition App from Gale Cengage Learning. The app allows you to access journals, articles, and other credible sources from your library's database.

Evaluate the information you find. Consider the scope and comprehensiveness of the information you find. Identify the source of the information and evaluate the reputation of the author. Is he or she an expert in the field? What sources did he or she use in his or her research? Take into account how timely the information is. Make sure you are using the most up-to-date information, especially if you are researching a topic that changes often.

RESEARCH PAPER CHECKLIST

Use this checklist to verify you have covered all your bases on your research paper.

☐ Have I covered all possible topics?

☐ Have I noted where all my information came from?

☐ Have I verified that my sources are all credible?

☐ Have I organized my notes?

☐ Have I cited all of my sources according to the style my teacher professor assigned?

ETHICAL DILEMMA

You've just stayed up all night working on a research paper, and you are exhausted. You realize you've cited most but not all of your sources. Rereading your paper, you realize you can't remember what information came from which source. What do you do?

Scan the code for additional information or visit: *http://bit.ly/TC6ED*

a.) Make an educated guess based on the main subject of the book. It's too late and you're too tired to stay up several more hours hunting down specifics.

b.) Make up sources for the ones you are lacking. Your professor will probably just be looking to see you have sources and not necessarily if they're real or credible.

c.) Go through your notes thoroughly to find the correct sources for the citations.

d.) Turn in the paper as-is with the few sources you do have cited.

Most teachers and professors will not accept Wikipedia as a legitimate source, so don't try putting that on your works cited page. However, articles within Wikipedia often have a works cited or bibliography section you can use to aid in your research.

Cite your source. Anytime you refer to information you did not originate, even if you are not directly quoting that information, you must cite your source. Your instructor may require you to use a specific style guide, such as *The Chicago Manual of Style*, American Psychological Association (APA), or Modern Language Association (MLA). The University of Purdue's Online Writing Lab offers excellent tutorials on how to cite sources, write a thesis statement, organize your information, and adhere to grammar conventions. The lab also has a section specifically for writing in engineering fields.

Organizing Your Research

It's important for you to keep your research organized and be able to trace your notes to the correct source for documentation purposes. Using a simple system each time you have a research project will make your assignment easier.

Number all of your sources sequentially. Use note cards to take notes from each source. Number each of your note cards with the number from the corresponding source, then subhead the card with an alphabetic character. For example, the first note card from source 1 would be 1A. On each note card, be sure to include the page number where the information was located in its corresponding source.

ON THE WEB

For information about citing your sources and organizing your paper, visit:

http://bit.ly/TC6owl

If you create an outline before beginning your paper, which is advised, write the associated note card numbers next to each point of your outline. For example, if one of your points is "History of Avionics" and your note card labeled 3C addresses this point, write it to the side. Now you will have a reference for locating your information as you organize your paper.

Finally, as you write your paper, place a big check mark on each card as you use the information from it. This way, you will know you have incorporated all of your information in the appropriate places.

If you would rather keep your research notes on your laptop computer than on note cards, you can use Microsoft Excel, the free Open Office Calc, or a similar spreadsheet program to set up a table with columns for each source, notes from each source, full publication information (include page numbers) for each source, and notes on when and where in your outline and in your research paper you used each note.

▶ WORKSHEET

Use the following worksheet to help organize your notes for a research project.

For the sample template, scan the QR code or visit:
http://bit.ly/TC6ws

	Location Found (URL/ Library/Etc.)	Full Publication Information	Notes	When/Where in Outline
Source A				
Source B				
Source C				
Source D				

Write a three-page research paper about your major. Use five sources. At least one source must be a professional journal and at least one source must be a book. You may not use Wikipedia or any encyclopedia as a source, although you may want to start your general research with either of those. Your remaining three sources can come from print or the Internet. Follow the citation style described in the MLA style guide (found at http://owl.english.purdue.edu) to cite your sources.

If you have trouble at any time during your research process, be sure to make use of your librarians' services. In the day of the super-fast information highway, many young people look at books and libraries as obsolete. The truth is, your librarian is trained in research methods and will be as comfortable searching the book stacks as the Internet for information. He or she will have ideas on how to narrow your search and hone in on exactly the information you need.

Research in Your Professional Career

> *"If we knew what it was we were doing, it would not be called research, would it?"*
>
> —Albert Einstein

You will find that the research and study skills you have developed on campus are just as necessary in the professional world, although for different purposes. Throughout your career, you will be confronted with situations you did not train for in college. The equipment you use in your technical laboratory sessions today may be outdated by the time you graduate. How will you be able to stay on top of your market once you have left the classrooms and laboratories of your college?

Staying connected to your professional field will be the key to your long-term success. Consider this: Would you want a surgeon who has never attended any continuing-education classes or seminars to learn about new surgical procedures operating on you? What about an anesthetist who has not learned to use the more technologically advanced anesthesia delivery systems? Would you want that person to be in charge of safely putting

you under for surgery? Many students feel that when they graduate from college, they are finished with learning. In reality, they're just beginning.

Professional Associations

According to a recent study published by Park University's International Center for Civic Engagement, it is the heart of a professional association's mission to improve the quality or conditions of their members' professions or organizations. Holding membership in a professional organization gives you a stamp of credibility. It indicates that you stay connected to new developments in your field and that you adhere to a certain professional code of ethics associated with your career.

Moreover, being a member of a professional association may offer you benefits, such as travel discounts, reduced insurance costs, and coupons. Many organizations offer conferences and seminars that will keep you abreast of changes in your field and, at the same time, provide fun getaways. Networking within your organization is important because you may find new job opportunities in your field. Additionally, some organizations offer professional certifications. Because certifications indicate you hold higher credentials and are willing to take the exams or classes required to hold that credential, your value as an employee increases. Some occupations have more than one professional organization available, so you'll need to use your research and critical-thinking skills to evaluate which association will best suit your needs.

Don't Put Off Until Tomorrow

You may be thinking you'll have to wait until you graduate to find a professional organization, but many associations offer student chapters. Joining a student chapter now may increase your chances of quickly finding a job in your desired field. Chapter membership also shows potential employers that you want to be part of a team, a quality more employers seek today than at any time in the past.

Meet people working in your field of interest. This is especially true when you join a group that has a chapter at your school or in your community. You'll get to know a host of people who could be potential mentors in your career development.

Learn about job or internship openings. Often, you'll find out about these opportunities before they're made public. By simply keeping your ears open at group meetings – or, increasingly, on group Internet-based discussion forums – you'll pick up leads on people and organizations that are hiring.

Understand trends in the field. Professional groups, because they have a vested interest in being so, tend to be on the cutting edge of issues affecting your field and thus you. By attending a professional organization's meetings and conferences, reading its publications, and networking with its members, you'll know more about what's going on in your field than most students and new graduates do.

Polish your communication and presentation skills. Your first job interview is not the place to learn the social skills you'll need to thrive in the world of work. Better to practice your interpersonal skills at more casual and less stressful professional association meetings.

Prove that your future career really matters to you. Relatively speaking, few college students join professional associations, and even fewer become actively involved in them. So when you do, you'll automatically stand out as someone who is truly motivated and genuinely interested in the field.

Joining a professional group is easy and, in many cases, quite inexpensive when you're a college student. It's just a matter of finding the right group, signing up, and participating when you can. You may not be able to attend the group's national conference, but you'll certainly be able to participate in campus and local events sponsored by the group.

To find a professional association matching your interests and career goals, do the following:

- Meet with a career counselor at your school.

- Talk to your professors.

- Contact people who work in your field of interest and ask them what local and national professional associations they belong to.

- Look on campus for professional organization sponsored campus-based student organizations.

- Use the Web.

Professional Journals

Subscribing to professional journals is a great way to stay on top of changes in your field. If you choose to become a member of a professional organization, you may receive a subscription at a reduced rate or perhaps for free. However, you don't have to be a member of an organization to subscribe to most professional journals. Many times your employer will pay for your subscription (and even your organization dues) because the company will benefit from employees who can change with the times.

Professional journals provide excellent research materials when you need help solving a tricky problem at work. No matter what field you go into, knowing where to easily find and how to efficiently use information specific to your field will make you a stronger employee. Check with the reference librarian at your campus library for a list of professional journals and magazines that fit your field.

Forums, RSS Feeds, and Email Discussion Lists

Another way to research changes in your field is to use the Internet. Forums, RSS feeds, and email discussion lists all provide up-to-date information provided by professionals and experts in various occupations.

Forums

If you have not previously used Internet groups, other than for social networking, you may be unfamiliar with some of the terms applied to the various groups. A moderator generally oversees the forum, and there are posted rules as to conduct and topics allowed. Messages within the forum will be divided into threads according to subject headings. Most forums require registration to be a member (most professional forums will fall into this category), and registration is quite often free. Typically, for each message you read, you will be able to post a reply. Then other people may reply to your post. If you have a specific question (for example, you need to know something about repairing a particular piece of equipment) you can begin a new thread by posting your question. Other people will then reply.

ON THE WEB

Visit Lifehacker for several free downloadable RSS readers:

http://bit.ly/TC6Lhacker

RSS Feeds

RSS (Really Simple Syndication) is a family of Web feed formats used to publish frequently updated content such as blog entries, news content, and headlines. The document content, called a feed, will contain either a summary of content or complete copy. RSS feeds are a great way to keep up with the news from your favorite websites and blogs, whether of professional or personal interest. Various websites offer RSS feeds, but you must subscribe to the feed and have news-reader software, which is free. Look for the RSS icon beside the URL of the site you're visiting.

Email Lists

A mailing list server manages email lists for groups of users. For instance, if you were a member of an organization devoted to graphic design news and information, being on the organization's email list means you will receive news and timely information directly in your email inbox from the email list and that you can reply to the entire list or to individual subscribers to the list.

Using the Internet, search for forums and RSS feeds that are related to your major. In your journal, make a list of five forums and feeds for your career.

Conclusion

As you review various websites, professional journals, and associations, you will begin to find the ones that are the best fit for you. If you can join or subscribe to any of these now, while you're still a student, you should. Since the Internet groups are free, you can easily unsubscribe later if you find that some of them don't fit your situation. Remember that even though your instructors will walk you through many technical scenarios during your laboratory assignments, there is no possible way to teach you everything you will ever need to know in your career field. Taking ownership of your career by investing time in continuing-education courses, staying current with changing techniques and technologies, and networking with other professionals will contribute greatly to long-term success and longevity in your career.

Further Reading

A Manual for Writers of Research Papers, Theses, and Dissertations, Seventh Edition: Chicago Style for Students and Researchers by Kate L. Turabian. University of Chicago Press: 2007.

The Craft of Research, 3rd Edition by Wayne C. Booth, Gregory G. Colomb, Joseph M. Williams. University of Chicago Press: 2008.

1. Why should you break the topic you are researching into manageable pieces?

2. How should you begin your research at the library?

3. What source can never be used in a research paper?

4. What are three kinds of style guides?

5. How can you organize your research?

6. Why should you join a professional association?

7. What are some benefits of joining professional associations as a student?

8. Why are professional journals helpful?

9. What are RSS feeds? How are they useful?

10. What is a benefit of joining a professional email discussion list?

Scan this code to access the puzzle online or visit: *http://bit.ly/TC6Crword*

Across

1. You may think you'll have to wait until you graduate to join a professional organization, but many associations offer ____. (2 words)

4. Evaluations, discussions, and/or interpretations of primary sources, such as biographies, history books, and journal articles (2 words)

10. What app helps you access journals, articles, and other credible sources from your library's database?

12. Gather general information from a book like an ____.

14. Your state ____ offers lawyer referral services and answers general legal questions.

17. A collection of primary and secondary sources, such as in encyclopedias, almanacs, and directories (2 words)

18. Most teachers and professors will not accept ____ as a legitimate source.

20. Who said, "Research is formalized curiosity. It is poking and prying with a purpose"?

Down

2. A periodical or magazine published by a professional organization, society, or group (2 words)

3. What app helps you compare millions of products for local deals?

5. What is a family of Web feed formats used to publish frequently updated content?

6. A mailing list server manages ____ lists for groups of users.

7. Holding membership in a professional organization gives you a stamp of ____.

8. Take into account how ____ the information is, especially if you are researching a topic that changes often, like technology.

9. A ____ generally oversees a forum.

11. ____ sources were created or written during the time under study by someone who experienced, was involved, or witnessed the event.

13. Who said, "Research is creating new knowledge"?

15. Information can change in ____ on the Internet.

16. Efficient ____ practices will help make sure your information is accurate in your personal life.

19. What should you do when you refer to information you did not originate when writing a paper?

STEVEN MOSS
English Department Professor & Assistant Chair

Scan this code for additional info
or visit: *http://bit.ly/TC6SMoss*

Looking for
Patterns When Researching

How do the NASA program and racial relations relate to one another? In 1997, Associate Professor and Assistant Department Chair Steven Moss explained the connection in his history thesis "NASA and Racial Equality in the South, 1961-1968."

"The popular and political influence of NASA affected Southern segregated states and communities in very different ways depending on the economic influence," Moss says. "No Southern state or community was willing to give up federal dollars or something as prestigious as NASA," he explains. Segregated communities accepted the integrated workforce that accompanied the NASA program.

Moss certainly didn't pick an easy topic. "Not only had the subject not been drained dry, it hadn't been drained at all," he says. "Apparently I was the only person who had ever written on this academically." He did, however, pick a topic that interested him, which Moss says is the first step in any research project.

"You must have some idea of what you want to write about. The shotgun approach will waste a lot of time." According to Moss, students should also be open to serendipity. "If you see a pattern developing on something, maybe that's where you should go."

While researching Project Gemini in graduate school, Moss began finding short one- and two-paragraph stories in newspaper articles connecting NASA, the South, and the Civil Rights Movement. He saw "a pattern developing" and dug deeper into the topic. The result was an original, extensively researched thesis.

According to Moss, another key to research success is time. "You have to be willing to spend time on it – whether it's in the library, in an archive, or online," he says. "You'll find a lot of material you'll never use, but maybe it will help you understand the stuff you do use."

Moss' research paid off. In 2008, he was contacted by radio documentarian Richard Paul to supply information for a three-part documentary, "Out of this World," which aired on NPR in 2010.

Outside of his thesis, Moss encounters research on a daily basis inside college classrooms or behind his desk. Moss has been teaching two developmental English classes that focus on reading. He has also conducted research for both the college and the English department in developmental education. "I find new ways of teaching and what other people are doing around the country," Moss says. His research involves such areas as campus operating procedures and state education guidelines and policy.

Moss encourages students to use the Internet as a resource, but not as a crutch. Look for authoritative websites such as those ending in .gov and .edu. "And don't trust Wikipedia," Moss warns. He also advises the correct documentation of sources, and above all, he encourages students to trust their instincts.

"Sometimes you find information that doesn't meet your preconception." In the end – whether you're a student or professor – Moss says, "It's not about the project; it's what you learn from creating it that's going to be important later on."

Notes

STUDENT DISORIENTATION

Organization had never been one of Carlos' strong suits. Unless things grew legs and walked from his desk, he generally knew where things were. He just sometimes had to look harder for it.

Lately, though, Carlos couldn't go five minutes without losing an important piece of paper from class or losing a quiz sheet he was supposed to turn in for a grade. His notes were a jumble of just random thoughts as he heard things in class. It was only two weeks until dead week before finals, and he couldn't find a single organized set of notes to get prepared. He didn't have any of his old quizzes or tests to go back through and hadn't recorded any of his lectures.

"Misha, please tell me you took notes," Carlos begged. "I just need to copy them down really quickly."

"Of course I took notes. You can have them, but I need them for tomorrow's class, so write quickly."

He copied down everything he could before she left to go to sleep. That took care of one of his multiple classes.

He brought the stack of notes he had taken from Misha's, and looked around his apartment hopelessly. Where was he going to put these notes? If he just set them somewhere, they were going to get lost in the piles and piles of junk and papers that he had lost beforehand. He was doomed. No materials to study, no way to get any more, and nowhere to keep what little he had.

CHAPTER OBJECTIVES:

- Keeping track of your records and documents

- Taking notes for class

- Writing in your field

Think back. What were you doing on this exact day two years ago? You don't remember? How about last year? If you're like most people, your life is so busy you barely remember what you did yesterday. What if you needed to be able to remember something you did or an event from your past? What if you needed to be able to produce important documents, such as tax records, bank statements, or a vaccination record? Keeping track of your personal life through written documentation and an organized filing system can save time and frustration, as well as help you remember important events in your past.

Personal Record Keeping

It's rather ironic that in the digital age, despite a stronger push than ever for our society to go paperless, our mailboxes are filled with more paper than at any time in the past – credit card offers, mortgage or rent invoices, bank statements, tax documents, payroll and benefits information, and junk mail. The stream of mail seems endless, and the temptation to toss it all is great. However, many of these papers are extremely important and must become a part of your regular personal record keeping.

> Can't find your passport? The warranty for your camera? The receipt for those too-small Jimmy Choos? Organized papers means less anxiety, less clutter, and more control.
>
> —Julie Morgenstern from *O, the Oprah Magazine* article "Wait! It Was Here a Minute Ago"

Why Keep Track?

Documenting important data from your life can prevent confusion or conflict later. Many of the documents in your mailbox – such as interest or dividend statements, mortgage statements, even utility bills if you use any portion of your home for business purposes – have tax implications. You'll need to be able to find these at the end of the year. Purchase receipts and charitable donation records are important for taxes too. If you're planning to buy a home, your mortgage company may require you to produce six months' worth of bank statements. If you want to rent a new apartment, you may be required to produce past rent receipts to prove timely payment. For your child to play T-ball, you'll need to prove he or she is current on required vaccinations. If you want a passport, you'll need to prove you are current on vaccinations.

Many people don't consider the consequences of poor record keeping and therefore face more stress and aggravation than necessary. For exam-

ple, let's say you have a credit card bill that you pay online. Every time you schedule the payment, you print the confirmation page and keep it in a file. One month, you receive a billing statement showing the company never received your last payment. Now you have a $35 late fee, plus an extra $150 in finance charges. Because you wisely kept a record of your payment confirmation, you can quickly pull it up and fax it to your credit card company, saving yourself the late fee and interest charges. If you had neglected to keep that record, you would only have your word the payment was sent electronically, and your word, in this instance, would not be good enough.

How to Keep Track

With all the record keeping you need to do, how do you keep from getting overwhelmed? It doesn't really matter if you keep a record of important data if you can't find the information when you need it. Remember the 43 Folders system of time management you read about in Chapter 2? You'll need a similar system for organizing your personal documentation, but this time instead of titling your files by the months, you'll need to label them utilities, rent or mortgage, auto insurance, credit card bills, bank statements, tax records, and family records. Let's take a close look at three of these – bank statements, tax records, and family records.

Although many people shred their bank statements once they've looked at them, this is a terrible practice. If there is ever a discrepancy between you and the bank as to your balance, you'll need your past statements to help prove your point. Mortgage and auto lenders may require a bank-statement history, and if you ever get audited by the IRS, you may need at least the last seven years' statements. Always check your statement to be sure everything looks as you expected, then file them in date order.

If you donate items to a nonprofit charity, make an itemized list and request a receipt for your file. You can use this for tax deductions. If you give money to your religious institution or favorite charity, they'll send you a charitable-giving record at the end of the fiscal year. Place it in your Tax Record file because you can claim it as a deduction. If you've received interest payments from investments, keep the form your institution sends you in December because you'll have to claim this interest as income. These are

ON THE WEB

For more information about tax records, visit:

http://bit.ly/TC7irs

just a few of the tax-related documents you may receive. Keeping them all in one folder will make your life much easier when April 15 rolls around.

Keep important documents for each person in your immediate family. You'll want to include vaccine records for your kids, as well as report cards and any important correspondence from your children's teachers or schools. Attach your children's Social Security cards (or a copy of the original if you prefer to keep the originals in your safe deposit box) to their birth certificates with a paper clip for handy retrieval later. In your

An official academic record from a specific school that lists the courses you have completed, your grades, and information such as when you attended

file, include your birth certificate, Social Security card, and passport. You should also keep your college **transcripts** and any reference letters former employers or teachers have written on your behalf. Do the same for your partner.

Regarding college transcripts, you need to know about the Family Educational Rights and Privacy Act (FERPA), a federal law that protects the privacy of your education records. Under this federal law, parents of students younger than eighteen have the right to review their students' education records and request corrections to them. Once you are eighteen or are attending a postsecondary education institution such as college, that right transfers to you. Under FERPA, schools are required to get written permission from you, or from your parents if you are underage, to release information about your education record, unless the following parties or conditions are concerned, according to the Family Policy Compliance Office of the U.S. Department of Education:

- School officials with legitimate educational interest

- Other schools to which a student is transferring

- Specified officials for audit or evaluation purposes

- Appropriate parties in connection with financial aid to a student

- Organizations conducting certain studies for or on behalf of the school

- Compliance with a judicial order or lawfully issued subpoena

- Appropriate officials in cases of health and safety emergencies

- State and local authorities, within a juvenile justice system, pursuant to specific state law

If you need a transcript of your student records, all you have to do is go to your campus' equivalent of an office of student records and fill out an official request form. Keep in mind if you are planning to mail the transcript to another college or university or other organization and have a deadline to meet, it may take some time for your transcript request to be filled. Records offices constantly receive similar requests from other students and organizations. Plan ahead.

Use Your Computer

Creating a Vital Information File on an Excel spreadsheet is a great way to help you keep up with all of your account numbers or passwords. List your accounts and credit cards on the left, and then across the top make the following categories: Account Number, Password, Date Opened, Date Closed, File Location, and Purpose. Use the File Location category to list where you store the documents from this account (for example, filing cabinet, second drawer). Use the Purpose section to record what this account is (for example, life insurance, investment account). To protect your privacy, set a password on this file. A secure password consists of a mixture of numbers, uppercase and lowercase letters, and symbols that do not include any of your personal numbers, such as your date of birth or Social Security number. In addition to having this file password protected, it's wise to have a password on your computer. Keep a backup on a CD that you store in a deposit box at your bank. Be sure a trusted family member has access to this CD in case you are ever unable to take care of your personal business.

▶ EXERCISE 7.1

Create a spreadsheet of your vital information. It's better to do this on a computer, but if you don't have access to your own computer, do not do this on an unsecured computer, such as a public library's or even a friend's. Instead, use grid paper on which to draw your spreadsheet. Review the instructions for creating a Vital Information File, and make your spreadsheet accordingly. Create a backup copy and store it in a secure location.

Make a Video or Photo Record

If you ever have an insurance claim because of fire or flood, or you are the victim of a home robbery, you'll need a record of the items you've lost. Take the time to create videos or digital photos of your belongings – such as furniture, electronics, jewelry, and any heirlooms – in each room of your house. Be sure to get photos or video of the serial numbers on your electronics and power tools. Once you've downloaded your video or photos to your computer, make a backup disk to store in your bank deposit box. It may seem unimportant today, but if you ever need an exact accounting of your personal belongings, you'll be glad you took the time.

All of these ideas for recordkeeping will take a little time to implement, and taking the first step toward organization is always the hardest. Once you've set your system up, however, you'll be able to maintain it quickly and easily by investing a small amount of time every few days. As you acquire new equipment, take photos to add to your record. Keep up with your filing system so it doesn't become a "piling" system. Maintain your Vital Information File as you add new accounts so you always have easy access to passwords and account numbers. Most importantly, remember to back up all of your data often and keep the copy in a deposit box.

Recording Your Private Life and Thoughts

Perhaps the journal you're required to use for this class is the first journal you've used for anything. Maybe up to this point in your life, writing down your thoughts, actions, or feelings was the furthest thing from your mind. The truth is, however, that keeping up with your daily life can help you solve problems, remember important details, stay focused on goals, and even resolve conflicts. In fact, this has been the case for hundreds of years.

Journaling as a pastime in the Western world did not take hold until the Renaissance when people became more interested in self-image and were drawn to literary pursuits by famous writers, such as William Shakespeare. From 1660 to 1669, Samuel Pepys (pronounced "Peeps"), a prominent London businessman and member of Parliament, wrote in his diary daily, chronicling both the Great Plague and the Great Fire in London.

Today, many people simply use a calendar that has a few spaces under each day to write down a couple of important events from that day – a doctor's appointment, a bill paid, or perhaps what the weather was like. Others will use a computer document to jot a quick recap of what they accomplished during the day. They typically want to explore their thoughts, using their journal as an outlet for emotions and developing ideas. Some use journals to record their spiritual journey, documenting prayers, scriptures, or revelations, while others use journals for healing past hurts or dealing with stress. Diarists usually keep a book near their bed to write a more extensive recap of the day, including their reactions to various events. Of course, others who are more technically inclined may use the Internet to blog their ideas and feelings. Whether you choose to blog, journal, keep a calendar, or recap your day with diary entries will depend on your personal preference. The act of documenting your life is as individual as you are.

▶ EXERCISE 7.2

Use your journal as a diary or log for the next fourteen days, including weekends. Create a record of your daily activities and write your reactions to some of the things you encounter during your day. At the end of the two weeks, pick a day you can share with the class, and be prepared for discussion.

The very act of writing your thoughts down creates a physical release. It can clear your mind, moving worries and concerns out of your head and onto the paper. It gives you the ability to test your thoughts, try solutions, brainstorm, and deal with your stress. Purists differentiate between journaling and other types of personal documentation by claiming that true journaling is a journey of healing. Tristine Rainer, author of *The New Diary*, describes journaling as a highly personal form of written self-expression. She states that it involves the process of writing one's thoughts and feelings to create an "active, purposeful communication with the self." Other writers and life coaches use the term journaling to mean any type of personal writing, whether strictly a recap of daily activities or an introspective exercise. For the remainder of this chapter, we will use the word *journal* to mean a generic recording of your personal thoughts, activities, or ideas.

What Is Blogging?

A blog may contain a person's opinions about and experiences with products, current events, or education concepts. It is normally updated frequently, if not daily, and the person who writes the blog is called a blogger. It's important to remember when reading blogs that you may be reading biased information presented as fact. If the blog offers external links as sources, click on them to check the validity of the information you're reading.

There are some very important things to keep in mind, however, if you plan to use a social networking site like a blog. Unless you set your privacy options to friends only and screen the people who request to be your friends, everything you post is open to the public. Chapter 3 discussed identity theft at length, but it bears repeating: Protect your personal information.

Wordpress

Scan the code for additional information or visit: *http://bit.ly/TC7Wpress*

Wordpress.com and Wordpress.org are two of the leading blog websites. The app for Wordpress.com is free, and once you set up a free blog, you can start blogging immediately from wherever you are. You can also include videos or photos in your post.

To participate in the online poll, scan the QR code or visit: *http://bit.ly/TC7Poll*

Would you ever consider starting a blog?

○ Yes, if I had a topic that was worthwhile and easy to write about on an ongoing basis.

○ No, few blogs are popular enough to make it worthwhile.

○ Yes, as a way to start a conversation about my career field and to show prospective employers I am dedicated to my work.

○ No, it's hard to keep up a schedule that will keep readers coming back.

Employers sometimes look at social networking sites for information on prospective employees. You may be tempted to blog about the crazy weekend party you threw last month, but resist the urge. Badenoch & Clark, an international recruitment firm that places thousands of professionals in jobs every year, admitted that checking Facebook and MySpace is routine for them as well as for many other professional recruiters.

As with any other discipline, practice and repetition creates habit. Once you have the habit of keeping track of your personal life, you'll begin to see how the habit helps you take charge of your thoughts, galvanize your purpose, and gain deeper insight into the motives that drive you. Don't be surprised if you find that journaling, in whatever form you are most comfortable with, becomes a primary part of your daily routine.

Education Success Through Effective Documentation

While note taking and journaling in your personal life is advisable, it's practically mandatory in your educational life. Unfortunately, most college instructors expect students to be already adept at note taking when they enter college. The truth is, very few college students know how to take notes effectively because the skill is not always emphasized at the high school level. Many students use voice recorders to capture their instructor's lectures, but depending on playback alone is a recipe for disaster and some professors don't allow recordings. It's also very easy to let your mind wander when listening to a recorded lecture.

Physically taking notes helps to cement facts in your mind. Education studies prove that students who see (reading in your text or what the instructor writes on the board), hear (listening to a lecture), and write their material down are far more likely to retain the majority of important facts. Still, for most students, knowing they need to take notes and actually having an efficient system of note taking are two very different things.

> **Even if you have a great memory, you won't be able to remember everything that the teacher says, unless you have a permanent written record for your reference.**
>
> —Esther Lombardi from the About.com article "Why Take Notes?"

Being Prepared

You can't take notes if you don't have supplies for recording and organizing them. Always make sure to bring with you to every class a spiral notebook; a folder with pockets for classroom handouts; writing tools, including pencils, pens, and highlighters; a laptop, along with a charger and power cord if your professor allows it; and the appropriate textbook(s) if your professor requires it. It will be easier to transport and keep track of these materials if you carry them in a backpack.

Knowing What to Write

Lifehacker (lifehacker.com), a website devoted to helping people find more efficient ways of getting things done, says that one of the reasons people have trouble taking effective notes is they're not really sure what notes are for. Class notes are not for capturing a complete record of everything your instructor says or of everything you read in an assignment. You must cultivate the skill to think while you're writing. This cannot be done if you are in a mad dash to record every word your teacher utters. Notes do not need to contain everything – just the important things.

NOTE-TAKING CHECKLIST

Before you get ready to take notes, make sure you have all of these:

- ☐ Two to three writing utensils that work and a manual (not electric or battery-operated as these are distracting to everyone) pencil sharpener if you use pencils

- ☐ Plenty of paper

- ☐ Two to three different colored highlighters

- ☐ Laptop with power cord if you choose to take notes digitally

- ☐ Textbook if the professor requires it

- ☐ Recording device to use in conjunction with your notes (make sure to get the professor's permission first)

"How do I know what the important things are?" The Lifehacker article "Advice for Students: Taking Notes that Work" recommends you ask yourself two questions: "What is new to me?" and "What is relevant?" There's no need to write down information you already know. For example, your instructor in American history may state that Columbus discovered the Americas in 1492. If you already knew that fact, don't waste time writing it down. Focus only on facts you did not already know.

You also must decide what is relevant. During a ninety-minute lecture, your professor will make many statements. Some will be relevant facts, some will be opinions, and some will be observations or supporting details. If you have read your assignment before class, it will be easy to pick out the relevant facts as you hear them. "Advice for Students: Taking Notes that Work" lists the following as the kinds of information to pay special attention to:

- Dates of events

- Names of people

- Theories

- Definitions

- Arguments and debates

- Images and exercises

- Your own questions

COACH'S CORNER

Truly listening can be more difficult than it sounds. In Coach's Corner, Coach discusses how listening is important for note-taking.

http://bit.ly/TC7CC

Organizing Your Information

formal outlining

Highly structured method of note taking

informal outlining

Unstructured note taking and a form of brainstorming

Cornell Method

Two-part method: information that you take down during a lecture and cues to help you remember the information

Organizing the relevant information from a lecture so you can quickly access it later is the second half to successful note taking. Through trial and error, you may tweak a system to make it work best for you, but if you aren't comfortable with note taking already, it's best to stick to the basics. There are several styles of note taking: **formal outlining, informal outlining,** and the **Cornell Method**. Because most students have had to use basic formal outlining skills for research paper assignments in high school, this type of note taking tends to be easiest for them. Like all organizational systems, the easier it is, the more likely you are to use it.

Lifehacker states that "whether you use roman numerals or bullet points, outlining is an effective way to capture the hierarchical relationships between ideas and data." For example, if you're a graphic design major, you'll have to study a certain amount of art history. If your instructor is lecturing on the life of Picasso and you are using formal outlining, you might begin with roman numeral *I* as "The Early Years." Next, you would switch to capital *A* for his birth and family. Under that, you would go to ordinal arabic numbers for relevant details.

▶ WORKSHEET

The following is a sample outline you can use for your notes. For example purposes, each level has notes about Picasso so you can see what kind of information goes where.

For the sample template, scan the QR code or visit:
http://bit.ly/TC7Outline

I. (Main Topic) The Early Years of Picasso

  A. (Subheading One) Birth and Parents
    1. (Detail) Born October 25, 1881
    2. (Detail) Born in Malaga, Spain
    3. (Detail) Son of an art and drawing teacher

  B. (Subheading Two) Education

    1. (Detail) Brilliant student
    2. (Detail) Passed exam for Barcelona School of Fine Arts
      a. (More specific details) Age fourteen
      b. (More specific details) Took only one day to pass exam
      c. (More specific details) Was allowed to skip first two classes

If you decide to use informal outlining, you'll find that this is a highly personal method, because each person does it just a little differently. This kind of outline does help you put information in order and organize your thoughts, but it doesn't use numbers of any kind or bullet points.

The Cornell Method has a built-in way to help you remember the important pieces of information from a lecture. This is how the method is described by Washington State University:

> "Rule your paper with a two-and-a-half-inch margin on the left, leaving a six-inch area on the right in which to make notes. During class, take down information in the six-inch area. When the instructor moves to a new point, skip a few lines. After class, complete phrases and sentences as much as possible. For every significant bit of information, write a cue in the left margin. To review, cover your notes with a card, leaving the cues exposed. Say the cue out loud, then say as much as you can of the material underneath the card. When you have said as much as you can, move the card and see if what you said matches what is written. If you can say it, you know it."

As you become more skilled with note taking, you'll find that you can develop a personal shorthand method. For example, use common abbreviations: *fed* for *federal*, *pres* for *president*, etc. Another idea is to leave vowels out of words when possible, or shorten words by using abbreviations. Ths wll hlp u bcz ur mnd wll read the mssng lettrs autmtclly. Use *thru* for *through*, *nite* for *night*, *u* for *you*, *ur* for *your*, for instance.

Quick TIP

If you have trouble keeping up with your notes during a lecture, consider investing in a "smart-pen" like Livescribe. The pen and special paper records your writing, which you can download to a computer, and records the lecture in an audio file, which you can associate to different parts of your notes.

▶ EXERCISE 7.3

Implement the formal outline method of note taking in all of your classes for the next two weeks. Then, for the following two weeks, use the Cornell Method. At the end of the time, evaluate whether either method has been beneficial to you, or whether one method worked better for you than the other. Be prepared to discuss the following in class:

a.) How did each form of note taking help you?

b.) Was there anything challenging to you in this exercise? If so, what?

c.) How likely are you to continue using either of these methods?

ETHICAL DILEMMA

You have a big test coming up next week. After reviewing the main topics your professor said would likely be covered on the test, you notice your notes are incomplete. You missed a couple of classes for various reasons during the semester. What do you do?

Scan the code for additional information or visit: *http://bit.ly/TC7Notes*

a.) Join a study group for the test. This way, you can get the missing notes and learn the information you missed in an interactive setting.

b.) Go to your professor. He will be able to help fill in the missing gaps and help you understand the information.

c.) Ask a classmate for the missing notes and copy them down word-for-word. Having the information available for the test and memorizing it is more important at this point than understanding and processing it.

d.) Focus on the elements you do know and don't worry about the things you missed. You were in class more days than you weren't, so it's really no big deal.

Whatever method you decide on for note taking, a few good habits will ensure your success in learning the material. Go to class; this cannot be emphasized enough. Copying someone else's notes is not the same thing as getting the information firsthand from your professor. As you listen to a lecture, your mind will form questions, and you'll have the opportunity to star those points for later discussion. If you're simply copying someone else's notes, you can write them down without actively engaging your mind. It's very possible to write what you see without absorbing it at all.

Go to class prepared. This means you read the assigned text to go along with the lecture before you got to class. You've already highlighted important information in your book as you read. You've used your note-taking method to outline the most important details from your reading. If you had questions as you read, you've written them down to make sure they get answered during the lecture. If not, raise your hand and ask the teacher to clarify the points you need help with. Make sure you have pencils, pens, highlighters, and a notebook with you in every class. Use only one notebook per subject so your notes stay chronologically and categorically ordered throughout the semester.

Pay attention in class. Purposefully keep your mind focused on what the instructor is saying. If your mind begins to wander, bring it back by stepping up your note-taking effort. Use various colored pens for note taking. Besides helping you stay focused by doing something unusual, it will help you remember the information you've written down. Additionally, associating certain colors with various blocks of text will help you quickly identify those sections later when you review your notes.

Rewrite or type your notes the same day you first write them. Taking the time to rewrite your notes, filling in details you remember from the lecture, will cement the concepts for you. You'll find you have much greater recall at test time if you practice this daily.

Getting It "Write" in Your Professional Life

If you thought your days of note taking, critical reading, and documentation would be over when you graduate, welcome to reality. Your education is preparing you for professional life in every way. From learning the ins and outs of your career to critical thinking to time management to goal setting and, yes, even to note taking and documentation, you will most likely draw on all of the college tools you have learned about to be successful in the professional world. While you let that news sink in, let's consider how you'll use note taking and documentation in your career.

Most companies require employees to attend weekly, or perhaps monthly, meetings where productivity goals, actual accomplishments, and company projections are evaluated. An efficient note-taking system will help you when later you need to refer to the details of something your manager discussed. Employees who pay attention during meetings and take the initiative to jot a few things down impress their employers by their willingness to interact and internalize company information.

You will also use note taking for project documentation. Imagine your company is sending you out to work on a piece of equipment that has just hit the market. You'll be the first technician in your company, maybe in your region, to work on that equipment. Once you've fixed the problem and returned to the office, your manager is likely to want a full report of what you did and how the machine responded. If you have a fully documented flow chart prepared, you're much more likely to be considered for future challenges and promotions than someone who is unprepared.

> 66 Blogging is good for your career. A well-executed blog sets you apart as an expert in your field. 99
>
> —Penelope Trunk

EDUCATIONAL JOURNALING

In addition to note taking during class and reading assignments, keeping an education journal can help you gain deeper insights, find further applications for your knowledge, and track your progress as you work toward your goal of graduation. Richard G. Scott, a Latter-day Saints teacher, once said, "Knowledge carefully recorded is knowledge available in time of need." The truth of that statement extends beyond simply recording notes in class. As you truly grasp a difficult concept, using a journal to write about the process and the insight you gained will give you later access not just to the information but also to the process you used in learning it.

You cannot absorb a complex concept simply by skimming the material about it. You must be able to think about it, turn it over in your mind, considering various applications and consequences, before you can take ownership of that idea. Roger Hiemstra, professor and program coordinator of adult education at Elmira College in New York, said in his article "Promoting Journal Writing in Adult Education" that one of the advantages of journaling about your education experience is being able

Quick TIP

If you keep a well-written professional blog about your particular career field, consider putting it on your resume. When prospective employers look at it, they'll see you are dedicated to your field and are interested in staying up-to-date with the newest information.

Most technical careers have magazines or professional journals associated with them. A sure way to get the attention of your managers, as well as of prospective employers, is to have your documentation published. Returning to the imaginary scenario just discussed, if you have documented your experience with complete details, you could turn that into a how-to article that other technicians would be interested in reading.

You may not have realized it, but blogging can provide added income for you. If you enjoy writing and can write about your field in a way that will help other people gain insight and understanding, then you might want to consider putting up a blog. In "Professional Blogs and Their Impact on Communications," Steve O'Keefe writes, "Product information and industry blogs are particularly attractive to blog publishing entrepreneurs. These tightly focused sites – like Gizmodo and Engadget in consumer electronics – have audiences that advertisers are willing to spend money to reach." O'Keefe continues by projecting that over the next few years, most industries will be covered by professional bloggers. "Corporations will need to identify professional blog[s] ... that cover their products and industry and develop programs for working with these bloggers. Customers and other stakeholders will increasingly use professional blogs as part of their product and company research efforts, and these blogs will impact corporations much like traditional media has done in the past." Bloggers make money when their blogs attract corporate sponsors, as well as when they host ads and banners for click-through revenue (meaning that every time someone clicks on an ad, the blogger gets paid).

to review or reread earlier reflections so that a progressive clarification of insights is possible.

Whether you are a young student, just out of high school, or an adult career-changer, you will find that the more education you have, the more your thinking will grow and mature. Journaling will help you document that personal growth. A very good practice is to use a journal specifically to record your growth within your major area of study. Undoubtedly your level of understanding (of your career field) today will be very small when you compare it with your understanding at the time of your graduation.

Journaling will help you in your professional development as well. As you write down your growing insights, you'll begin to see future applications for the knowledge you're gaining. If you want to be able to share these ideas with other people in your field, consider publishing your musings as a blog. This will encourage interaction and networking with other people in your career.

The whole idea of writing about your field may seem daunting now, but as you gain understanding and maturity in your field, you might find you actually have a gift for sharing relevant information. The Internet offers rich and diversely complex information in an easy-to-use environment that 73 percent of Americans access. Before you assume you could never write anything that someone else would want to read, consider the financial and career development implications that you could be passing up. Again, publication offers instant credibility. A professional blog could take your career places that you would never have imagined.

▶ EXERCISE 7.4

Take one technical aspect of your career field – a theory, a piece of equipment, etc. – and write a blog post about it. Your blog post should be about 250 words and needs to include any sources you quote. Remember, a blog post isn't just the facts; it's also your evaluation or opinion. Keep a copy of your blog posts in your journal, as well as on your hard drive. Do an online search for blogs that have to do with your career field, then see how your style of blogging matches the pros.

Social and Professional Networking for Career Growth

While plenty of bad press exists about social network sites, these websites also have their redeeming qualities. Many professionals use MySpace and Facebook to network with others in their industry and search for new job opportunities. However, you still need to be careful about what you post and what others post about you. Larry Rosen, author of *Me, MySpace, and I: Parenting the New Generation*, writes, "You have no control over what other people write about you and what other people choose to say." Postings from your friends could inadvertently cause employers or future employers to view you negatively.

Internet Duct Tape is a blog that offers insights into lifehacks (ways to make your life easier) and a "Frankenstein-like philosophy of making things work together." One article on the blog, "How to Use Facebook Without Losing Your Job Over It," offers some very good advice: If you're going to use Facebook (or any other social network site, for that matter), have two accounts, one for your professional life and one for your personal life.

Your professional-life profile:

- Show your full name, job history, and schooling.

- Add only work-related email and instant-messaging accounts.

- Add only industry contacts as friends.

- Join networks related only to school and work.

- Have one professional-looking photo or do not include a photo.

Your personal/private profile:

- Show your first name or nickname, plus your last-name initial.

- Don't join networks related to school or work.

- Don't list your work experience.

- Don't ever use your work email address or work instant-messaging account.

- Do whatever you want with it.

"Obviously, don't link your personal and professional account as friends. Since you have two Facebook accounts that are unrelated to each other you can switch accounts to test how much information is publicly available on the other account," the article says.

LinkedIn

Scan the code for additional information or visit: *http://bit.ly/TC7LinkedIn*

Some social network websites offer apps to allow you to use them on the go. One such site is LinkedIn.com, the professional networking website. Keep up to date with the professionals you know in your field. You can also join groups and interact with other professionals. Remember, it's who you know.

Alternative Social Networking Sites

While Facebook dominates the social network scene, there are professional alternatives. Mediabistro.com provides news and networking for professionals who work in creative fields such as graphic design and media-content production. LinkedIn is a networking site for connecting to professionals in your field or to find alumni from your college. "It's who you know" rings true when it comes to networking. You may already know someone who has connections at your dream company; you just need to find that person. The following is a list of alternative social networking sites you can use.

Artbreak: An artist community for sharing and selling artwork

Blogtronix: A site that promotes corporate social networking, enterprise 2.0, and wikis

DoMyStuff: A good site for working professionals looking to find online assistants

Doostang: An invitation-only career community for professionals

iKarma, Inc.: A specialist in providing customer feedback for organizations and professionals

ImageKind: A community and marketplace for professional artists

Jigsaw: An online business-card networking directory for users to establish contacts with one another

Konnects: A site that enables members to create their own professional networking communities

LinkedIn: A professional social networking website for business users; one of the most popular such sites out there

Mashable.com: A blog dedicated to providing information on social network sites

Mediabistro.com: A site for professionals in the media or other creative media-related industries, including publishing

Ryze.com: A site for establishing new connections and growing networks; connections for jobs, career building, and making sales

Spoke.com: A site that offers access to a business network of over 40 million people worldwide

XING: A networking directory of business contacts powering relationships between business professionals, allowing users to connect with one another

Joining a professional social networking site will give you the opportunity to practice your blogging skills while you develop important, career-promoting networks.

Conclusion

Emotional journaling won't be for everyone, but everyone will have a need at some time in their lives for accurate note taking, record keeping, and, perhaps, report writing. The techniques you've learned here will definitely help you get started. Chapter 10 will build on your skills by offering some nuts-and-bolts ideas for stronger written communications. The sooner you get started practicing with note taking, blogging, or journaling, however, the faster you'll benefit from the habit.

Further Reading

How to Study in College by Walter Pauk and Ross J. Q. Owens. Wadsworth Publishing: 2010.

How to Organize (Just About) Everything: More Than 500 Step-by-Step Instructions for Everything from Organizing Your Closets to Planning a Wedding to Creating a Flawless Filing System by Peter Walsh. Free Press: 2004.

1. Why is it important to keep track of official documents?

2. How can the 43 Folders system be applied to organizing your bills and documents?

3. What do people use journals for?

4. What are some key types of information to pay special attention to when taking your notes?

5. What are three kinds of outlining for your class notes?

6. How is the Cornell Method applied?

7. How can effective note taking help in your professional career?

8. Why is blogging possibly a good idea for you career-wise?

9. Why should you have two accounts for certain social networks? What should they be used for?

10. What are some alternate social networking sites?

▶▶ Are you puzzled?

Scan this code to access
the puzzle online or visit:
http://bit.ly/TC7Crword

Across

1. Under ____, schools are required to get written permission from you, or from your parents if you are underage, to release information about your education record.

6. It's wise to have a password on your ____.

7. An artist community for sharing and selling artwork

9. If you already ____ a fact, don't waste time writing it down.

10. Two part method: information you take down during a lecture and cues to remember the information that you took down (2 words)

13. It doesn't matter if you keep a record of important data if you can't ____ the information when you need it.

14. Use only ____ notebook per subject so your notes stay chronologically and categorically ordered.

15. An official academic record

16. Keep up with your filing system so it doesn't become a "____" system.

18. This method of note taking is not structured and is a form of brainstorming. (2 words)

Down

19. A networking directory of business contacts powering relationships between business professionals, allowing users to connect with one another

2. Protect your ____ information.

3. What app helps you set up a free blog?

4. ____ important data from your life can prevent confusion or conflict later.

5. Keep important documents for each person in your immediate ____.

8. This method of note taking is highly structured. (2 words)

11. While note taking and journaling in your personal life is advisable, they are practically ____ in your educational life.

12. Take time to create videos or digital photos of your ____ for insurance purposes.

14. You can't take notes if you don't have supplies for recording and ____ them.

17. ____ to class.

FRED HILLS
College Program Director for Computer Information Systems and Multimedia

Scan this code for additional info
or visit: *http://bit.ly/TC7FHills*

Staying Organized for Success

Students face several deadlines and responsibilities ranging from class assignments to after-school jobs. It's essential for students to be organized because of the many new ideas and opportunities that will come their way in college, according to Fred Hills, a college program director for computer information systems and multimedia. If students are not organized, "multiple opportunities will slip by," he says. "It is important to be organized so as to take advantage of these opportunities and maximize your time."

With his myriad of responsibilities and roles, Hills must maintain organization and balance to accomplish and fulfill each obligation. He is working on his dissertation to complete a PhD in education from the University of North Texas. As program director for Computer Information Systems and Multimedia, he manages a team of eight full-time employees, an adjunct staff, and lab assistants. He also teaches computer systems classes, oversees the CIS Open Lab, builds class schedules, and makes sure faculty and staff have the technological resources necessary to teach effectively. In addition to these duties, Hills is also an advisor for the Phi Theta Kappa honor society, serves on the college's sustainability committee, and teaches workshops to professors and employees about the benefits of Web 2.0 (blogs, social networking, video sharing, etc.) in the classroom.

Accurate note taking is a key component of good organization and study skills. When students are first learning how to take notes, Hills suggests they use a tape recorder to ensure they have every point from a class lecture. They can listen to the recording later to pull out important points for study and review. He also says students should compare notes and ask the professor after class if they've written down all of the significant information.

One of the most important habits organized, successful students practice is asking for help when a problem or issue arises, Hills says. Students who read ahead, manage their time effectively, and take accurate notes will recognize if and when they need help long before a test or assignment is due. "Don't hesitate to ask for advice – we have all been there and have had to learn the skills you are now embarking on," he says. "All of us are here to help you be successful in the classroom and beyond."

CHAPTER **8** Dealing with Tests

STUDENT DISORIENTATION

Misha knew college would be hard, but she never anticipated spending an entire week at the library. Midterms were killing her. She had to beg friends to bring her food. Her sleep was cut down to an hour power nap whenever her eyes just wouldn't stay open anymore. She just needed to struggle through forty-eight more hours and then her midterms would be over.

She hated that everyone else never seemed to have to study as much as she did. Aaron was looking through Steve Jobs videos. Brad and Kristen were giggling over some stupid YouTube video of a sneezing panda. They had midterms tomorrow, too! Misha rested her head on her arms and mumbled about how it just wasn't fair.

Someone shook her arm. She raised her head to see Aaron looking at her worriedly. "You've been sleeping for two hours. Your test is in thirty minutes. Shouldn't you be studying?"

Misha thought her head had been down for thirty seconds max. She looked at the whiteboard. Everything looked like gibberish.

CHAPTER OBJECTIVES:

- Establishing your values and ethics

- Discovering what test anxiety is

- Determining your learning style and acquire successful test taking skills

- Surviving performance reviews and workplace tests

What does everyone have that nobody wants? Tests! We all face a test of some sort every day. Some tests are emotional, while others are ethical. Some are educational and still others are professional. No matter what area of life you consider, you will be faced with tests. How well you deal with your tests and how much integrity you use or lose on any given test all combine to help form your character.

It's not pleasant to think about, but the fun, easygoing times we experience are not what shape us. They are the times we like best, no doubt, but they aren't the times we look back on and say, "I really stepped up to that challenge. I'm a better person for it." Of course, the challenges you, as a student, are mostly concerned with right now are probably actual academic tests. Midterms, final exams, quizzes – these determine your grade point average (GPA). Chapter 8 will address successful test taking to ease anxiety and help you strengthen your skills. We'll also look at ways to pass other tests, the tests that may eventually matter most in life. From education to business to personal relationships, taking charge of your life means handling the challenges that come your way with integrity, common sense, and confidence.

Making the Grade in Your Personal Life

Many people never give a moment's thought to the values that are most important to them. However, as you learn to think critically, you will find you begin to analyze certain situations you are faced with based on the value system you believe in. A hallmark of mature thinking is the ability to dissect information, situations, and concepts and look at the individual pieces in light of your own motivating beliefs. People who have not learned to think critically tend to react emotionally when situations take them by surprise. Having a set of well-defined values will help you stay on course as you meet your personal challenges.

> " Always do right. This will gratify some and astonish the rest. "
>
> —Mark Twain

What Are Values?

A value is a guiding principle that helps you make choices in life, and not just the big choices. When you decide to hold the door open for the person behind you, even if that person is perfectly capable of opening the door, you've made a value-based decision, with politeness being your value. When you return the extra fifty cents in change that the cashier at Starbucks gave you, you are acting on the value of honesty.

Conversely, you could hold negative values. Some examples are selfishness, self-centeredness, and apathy. Whether you hold positive or negative values, these are the qualities by which you live your life. Additionally, your reputation is primarily built on the values you hold, because people associate you with your actions.

What Is the Difference Between Ethics and Values?

The dictionary defines ethics as a group of morals that characterizes certain actions as either right or wrong; in other words, ethics embody a set of basic principles that guides a person's or group's actions.

How is this different from values? Ethics are something you either have or you don't, whereas everyone has values. The value choices you make indicate whether you are an ethical person. In *Three Dimensional Ethics: Implementing Workplace Values*, Attracta Lagan and Brian Moran write, "Individuals have an innate need to make sense of the situations in which they find themselves." When a deeply rooted, positive value system is combined with ethics, a person has a strong model through which to filter his or her responses before taking action in a situation.

Integrity, the Secret Ingredient

Some studies have shown that even people with strong values may choose to behave unethically in certain situations. That's where integrity comes into play. Integrity is the adherence to values and ethical principles even when it's not convenient or, possibly, when no one would know the difference; it is what you are when no one is looking.

▶ EXERCISE 8.1

In your journal, identify the top four values you use when making decisions in your personal life.

a.) What will you never compromise?

b.) Which value might you change in a different context?

c.) Ask a friend who has known you for a long time to identify the top four values they associate with your character. How does your answer compare with your friend's?

Know Thyself

Chapter 5 introduced the Socratic Method, which is based on the teachings of the Greek philosopher, Socrates. One of his most famous directives is still quoted regularly today: "Know thyself." If you know who you are at your deepest level and if you know the values and ethics that guide you, you can live with the confidence that few situations can catch you off guard. You won't be disappointed with yourself when crunch time comes, and it will inevitably come.

THE STAGES OF MORAL DEVELOPMENT

Moral development is much like the process of physical maturity. We begin at baby steps and move through stages toward adulthood. Lawrence Kohlberg, a well-respected psychologist, studied the stages of moral development for his doctoral dissertation in 1958. He later published his findings in the book *The Psychology of Moral Development*, in which he proposed six stages of development. As you read, try to decide which stage best describes you:

Stage 1: "Please the authority figure." In this stage, an act is considered bad if the person committing the act gets punished for it. The individual is not acting so much on what is right or wrong as on what he or she can get away with.

Stage 2: "You scratch my back, I'll scratch yours." This is a "what's in it for me" philosophy in which a person is mindful of other people's feelings and well-being only when it is in his or her own best interest. This is a very limited form of moral development because the ethical behavior stops when it's no longer beneficial to the individual.

Stage 3: "Self-consciousness." In stage 3, a person makes moral decisions based on societal norms, such as the Golden Rule and his or her personal relationships. The circle of influence and respect is still very small, as opposed to taking a world view. The desire to conform is based solely on maintaining stereotypical roles.

Stage 4: "Keep the status quo." At this stage of development, a person has become more mindful of societal rules and regulations, whether spoken or implied. The individual feels a need to conform and obey laws for the good of society, not just

Review Kohlberg's six stages of moral development. Record your answers to the following questions in your journal and be prepared for class discussion.

a.) Which stage do you think you are in? Why?

b.) Which stage would you like to be in?

c.) What can you do to help yourself get to that stage?

when it's convenient for him or her, as in stage 2, or when it's good for the group, as in stage 3.

Stage 5: "Personal empowerment and social contracts." At this stage, people begin to view laws as "social contracts" that need to be changed when the greater good of the people is not met. Individuals also become more aware that not all people share the same ethical standards. People look for "majority rule," common ground, and the greatest good for the greatest number of people.

Stage 6: "Do the right thing precisely because it is the right thing." At the final stage of moral development, individuals think in the highest abstract order possible – projection. "What would it be like for me to be in that person's shoes?" Laws are valid only when based on justice; unjust laws must be disobeyed (for example, Martin Luther King, Jr.'s civil disobedience and Rosa Parks' refusal to go to the back of the bus). People in this stage invest time in clarifying their personal values and principles, even when others disagree. A person acts because it is right, not because it is expected, lawful, or previously agreed on.

As you read these stages, did you recognize yourself in one of them or perhaps a combination? Using this scale as a measuring rod. Are your morals and ethics developed as highly as you'd like them to be? Fortunately, as adults, we have the ability to think abstractly and critically. If you did not like the stage you discovered yourself to be in, you have the ability to attain a higher stage simply through self-discipline, analysis, and practice.

Ethical Models and Tests

An ancient Japanese proverb holds that "the reputation of 1,000 years can be built on the act of one hour." Consider some of the major political decisions made centuries ago. History books today still record the actions of the leaders who made those decisions.

To help individuals attain higher moral development stages, psychologists have developed various ethical models and tests. The Mary Guy model, proposed in 1990, is probably the most popular among advocates of corporate social responsibility. Although the Mary Guy model was written for the workplace, it also is valid in our personal lives.

The Mary Guy model has several steps. You must consider the well-being of others, including nonparticipants (in any given agenda, situation, etc.). You need to think as a member of the community, not as an isolated individual. This emphasizes loyalty, integrity, respect for others, and responsible citizenship. Obey but do not depend solely on the law. This point emphasizes integrity and social responsibility. Ask "What sort of person would do such a thing?" anytime you are confronted with an ethical dilemma. Finally, you must respect the customs of others, but not at the expense of your or your organization's ethics. This emphasizes accountability, fairness, integrity, and respect for others.

When you are confronted with an ethical or moral decision, whether great or small, there are a few tests to help you stay on the right track. In the "sunlight test," you ask yourself how you would feel if this decision was made in front of the public or in front of those you admire. The "newspaper test" takes this one step further by asking how the decision would look on the front page of a newspaper or how you would feel defending yourself on, for instance, *60 Minutes*. In the "test of time," ask yourself how your behavior would be viewed in five, ten, or twenty years.

DECISION EVALUATION CHECKLIST

- ☐ Is it legal?
- ☐ Is it right according to your personal values?
- ☐ Is it fair?
- ☐ How will I feel about myself?
- ☐ Is this a special situation? Or am I only pretending it is?
- ☐ Would I be prepared to have my behavior reported in the news?
- ☐ How will this behavior be viewed in five years, ten years, and twenty years?
- ☐ What are the possible negative and positive outcomes of this decision?
- ☐ How would I feel making this decision in front of someone I admire?

If you filter your actions through these questions, you are sure to make good, healthy decisions. Before we move on to the types of tests and ethical decisions you will make in your education life, consider these five ethical principles, published by the North Carolina State University Center for Student Leadership, which will guide you in all areas of life:

- **Respect individualism.** Everyone has a right to their own beliefs, customs, and opinions, as long as their actions do not interfere with the welfare of others.

- **Do no harm.** We all have a social responsibility to avoid inflicting harm or damage, either physically, psychologically, or environmentally.

- **Benefit others.** We each have an obligation to do good when we can.

- **Be just.** Treat others with the fairness you desire.

- **Be faithful.** Keep your word. Tell the truth. Be a person others can count on when they need someone to help them. We can only be seen as trustworthy when we are faithful.

Making the Grade in Your Education Life

Few things strike fear in the heart of a college student the way midterms and final exams do. The pressure of knowing your final grade rides only on two, or possibly three, exams can induce anxiety, stress, and even physical illness. Knowing how you learn best and having a strategy for building strong study habits will lessen your concerns, help you overcome issues such as test anxiety, and give you a greater chance at academic success.

What Is Test Anxiety?

Test anxiety is a very real psychological condition that many students experience. Symptoms include the following:

- Profuse sweating, especially on the palms

- Shallow breathing

- Dizziness

- Rapid heartbeat

> **"**School has helped me to study better and not be afraid to take tests.**"**
>
> —Christopher F., Digital Media Design Student

- Nausea

- Racing thoughts, a feeling of "going blank," or inability to recall information

If you experience any of these symptoms during or before exams, you have test anxiety. Sometimes this type of anxiety can be linked to previous negative experiences in the classroom or to a deep-rooted fear of failure. Sometimes students need professional help from a psychologist or counselor to conquer test anxiety.

There are several ways to manage text anxiety, and each works differently for every person. When you feel overwhelmed, there are some techniques you can use. Keep a realistic perspective. Take a step back and consider the consequences from a realistic viewpoint. It is important to recognize that one mistake, one low grade, or one bad performance does not equal failure or mean that you're worthless.

Practice deep breathing. Breathing deeply has been proven to regulate heartbeat, reduce sweating and nausea, and relieve anxiety. Inhale deeply with your mouth open. Hold the breath for a few seconds, and then exhale slowly through your nose, letting your stomach sink inward. Repeat this ten or fifteen times, or until you feel calmer.

Use progressive muscle relaxation. Tension causes us to tighten our muscles unconsciously. Focus on one particular muscle group at a time, such as your shoulders, tightening as you breathe in and relaxing as you breathe out. Move progressively to your arms, torso, and lower body with each breath.

Proper preparation is the best relief for test anxiety. According to a study conducted by Questia, 79 percent of students reported that they would most likely procrastinate on their next assignment, even though 72 percent of them agreed that procrastinating did not help their grades. Studying at the last minute makes you feel less confident of your ability to recall important information, but being able to anticipate what the exam covers and knowing that you gave yourself enough time to study will help you feel more relaxed at exam time.

Being well prepared also will lessen the temptation to compromise your values. We cannot stress enough the importance of behaving ethically when it comes to your exams and projects. Most schools view cheating as grounds for expulsion. Simply put, keep your eyes on your paper, do your own work, and stick to your values and ethics.

Learning How to Learn

"If a student has done everything possible to prepare for an exam including attending class, taking good notes, studying well, and being well rested when they test, they will feel less anxious and are likely to do much better because they are able to relax."

– Michelle J., college testing center director

Quick TIP

If you're feeling overwhelmed with tests and school in general, consider taking up meditation or yoga. You will improve your health and create a means to calm down.

If you understand a bit about how students learn in general and the way you learn best in particular, you will retain more of the material that your instructors cover.

Bloom's Taxonomy of Learning

In the mid-twentieth century, Benjamin S. Bloom developed his taxonomy of learning, which involved three domains, each with several levels. It was his belief that we can't address a higher level within a domain until we have covered the lower levels.

The cognitive domain refers to the way you deal with knowledge and events intellectually. In this domain, you process things by remembering, understanding, applying, analyzing, evaluating, and finally creating new knowledge based on what you have learned.

The affective domain refers to the way you deal with knowledge and events emotionally. In this domain, you approach things by receiving, responding, valuing (assigning a value to it), organizing and conceptualizing, and characterizing them by value or value concept.

The psychomotor domain refers to the way you deal with knowledge and events physically. Bloom didn't finish his work on this domain; several researchers have come up with a more complete version. In this domain, according to R. H. Dave's book *Developing and Writing Behavioral Objectives*, you approach things by imitating, manipulating, refining (achieving precision), articulating, and naturalizing them (performing it at such a high level that it comes naturally to you, almost without thought).

Depending on your learning style, you may find you process new information better in one domain than in the others. Once you discern which learning domain helps you retain new information the best, go with it every time.

ON THE WEB

Go to Human Metrics to find out your personality type and what careers or degrees best suit your personality type. This will help you determine which learning style works best for you.

http://bit.ly/TC8jung

Learning Styles

Different people learn best in different ways because of the way their brains are wired. Do you recognize your learning style in the following list?

Visual (spatial): Images are the best way to convey information to you. Add images to your class notes, including maps and diagrams, to use as memory cues.

Aural (auditory or musical): Sounds and music help you remember things. Reread your notes out loud to yourself. Fit facts to a short, familiar tune and sing it to yourself several times.

Verbal (linguistic): Spoken and written words help you lock in information. Review your notes and then rewrite them in longhand or type them and in your own words, as if you had to explain the information to a friend.

Physical (kinesthetic): When you can do it, you know it. Sitting still for long periods isn't for you. That new routine you learned in dance class? Don't just look at your notes – perform until you get it down. Listen to a recorded classroom lecture on headphones while you go for a walk. Whatever you're studying, take frequent breaks to get up and move around.

Logical (mathematical): Analyzing information logically and categorizing it cements new knowledge for you. Reorganize your class notes as a table, graph, or diagram. Seek out online simulators where you can practice the tasks you've been learning in laboratory assignments.

Social (interpersonal): You like to learn in groups, not on your own. Put together a study group after classes; have members take turns explaining the study material to the entire group.

Solitary (intrapersonal): You like to learn on your own. Study in a quiet place away from other students, such as a library study carrel, and wear noise-masking headphones. Keeping a journal for each class will hone your analysis of the subjects you're studying.

Learning Disabilities and Multisensory Teaching and Learning

You may be surprised to find out that 4 to 6 percent of all students in the United States have some kind of learning disability, including attention-deficit hyperactivity disorder (ADHD), auditory processing disorder, dysgraphia (a disability that affects written expression), and dyslexia (a reading disability). The Learning Disabilities Association of America (www.ldanatl.org) defines learning disabilities as neurologically based processing problems that can interfere with learning basic skills, such as reading, writing, and math, and/or with higher-level skills, such as organization, time planning, and abstract reasoning.

If you have a learning disability, you may benefit from multisensory teaching and learning. In this setting, the instructor engages students' three learning senses: auditory (hearing and speaking), visual (seeing and perceiving), and kinesthetic (touch and movement). You can use multisensory learning techniques to help yourself better understand new information and retain knowledge.

If your learning disability affects your organization and time-planning skills, it is imperative you use a master schedule and daily planner. Many students like you find that their lives are transformed by conscientious use of an online calendar or cellphone that allows them to set reminders for upcoming events. After all, who wants to forget to study for an exam or to show up for a class?

Overlearning

One way to lessen test anxiety is to increase your confidence through overlearning. This learning technique involves continuing to study or

learning disability

Neurologically based processing difficulty that can interfere with learning basic skills, such as reading, writing, and math, and/or with higher-level skills, such as organization, time planning, and abstract reasoning

multisensory teaching and learning

Techniques that use several senses to teach and to learn new materials

overlearning

A learning technique that involves continuing to study or practice material that you've already mastered practice material you've already mastered. German psychologist Hermann Ebbinghaus conducted several experiments in the late nineteenth century on how the human mind works. He discovered that overlearning increased how much information people retain.

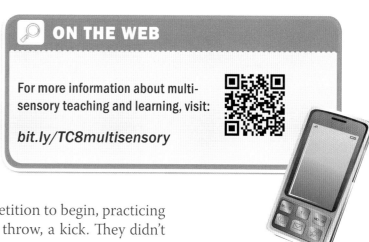

ON THE WEB

For more information about multi-sensory teaching and learning, visit:

bit.ly/TC8multisensory

Think of amateur and professional athletes: Do they stop practicing a particular skill or maneuver once they've learned it? No. You'll see them waiting for a game or competition to begin, practicing a lunge, a jump, a back flip, a pitch, a swing, a throw, a kick. They didn't learn these maneuvers just before the game or competition; they've been practicing for weeks, months, or even years. If you repeat to yourself – aloud, on paper, on a computer screen, or by performing – the materials you've already learned, you'll know them so well your confidence will shoot up at test-taking time.

The popular **SQ3R** – which stands for survey, question, read, recite, and review – reading strategy will help you remember the material from each reading assignment:

Survey: Before you start reading, survey the chapter or material by looking at all of the elements – the title, headings, subheadings, captions, illustrations of all kinds, review questions, study guides, beginning and ending paragraphs, and summary. This will help you get an idea of what you will be learning.

SQ3R

A reading strategy that helps you learn new reading material; stands for survey, question, read, recite, and review

Question: While you are surveying, think of questions. Turn the title and all subheadings into questions. Read the end-of-chapter or end-of-section questions. Think, "What did the instructor say about this material? What do I already know about this topic?" Write down or type these questions for later use in studying.

Read: Begin reading. As you go along, be alert to material that answers the questions you developed. Answer the questions at the end of the chapter or of each section or on the classroom study guide. Pay attention to words and phrases that are treated differently than others; if they're italicized, bolded, or underlined, they are pointers to especially important information. If you reach a difficult or unclear section, slow down and reread until you understand it.

COACH'S CORNER

Test anxiety can make all the hard work you did studying null and void. In Coach's Corner, Coach gives you some tips on how to beat the anxiety and do your best.

http://bit.ly/TC8coachscorner

Recite: After you read each section, stop and ask yourself – aloud – questions about what you've just read. Summarize it in your own words. Now write down notes about what you've read, but use your own words. As you go, use a highlighter to mark important points.

Review: Now it's time to review what you've read. As with many other learning-retention methods, this is an ongoing process to help you retain your new knowledge.

On the first day of your review, write questions next to terms you've highlighted in the margins. Now go back to the notes you wrote as part of the reciting process. Review them and write questions in the margins of your notebook.

On the next day, skim the chapter and your notes to remind yourself of the relevant information. Then put away the textbook and the notes and ask yourself questions about the material. Answer aloud. Next, make flashcards for the questions you have trouble answering, and then create mnemonic devices to help you memorize information.

▷ WORKSHEET

This worksheet provides basic questions to help you analyze and absorb material while you are studying a new subject.

For the sample template, scan the QR code or visit:
http://bit.ly/TC8wsht

What is the general topic?	
What did you know about the general topic before you read the chapter/section?	
What are the main points presented (headlines, subheadings, and other important elements)?	
Write out the main terms and define them in your own words.	
What do you want to know more about or need more information regarding?	

On days three through five, switch back and forth between using your flashcards, mnemonic devices, and notes to test your knowledge of the material. If you need to, make more flashcards.

On the weekend, use your notes and the text to create a table of contents of all of the major and minor subjects you must learn. Use this to create a study sheet or diagram. Say the information aloud as you assemble your study sheet, using your own words. Until the exam, go over your study sheet every so often to keep the material fresh in your mind. That way, you won't feel the need to pull an all-night study session before the exam.

APT APPS!

Soshiku

Scan the code for additional information or visit: *http://bit.ly/TC8aasoshiku*

Having trouble keeping up with all those homework assignments? Soshiku helps you keep track of what assignments are due and when. This tool also allows you to set up group projects. You can chat, exchange notes, and share files with group members. It will even notify you via email or text message to let you know what's coming up on your schedule.

More Study Strategies

- Stay up-to-date on class information, keeping up with your syllabus assignments. Review your notes as you go along.

- Make sure you understand the information. If you don't, ask your instructor.

- Read and study information in meaningful chunks (sections or chapters) so you'll be able to file and retrieve related information.

- Break your study times into manageable time segments so you don't become overwhelmed with information. You'll remember more by studying for shorter times (forty-five minutes to an hour) over a period of a week than by studying everything in one all-nighter.

- Use mnemonic techniques to memorize lists, definitions, or other specific facts. An example of a mnemonic device is ROY-G-BIV, an acronym for the colors of the rainbow – red, orange, yellow, green, blue, indigo, and violet.

- Practice healthy habits. Get plenty of sleep and make sure you aren't filling up on sugars and other junk foods that will give you sugar rushes and leave you feeling sleepy and groggy in the middle of your exam.

- If you've taken time to prepare effectively, using all of these suggested techniques, you should be able to approach your exam with confidence.

🔍 ON THE WEB

For more study tips and strategies, visit Test Taking Tips – Study Skills:

bit.ly/TC8testtakingtips

Memory and Your Body

Your memory functions best when you treat your body well – getting enough sleep, getting enough exercise, and eating well. Getting less than six and a half hours of sleep a night can decrease your academic performance. Keep the same bedtime and rising time each day; don't consume caffeine, nicotine, or food within two hours of your bedtime; and limit your alcohol intake or don't drink it at all.

> ▶ **EXERCISE 8.3**
>
> ## What learning style do you have?
>
> a.) In your journal, describe your current study strategy.
>
> b.) Have you used any of the learning techniques discussed in this chapter?
>
> c.) How likely are you to change your study habits after having read this chapter?
>
> d.) During class discussion, explain how the learning technique(s) you use fit with the kind of learner you are.

Quick TIP

Feeling drowsy while studying? Get up every hour and do something physical, like jumping jacks, push-ups, jogging in place, or stretching. That brief bit of extra blood flow will help clear the fog from your mind and keep you from getting too stiff while studying.

Exercising regularly will give you more energy and help you focus. Exercise improves your focus by increasing blood flow to your brain. It also decreases your stress level, which is a very good thing at test time. Get out there and get moving for a minimum of sixty minutes – whether all in one stretch or in shorter spurts throughout the day – every single day.

Finally, keep your memory humming along by giving your brain the proper fuel – nutritious foods and plenty of water. You need the natural sugars and energy of fresh fruits and vegetables, fiber, and protein. You even need a little fat in your diet, but don't go overboard. If you take care of your body – and study, of course – your memory will take care of you at exam time.

Make every effort to earn the highest grades possible, but don't lose sight of the whole purpose of your education – for you to learn. If you don't make a straight 4.0 GPA, it does not mean you have not learned the information you will need in your career. You will leave college with a wide variety of knowledge, and when you apply it with careful, critical analysis, the final test question will be, "Did you learn how to do the job you set out to do?"

Making the Grade in your Professional Life

Your career will bring many challenges and opportunities for personal growth and development. From continuing-education requirements to maintaining various certifications to on-the-job training and evaluations to performance reviews, your test-taking days are certainly not over when you leave college. For many careers, it is important to pursue continuing education in order to stay up to speed with changing technologies, policies, and procedures. You may find you need to take a course or two or even return to school for another degree in order to stay up-to-date with the skill sets necessary for your career.

Why Do I Need Continuing Education?

Continuing education refers to classes you take once you have earned your degree or certain certifications associated with your career. Many teachers, for example, are required to attend ongoing classes and update their certifications every two years, depending on when they first earned their teaching certificates. Various engineering and technological jobs also require their certificate holders to engage in ongoing education.

Typical continuing-education unit (CEU) requirements are ten hours of education completed every two years, often followed by an exam, but this can vary from career field to career field. This ensures the professional stays abreast of changing technologies, techniques, and compliance issues. Many times your employer will pay for your CEUs and/or for your exam, but this is not always the case. You should ask any potential employer during your job interview about their policies regarding CEUs, as this can be part of your total benefits package and may be a point of negotiation.

There are numerous CEU accrediting bodies, depending on the type of work you are engaged in. The instructors for your major courses will serve as excellent information sources on specific continuing-education requirements in your field. Additionally, various product manufacturers offer continuing training courses and certification exams. Many of the positions that graduates of two-year technical colleges hold may require this kind of training.

On-The-Job Training

Earning a college degree means you have an extensive amount of general knowledge about a variety of subjects. It does not make you a specialist. Most employers put new employees through on-the-job training to ensure the employee has the company-specific, or product-specific, knowledge needed to function within that organization.

> " The illiterate of the twenty-first century will not be those who cannot read and write, but those who cannot learn, unlearn, and relearn. "
>
> —Alvin Toffler

continuing education

Classes that you take once you have earned your degree or certain certifications associated with your career, to ensure that your knowledge of your profession remains current

Make time to meet with your adviser or lead instructor in your major area of study. Ask what types of on-the-job training you can expect in your career field. Document the answers in your journal.

This shouldn't make you feel as if you just wasted two years at college. In fact, the complete opposite is true. Most likely, you would not have been able to get the job without the educational background you received in college, but now your employer needs to fine-tune the information you learned to help you apply it accurately for the organization's specific needs.

In technical fields, some employers send their new employees to several months' worth of manufacturers' schools to learn how to work on the equipment used in that company's operations. Most OJT is followed by a formal exam or set of exams. You'll need to study for these exams just the way you did for any college exam, using the strategies outlined in the learning and test-taking section of this chapter. Showing your employer you are eager to learn will go a long way at performance review time.

How Do Performance Reviews Work?

Performance reviews are the way employers measure their employees' productivity, attitudes, and accomplishments during a given time period. Typically, your performance reviews will be tied to the timetable used in your company for calculating raises. Some companies conduct reviews quarterly, some every six months, and some annually. You can expect at least one review annually.

You can expect your evaluation to begin with a review of the goals that were set when you started your job or during your last evaluation. Then your reviewer (typically your supervisor) will go over how well you have met those goals and which goals you still need to work on. Much of your review will be subjective – that is, based on opinion of how well you've done your job – but other sections will use concrete facts such as sales numbers or number of service calls. You will probably be asked to evaluate your own performance as well. Be honest but not self-deprecating. Point out the things you did well, downplay but don't ignore your weaknesses, and, above all, do not inflate numbers or outcomes. At the conclusion of your review, your manager will work with you to set future goals and determine which current goals you should still try to reach.

Quick TIP

Instead of waiting for a performance review to evaluate your performance, routinely evaluate yourself. On a daily, weekly, or monthly basis, examine your work habits and how effective you are. Find places to improve and keep track of them in a journal or notebook.

Ethics on the Job

One thing most employers look for in employees is a high standard of ethics. In high-pressure careers, the temptation to fudge facts and numbers for your own benefit can become very tempting. Most likely, you will find other employees at your job who do it regularly and never get caught. Personal accountability is the highest measure of ethics and has nothing to do with whether you might get caught. Personal accountability means you do what is right because it is right. You tell the truth and take the consequences. You don't make promises you can't keep just because the pressure to do so is great.

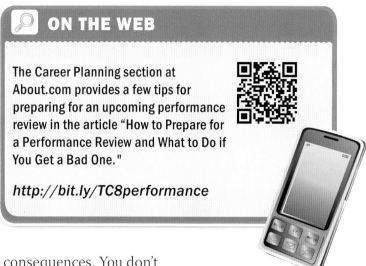

ON THE WEB

The Career Planning section at About.com provides a few tips for preparing for an upcoming performance review in the article "How to Prepare for a Performance Review and What to Do if You Get a Bad One."

http://bit.ly/TC8performance

Even though you have a high standard of ethics, it doesn't mean everyone around you will also have the same standards. There may come a time in your professional life when you see someone being harassed at work, or perhaps you may even be the victim. Too many times, victims of harassment don't speak up because they fear they will lose their job. Knowing how to use a "ladder of escalation" can empower you to speak out when you need to, whether on your behalf or on someone else's.

Speak up. If you see someone at work being discriminated against or harassed, approach the person and encourage them to speak up. If they feel supported, they may garner the courage to confront the issue. If you are the one being harassed, confront your persecutor. Bullies will bully as long as no one calls them out.

If the inappropriate behavior continues, take the issue to the next person in authority. This would normally be the immediate supervisor, unless that person is the one causing the problem, in which case, speak with his or her supervisor.

Make a formal complaint. If the issue cannot be resolved at the management level, consider filing a formal complaint with your human resources department. However, different companies have varying views of whistle blowers. You must decide whether you are willing to risk your job, or possibly future promotions, to help someone else who is being harassed.

Seek independent counsel. Many companies have ethics committees for reporting abuse or breeches of company principles. Additionally, in some states you can contact a special state workforce organization, which acts as a mediator between employers and employees with ethical conflicts. The Equal Employment Opportunity Commission (EEOC) also handles such cases.

ETHICAL DILEMMA

You are a sales professional at your company. Your job, as well as that of your manager, depends solely on your outcomes. You are judged on your number of touch points (how many times you contact prospects). Your manager knows you have been low on phone calls and personal visits this month, but he needs to turn in a good report or his job will be on the line. He comes to you and asks you to inflate your numbers by reporting twice the amount of touch points compared to what you actually made. There is no way for his supervisor to know you fudged the books. What do you do?

Scan the code for additional information or visit: *http://bit.ly/TC8ED*

a.) Tell your supervisor you will not inflate your numbers, but you will endeavor to improve them before his report is due.

b.) Ignore him. Turning in a bad report will primarily affect him, and you've been doing the best you can.

c.) Agree to inflate the numbers this time, but try to improve your numbers honestly by the next report.

d.) Speak to your supervisor's boss and explain the issue that has been presented.

Conclusion

Personal accountability teaches that the burden of your success or failure is primarily on you. Yes, we are often shaped by our circumstances, but the fact remains that we can rise above our circumstances. Many of the challenges you will face will be tests of character or knowledge, whether personal, educational, or professional. The way you choose to meet those tests will determine your success in all areas of your life. Planning ahead, having a study strategy that fits your particular learning style, knowing what you stand for, and flexing your ethical muscle whenever possible will help you overcome virtually any challenge life throws your way.

Further Reading

Test-Taking Strategies, by Judi Kesselman-Turkel and Franklynn Peterson. Wisconsin University Press: 2004.

Pocket Guide to Study Tips, by W. H. Armstrong. Barron's Educational Series: 2004.

REVIEW QUESTIONS | What did you LEARN?

1. What is the difference between ethics and values?

2. Identify and explain Lawrence Kohlberg's six stages of moral development.

3. What are some methods to deal with text anxiety?

4. What is Bloom's Taxonomy?

5. Identify and explain the seven different learning styles outlined in this chapter.

6. What is overlearning and how is it helpful?

7. What does SQ3R stand for? How is it applied?

8. Why is continuing education beneficial?

9. What is a performance review?

10. What should you do if you witness harassment or are a victim of it yourself?

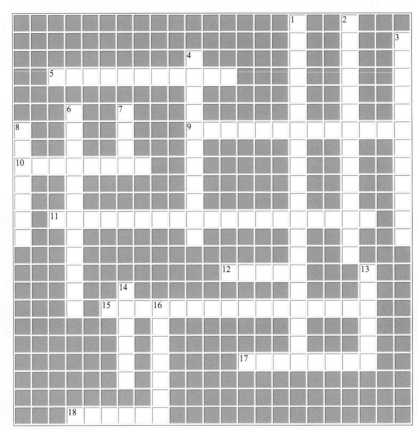

Scan this code to access the puzzle online or visit:
http://bit.ly/TC8Crword

Across

5. A very real psychological condition that many students experience

9. The way(s) in which you learn best

10. You like to learn on your own.

11. Classes you take once you have earned your degree or certain certifications associated with your career to ensure that your knowledge of your profession remains current (2 words)

12. Sounds and music help you remember things.

15. Chapter 8's title (3 words)

17. When you can do it, you know it.

18. You like to learn in groups, not on your own.

Down

1. Neurologically based processing difficulties that can interfere with learning basic skills (2 words)

2. A system of three domains, or areas, of learning, each having several levels

3. A learning technique that involves continuing to study or practice material that you've already mastered

4. Stages of moral ____

6. Who said, "The illiterate of the twenty-first century will not be those who cannot read and write, but those who cannot learn, unlearn, and relearn"?

7. Reading strategy that helps you learn new reading material

8. This tool allows you to set up group projects. You can chat, exchange notes, and share files with group members.

13. Images are the best way to convey information to you.

14. Spoken and written words help you lock in information.

16. Analyzing information logically and categorizing it cements new knowledge for you.

APRILSUE GRULICK
Director of Educational Technology & Faculty Professional Development Officer

Scan this code for additional info or visit: *http://bit.ly/TC8grulick*

Overcoming Test-Taking Anxiety

Professional and Olympic athletes do not become stars overnight. By constantly practicing and disciplining their bodies, athletes are able to excel in their sport of choice. The same is true for students, says Faculty Professional Development Officer Aprilsue Grulick.

"Learning happens by doing something repeatedly with concentration," Grulick says. Challenging school subjects cannot be mastered overnight either. By taking the extra time to practice and study new things, students exercise their brains and become smarter. Learning new concepts causes new neuron connections to form in the brain, Grulick says. Continued practice and repetition of these concepts creates stronger connections and improves long-term memory.

Grulick's role involves training new faculty how to use the latest teaching and learning strategies to optimize student success, helping professors revise and improve their syllabi and course materials, and supporting instructors by offering various workshops. She also hosts math anxiety workshops for students.

Because of her love for math while earning her degrees, Grulick's college professors and mentors encouraged her to study engineering. Throughout her educational and professional career, Grulick displayed her determination to succeed by overcoming a slight issue with dyslexia. She received her associate degree in robotics at a local community college and then at the University of Akron in Akron, Ohio, she also earned her bachelor's degree in technical education and a master's degree in curriculum development. Her love of math and the "visual and tactile nature" of robotics led her to a career teaching the subject and Programmable Logic Controllers (PLC) for several years.

Grulick says she developed a passion for education while in college. "I like everything about education and wanted to be a math teacher all my life," she says. The only female in many of her math and engineering classes, Grulick says math was always easy for her until she failed her first calculus. She retook the class twice because she was determined to succeed in learning the material.

After finding an isolated spot in the library she began to read and copy examples from her textbook. She repeated this several times until she began to understand the examples. After she understood the concept, she closed the book and tried to work the problems by herself. By practicing math problems in this way and reviewing before the professor's lecture, Grulick went from Fs to As on her calculus tests. Several of her classmates saw her success and asked her to tutor them. She discovered her interest in teaching when she began tutoring the guys in her class and helping them improve.

Tests are necessary in college for professors to determine what students have learned. Tests also enable instructors to give students accurate feedback. However, many students suffer from test anxiety. To overcome anxiety, Grulick says students need to change their negative thinking. "Attitude is everything," she says. "Stop telling yourself you're dumb and can't do it."

"Negative self thoughts" prevent students from having confidence in their potential, limiting how much effort and concentration they put into learning new material. Grulick believes every student has the ability to learn new concepts and encourages them to strengthen their minds by using proven strategies to overcome math anxiety.

Students also can take practical steps to minimize the anxiety of test taking. Beginning to study a week before the test and getting a good night's rest the night before will lessen stress and help students feel prepared. Eating a wholesome meal before a test also will give students energy to perform their best. Grulick says students who cram the night before a test or try to "wing it" weaken their confidence and become anxious. Cramming puts information into short-term memory. Stress causes blood vessels in the brain to shrink, causing short-term memory loss, she says.

Grulick says there are a variety of support systems that provide free assistance to students. Asking instructors for help, getting a tutor, and attending a math lab are just some of the options available. Grulick says if students want to excel at a subject, they need to realize the work involved and be willing to put in the time and effort.

"We can be as good as we want to be at almost anything if we try hard enough," she says. "If I can succeed while having a learning disability, others can, too."

Notes

STUDENT DISORIENTATION

Aaron started off the project's presentation to the class. His debate group had all agreed on doing a biography for Steve Jobs to honor him postmortem, but they couldn't ever really figure out how to have the design of the video reflect the technological contributions of Jobs and his company while adding their own touches and styles. It felt like a crime to even compare what they had worked on up to the legend himself, but *que sera sera*. They just had to show the film, and then discuss why they chose their topic. They showed the film and then Aaron stood up to go first.

"This truly shows why Steve Jobs is the master, and his loss is a blow from which technology may never fully recover." Aaron ended his part of the presentation.

The one girl Aaron had not gotten along with during the project got up to present her part. They had disagreed throughout the assignment, and Aaron knew she was going to say something contrary.

She began to discuss Jobs and what he contributed. "Steve Jobs was a very powerful person in technology, but his effects are limited to those who can afford Apple's creation. While many people can afford an iPod or iPhone, the iPad, which arguably is Apple's best creation yet, is extremely expensive. There are tablet alternatives on the market that are just as good at a more reasonable price. It was a terrible loss, but to say that he is the end all of technology is a bit narrow-minded."

Aaron butted back in to usurp her final statement. "Narrow minded or dead-on? No tablet will ever match up to the iPad and its subsequent generations. To believe otherwise is just stupid."

"Let's just finish the presentation." She sighed and nodded for their partner to go.

CHAPTER OBJECTIVES:

- Learning to communicate effectively

- Communicating with teachers

- Managing coworker conflicts

Humans have long searched for a way to communicate with each other. The earliest known form of writing, cuneiform, dates back to 2,000 BC. Certain Native American tribes used smoke signals to alert other tribes. The indigenous tribes of Australia and Africa used, and in some cases still use, drumbeats to communicate over distances. In 1837, Samuel Morse invented the first practical telegraph, and in 1876, Alexander Graham Bell invented the telephone.

Throughout the twentieth century and into the twenty-first, scientists have steadily worked to improve communication capabilities to the point that, today, you can choose from text messaging, faxing, instant messaging, and emailing. That's not to mention blogging and sending messages or bulletins over social networking sites such as Facebook. The speed and accuracy of our delivery systems has led to the era we now live in being termed "the Communication Age." Connection is everything in the global economy in which millions of dollars can be made and lost in mere seconds.

In spite of the many choices available for communicating technologically, these are simply the means of getting a message across. On the personal level, effective communication relies on physical cues such as voice inflection, body language, listening skills, and eye contact. Personal interaction enriches our relationships in all areas of our lives. While the need to communicate is as inherent as breathing for most people, not everyone is equipped to handle communication well. Effective communication can defuse arguments, avert misunderstandings, create relationships, and lead to greater personal and career satisfaction and fulfillment.

> " To be able to ask a question clearly is two-thirds of the way to getting it answered. "
>
> —John Ruskin

Everyday Personal Communication

We all employ communication skills every day. Simple greetings on the street, phone conversations, asking for directions – not a day goes by that we don't speak to numerous people throughout the day. Professional speaker and life coach Susan Fee says, "You have thirty seconds or less to make a first impression. The clock starts the moment someone encounters you. That could be your voicemail message, noticing you in a waiting room, or overhearing you on your cellphone. Whatever happens in that time sets the groundwork for future interactions."

What kind of perception do you want other people to have of you? The words you say, combined with the way you say them, the way you listen – or don't listen – when others speak, how often you make eye contact, combine to create your personal communication style, and it is as unique to you as your signature.

Some Tips for Effective Communication While Speaking

The Princeton Review website offers many tips to help you make a better impression while communicating. **Have an appropriate expression.** In other words, be sure that your facial expression matches your words. If you're not angry, don't look angry. A study from the University of California at Los Angeles found that up to 93 percent of communication is nonverbal. The people you speak to watch your facial expression and body language for cues to your sincerity. Don't put out unintentionally misleading cues by looking angry when you're not or, conversely, by looking happy if you aren't.

Voxer
Scan the code for additional information or visit: *http://bit.ly/TC9Voxer*

The Voxer app takes communication to a whole new level. Push a button to talk (like using a walkie-talkie), text, send photos, talk to groups, and much more.

Moderate your speaking speed. Speaking either too rapidly or too slowly can be annoying and turn off listeners. If people ask you to repeat what you just said or seem unable to follow your train of thought, you most likely speak too fast. On the other hand, if you encounter many people who tend to finish your sentences or get impatient and interrupt you, you may be speaking too slowly. Practice speaking into a voice recorder and listen to yourself. If you need to adjust your speaking speed, practice reading aloud at the speed you want to speak. Consciously listen to yourself during your conversations. When you find yourself falling into the old habit of running all your words together breathlessly, or of drawling out each syllable, change your speed accordingly. You will find people want to listen to what you have to say when they can listen at a comfortable speed.

Eliminate fillers. Try not say umm or uh. In today's casual conversations, the word like has taken on a life of its own. It's like, every word, like, has to be punctuated, like, with like. Not only is this distracting, but it also makes the speaker sound like a character straight out of a 90s teen movie. *Like* is a word for comparison (that dog is like mine) or to be used as a verb for stating preference (I like ice cream). If you want to be perceived as professional, be sure your words and delivery style convey that image.

Speak loudly enough to be heard, but don't be overbearing. Speaking in a whisper or hushed tone is annoying and can be seen as condescending, as if you were speaking to a little child. On the other hand, speaking so loudly that people step back from you or ask you to lower your voice is also annoying. Practice modulating your volume so you can be easily heard at a pleasant decibel level.

Smile while you're speaking on the phone. Telephone conversations don't afford the opportunity for body language to come into play. Words and tones can be easily misunderstood when a person can't see your facial expressions. To keep this from happening, remember to smile and keep a pleasant expression on your face while you talk on the phone.

Watch your diction. Completing words makes you sound smarter. Adding the "-ing" ending to words, rather than ending with an "n" sound, makes a huge difference in how you are perceived. If you enunciate clearly, you'll be easier to understand.

Effective communication is often an outgrowth of a positive self-image. People who are self-conscious may speak with their hands covering their mouths, avoid eye contact, shuffle their feet, shove their hands in their pockets, or slouch as they speak. In the general American culture, all of these things send a message of "I don't feel good about myself, so you shouldn't feel good about me either."

 WORKSHEET

This worksheet will help you assess what areas of communication you should work on. Take either a speech you've prepared for class or explain how to do something, step by step. Record yourself with your phone or some other recording device. Play it back and make notes on the worksheet about things you notice as you listen to yourself.

For the sample template, scan the QR code or visit:
http://bit.ly/TC9CommWS

How fast or slow did you speak?	
How many times did you pause?	
What fillers did you use and how often?	
How loud or quiet was your voice?	
Did you enunciate your words properly?	

However, in some other cultures, making frequent direct eye contact may be seen as arrogance. If you come from such a culture, it's important to be aware that many Americans may misinterpret your avoidance of eye contact. Even if it's a challenge for you, work on changing your interaction body language.

Use positive internal self-talk if necessary. Stand up straight when you talk to yourself in the mirror, then do the same when you talk to other people. Practice making eye contact with yourself first, and then try it on someone you meet at the coffee shop. Smile; it will make you look confident even when you aren't. Try to keep your feet and legs still when you talk, and let your hands gracefully punctuate your conversation, rather than keeping them shoved into your pockets or flailing about wildly.

To participate in the online poll, scan the QR code or visit: *http://bit.ly/TC9Poll*

What part of communication do you need to work more on?

○ Diction and speaking more clearly

○ Avoiding using fillers like "um" or "uh"

○ Speed of speaking, whether too fast or too slow

○ Loudness or softness of tone

Body Language Cues

Scan the code for additional information or visit: *http://bit.ly/TC9BodyCues*

Need help deciphering body language? The Body Language Cues App includes interesting facts about gestures, expressions, and body language and can help you communicate better with others.

Listen and Learn

Communicating isn't just a matter of knowing what to say and when to say it. It's just as important to know when to stop talking and listen. No one likes to have a one-sided conversation, except maybe for the person doing all the talking. If you ever walk away from a conversation feeling as if your friend didn't really say anything, maybe it was because you didn't give him or her a chance. Being a good listener is an important skill in all areas of your life.

There are two types of listening, and you'll need to know which one to employ when, depending on the type of conversation you're having. **Passive listening** is for when you are involved in a conversation that may be emotional, confidential, or of an otherwise personal nature. It means listening to another speaker without jumping in with your own comments. In a flowing give-and-take conversation, such as at a party, the story one person tells may set off a string of stories told by other listeners. This is called **active listening** and is used for interactive conversations. This type of conversation is lively and fun, but people may not be truly listening to the speaker because they are thinking about what they want to say.

Let's look at passive listening first. In "Interpersonal Communication" (published at www.ststephenanglican.com), Ed Swayze writes that passive listening "communicates acceptance to the speaker." When you give someone your full attention, without interrupting, without letting your

passive listening

Listening without interrupting; paying full attention to just the speaker

active listening

Listening but also interacting in the conversation

thoughts and eyes wander away (signaling boredom), you essentially tell that person what he or she says matters to you. Of course, at this point, the listener only knows you've "heard" and has no idea whether you've understood. Interjecting comments, such as "Uh-huh" or "I see," lets the speaker know that not only are you listening attentively, but you also are absorbing the information. The time will come in the conversation for you to speak, but sometimes, when a person is really struggling with a problem, they just want someone to hear and understand, not offer advice. When you can demonstrate passive listening ability, you deepen your relationship with that person.

Communications experts and psychologists often use the acronym SOLER to teach passive listening skills:

- **Sit** squarely facing the other person.

- **Open** your posture toward the speaker. Don't cross your arms or hunch your shoulders. Be in a receptive position.

- **Lean** forward.

- **Eye** contact is important. Don't stare intently, but maintain good eye contact.

- **Relax.**

▶ EXERCISE 9.1

In your journal, describe a situation in which you have had to use passive listening skills. Do you think you did a good job? Why or why not?

These suggestions show your conversation partner that you are truly listening and can also deflect argument or tension. As you listen, try to be empathetic. Ask yourself, "How would I feel in this situation?" When you listen sympathetically, you can feel sorry for a person about a difficult situation, but when you listen empathetically, you allow yourself to feel some of that person's emotion, creating a stronger bond between the two of you. This is more applicable in personal relationships than in business or education situations. However, being able to empathize with a teacher or manager will give you greater insight into what that person is asking of you, helping you to better perform to expectations.

Avoiding Conflict with "I" Messages

Conflict is an inevitable part of any relationship dynamic, whether at home, at school, or at work. As individuals, we all have creative ideas that we naturally prefer over others' ideas. Sometimes, in an equal relationship, as with friends or a life partner, there can be an unconscious fear of "losing face," or status, when the other person rejects your ideas or acts in a way that hurts your feelings. No two people will get along all of the time, nor will they agree on everything.

It's important to be able to voice your feelings when conflict arises, but how you get your message across can make or break a tense moment. When you use "you" messages, such as "You make me so angry when you say that," you are essentially attacking the other person. It causes your conversation partner to put up natural defenses that then have to be broken through for constructive dialogue to happen. Instead, try "I" messages, such as "I feel angry when I hear you say…" Now the responsibility for how you feel is on you, not on the other person, allowing them to feel emotionally safe in responding to your statement.

Additionally, try to avoid generic, wide-sweeping accusations such as "This always happens," or "We never get along." When disagreement arises, gentle words and cool heads can avert a heated argument and defuse smoldering tempers.

When you're angry, even if you're trying to use "I" messages, your body language can become the tipping point that escalates an argument. Make sure your eye contact is just that, not a glaring contest. Don't cross your arms, a sure defensive signal, and keep your hands relaxed at your sides and unclenched. Regulate your breathing so you stay as calm as possible. If necessary, step away from the situation for a few moments to let your temper subside. Don't just stalk away without a word. Tell the other person, "I need a few minutes to think about this. Please excuse me." Go outside, take a brisk walk, pull a few weeds, or do some other activity to release pent-up tension. You'll find you're both better able to discuss your issue when you return.

A final note about personal communication: Ria Angelia Wibisono writes in her article "A Glance of Interpersonal Communication" that "communication is irreversible. You can't undo your spoken words just like you edit your file in Microsoft Word. You have to manage your communication so that it won't bring a bad effect to anybody." Words can hurt a person or a relationship beyond repair. An old children's nursery rhyme says, "Sticks and stones may break my bones, but words can never hurt me." Nothing could be more untrue.

Quick TIP

Control your breathing when you get nervous or excited. This will help lower your pitch and keep you from coming across as hysterical.

Better Communication for Education Success

Now that you understand some of the basics of more effective personal communication, let's consider how you can benefit educationally from implementing your skills. Students often feel intimidated by college faculty members, including instructors, advisers, deans, and bursars. Because you are the student and they are the authorities, you may feel automatically at a disadvantage. The truth is, your college faculty members want you to feel you can approach them when you have questions or concerns. The way you approach a faculty member will determine your success or failure at initiating a constructive conversation.

> ❝The single biggest problem with communication is the illusion that it has taken place.❞
> —George Bernard Shaw

Classroom Communication

At a two-year technical college, much of the learning activity is interactive, taking place in the classroom or the laboratory. University environments foster more of a listening and absorbing environment, with the primary classroom sounds being the instructor's lecturing voice and the scratching of students' pens on paper as they take notes. Occasionally, a student may ask a question or answer if called on.

In an interactive learning environment, where the majority of class time is spent in a laboratory, students interact openly and often with each other and with teachers. A class setting such as this tends to be more casual, and it's easy to get sidetracked in personal conversations. Students who were naturally class clowns in high school may find this the perfect opportunity to continue entertaining their friends. This is not acceptable at the college level. It's important to remember that you and all the other students in the room are there because you all *pay* to be there.

Respect your own education and financial investment, as well as those of your classmates. Be on time. When you're late for class, you can miss vital information. You also disrupt class by pulling everyone else's attention away from what was going on before you arrived.

Arrive prepared. Know what is to be covered on the syllabus. Make sure that you've completed any assigned reading or homework so that you don't waste time asking questions that have already been covered. Also, bring with you any materials that will be needed in class.

Sit at the front of the class and away from any windows with eye-catching views. You'll be more likely to stay focused on what your instructor has to say than to get distracted by the beauty of the shady courtyard outside the window or fall asleep because of the quiet of the back of the room.

Keep even more distraction at bay by turning your cellphone off; then, put it away and leave it there. Don't take out calculators (unless they're needed during class), electronic gaming devices, or digital music devices. How well you do in your future career depends a great deal on how much you learn now and how well you learn it, not on how quickly you can send a text message.

Keep your conversations on task. If you're working in a laboratory situation, make sure your conversation focuses on the project at hand. Save chitchat for after class. During classroom discussion, avoid bringing up off-task subjects that will set the whole class off in the wrong direction.

Don't dominate the classroom discussion. When a concept is truly interesting to you or easy for you, you may be tempted to unconsciously dominate the discussion, simply by asking too many questions or making many comments. After a few of your questions are answered, let others have a turn. Approach the instructor after class and ask if you can have some one-on-one time to discuss the concept further. Teachers appreciate active learners, so your instructor will most likely be glad to give you more time.

Get involved in class discussion. While some students tend to dominate open discussions, other students will often sit through a whole semester without saying a word. Try to involve yourself every day in class discussions. Not only will this help you grasp important concepts and show your teacher you are engaged in the lecture, but it will also give you confidence for later on in the workplace when you may be called on to give presentations.

Save the clowning around for the weekend. Few teachers appreciate a class clown, and certainly not in a postsecondary situation where people have paid money to be educated, not entertained. If you want to be the life of the party, do it at the party, not in class.

Handle disappointment and mistakes maturely. If you learn during class that you got a lower grade than you wanted on a recent assignment, don't protest out loud during class. After class, speak with your instructor to schedule a time to discuss the grade. If you make a mistake during laboratory work, don't take it personally or let it affect your level of participation. Everyone makes mistakes; in fact, making mistakes is an important way that humans learn. Ask questions to get information that will help you learn from your mistakes.

Knowing how to use the dynamics of communication effectively in your education life will help you enjoy greater success academically and prepare you for the challenges you'll meet in the workforce. Knowing how to avert conflict, how to communicate openly with superiors, and how to present your ideas and concepts effectively will give you greater confidence when the occasion arises to use these interpersonal skills in any area of your life.

COACH'S CORNER

Many teachers require in-class participation, but how important is it? In Coach's Corner, Coach discusses why you should contribute to classroom discussions.

http://bit.ly/TC9CC

Quick TIP

Turn your cellphone all the way to silent, not vibrate. Don't kid yourself into thinking no one can hear your phone go off when it vibrates. Better yet, set your phone to airplane mode so you don't risk incoming calls or messages causing a distraction.

Recent polls of employers indicate that one of the most important "soft skills" – people-oriented skills rather than job-specific skills – they look for is the ability to work in a team environment. Dr. Randall S. Hansen and Katharine Hansen wrote in "What Do Employers Really Want? Top Skills and Values Employers Seek from Job-Seekers" that "[b]ecause so many jobs involve working in one or more workgroups, you must have the ability to work with others in a professional manner while attempting to achieve a common goal."

Learning how to work in a group effectively means knowing how to communicate within that group. The University of Reading in the United Kingdom offers the following points to help facilitate group collaboration and communication:

- Make sure everyone in the group feels equally valued.

- Listen actively.

- Be responsive to each other, directly acknowledging each other's contributions.

- Be curious and ask for clarification when needed.

Approaching a Teacher about Your Grades or Other Issues

Your instructors and other faculty members are considered experts in their field and deserve the respect their position brings. While you do not need to approach them in a subservient manner, you do need to be respectful. If you have an issue with something your teacher does, make sure you use appropriate communication techniques.

Assess responsibility for the problem. Think through the situation. When there is a problem between two people, it usually isn't all one person's fault. Do you share responsibility for this particular problem? Have you been putting enough time into studying? Have you been asking enough questions in class to ensure that you understand the course material? Once you clearly see ways you can improve the situation, then it's time to speak with your instructor about any remaining issues. Never go above your instructor's head without first attempting to work with him or her. Doing otherwise will set up your

Additionally, the University of Reading offers these principles for effective group work:

- Establish clear, common goals and identify specific roles for every group member.

- Commit to attend, prepare, and be on time for group meetings.

- Take responsibility for a share of the tasks and carry them out on time.

- Value multiple points of view. Respect others' alternative views.

- Pull together related ideas after they have been fully discussed. Have a group decision about whether to reject or accept the ideas.

- Keep minutes on group meetings. Make sure everyone is aware of the group's decisions and progress.

Be aware that negative attitudes will impair your group's ability to work together. Critical comments and judgments will create tension and keep the shyer members of the group from speaking up. Try to keep everyone participating equally and conversations on task for quicker results.

instructor as your adversary from the start, which will make resolving the situation more difficult.

Set an appointment, prepare for the meeting, and be on time. Check the class syllabus for information on your instructor's office hours, and then go to your instructor at the end of class and ask for an appointment to discuss your grades. Don't expect your teacher to make time for you right then, although the teacher may be able to do so. Busy teachers who are trying to maintain a schedule don't like to be ambushed by disgruntled students. Showing your teacher you respect his or her time will go a long way toward establishing a feeling of goodwill when you meet with your instructor.

Be prepared for your meeting. Before the meeting, make notes about the points you want to cover, so you don't forget something during the discussion or waste your instructor's time trying to remember an elusive point. Gather any materials you will need to document your case, and don't forget to bring them with you to the meeting. Make sure you're punctual to the appointment, as your instructor will most likely fit you in between other pressing matters.

Use polite conversation to set the tone. Even though you may be upset about a grade or some other classroom issue, jumping right into the problem will immediately bring up your instructor's defenses. A few moments of ice-breaking conversation with starters such as "How was your day?" or "How's the semester going for you?" will keep tensions low. Don't overdo it, however. Make a few polite comments only, and then move on to the reason you're there. Throughout the meeting, use your best manners. You'll get much further by showing respect than by being whiny or rude.

ETHICAL DILEMMA

Your teacher has just given you a D on a paper that you spent quite a lot of time working on. You want to confront the teacher and ask how he could've given you such a grade for all that work. Upon closer inspection, you begin to see numerous errors, but you're still not sure why you got the bad grade. What do you do?

Scan the code for additional information or visit:
http://bit.ly/TC9Ethical

a.) Confront your teacher. Don't worry about the errors you found. You put a lot of work in the paper, and your teacher should adjust the grade to reflect the effort.

b.) Go to your teacher and tell him you do not understand the grade, but not in a threatening way. Ask him for practical advice on how to improve for future papers.

c.) Take the paper to your school's writing center or a writing tutor to find ways you can improve your writing or research skills.

d.) Go to your teacher's superior and demand a better grade. You were obviously graded unfairly, and the superior has a right to know.

Use your "I" messages. Don't start the conversation with accusations. "You failed me on this paper" is one comment teachers don't appreciate but hear way too often. The reply is usually something such as "No, you failed yourself by not doing good work." Approaching a teacher like this sets up a losing situation, because the teacher possesses all of the power – in this case, control over your grades. It's better to approach the situation by putting responsibility on yourself first: "I don't understand why I received this grade." Or you could say, "I need to understand how you came to this conclusion about my grade." Teachers are human – they are extraordinarily busy, and they even make mistakes at times. It could be you actually got something correct that your teacher mistakenly downgraded you on. Perhaps, once you open a constructive dialogue about your essay, your teacher will see it in a different light. By not putting your teacher on the defensive from the start, you've given him or her the opportunity to reevaluate your grade without feeling as though he or she is giving up authority.

▶ **EXERCISE 9.2**

Role-play: You just spent two weeks writing the best research paper you've ever turned in. Your instructor gave you a C, but you felt it was at least worth a B. Have a classmate role-play the instructor's part, and walk through the suggestions in the section "Approaching a Teacher About Your Grades or Other Issues."

Don't argue. If your teacher hears you out but still maintains that you were graded fairly, do not escalate the situation by arguing. If you truly feel your grade is unfair, take the situation to the department chair. Engaging your instructor in an active argument will put you on the losing side every time, and you'll have to sit in class under a teacher who now views you as an adversary.

Show gratitude. If you and your instructor can come to an agreement that suits you, politely thank him or her and take your leave. Even if you don't agree, politely thank your instructor for his or her time anyway. "Thank you," "please," and "you're welcome" can open many doors of opportunity and create bridges of communication.

> ❝ Courage is what it takes to stand up and speak; courage is also what it takes to sit down and listen. ❞
> —Winston Churchill

Interpersonal Communication on the Job

The workplace is a dynamic environment with a variety of fluid relationships, some of which will be long lasting and some of which will exist only for a short time. Employees with strong interpersonal skills will enjoy greater success and longevity in their careers than people who don't develop these soft skills. Whether you are communicating with

your manager or with a customer on the phone, it is important to know how to handle your interpersonal communication in a way that opens doors, rather than shuts them.

In "Play Well with Others: Develop Effective Work Relationships," Susan M. Heathfield writes, "You can submarine your career and work relationships by the actions you take and the behaviors you exhibit at work. No matter your education, your experience, or your title, if you can't play well with others, you will never accomplish your work mission. ... How important are work relationships? Work relationships form the basis for promotion, pay increases, goal accomplishment, and job satisfaction."

For some people, knowing how to communicate interpersonally is intuitive. For others, it is a learned skill that has to be honed every day. Heathfield offers these suggestions for getting along at work:

- Bring suggested solutions, along with the problems, to the meeting table.

- Don't play the blame game; take responsibility for your own actions and don't place blame on others.

- Remember that verbal and nonverbal communication matter.

- Never blindside a coworker, boss, or reporting staff member.

- Keep your commitments. If you fail to meet your deadline, you affect deadlines of other people.

- Share credit for accomplishments, ideas, and contributions.

By employing these strategies, you will find that you build many rewarding relationships with coworkers as well as managers, contributing to your success, and often to the success of others, which can be just as satisfying.

Dealing with Difficult Coworkers

Even when you employ the strategies just discussed for better workplace relationships, conflict is unfortunately bound to come along. Jonathan A. Hess, author of the article "Dealing with Coworkers We Don't Like," calls work relationships "non-voluntary" because, as long as you hold a particular job, you have no choice about whom you interact with on the job. You can pick your friends, but you definitely don't get to pick your coworkers.

When a conflict comes up, there are some steps you should take to resolve the issue calmly and effec-

tively. First, clarify what's in conflict. Understand what the sticking points at the root of
the conflict are and be prepared to negotiate
on other issues. Then, find common goals.
Remind yourself and your colleague that
you're all working toward the same goals.
Put yourself on the same side, rather than
on opposing sides.

ON THE WEB

For information about work
relationships, visit:

http://bit.ly/TC9DiffPpl

Try not to take things personally. Just
because someone disagrees with you does
not mean it is a personal issue. Also, stick to the issues at hand. Don't
allow the argument to dissolve into a fault-finding expedition. Keep the
discussion relevant and focused on the present issue only. Remember to
be polite but not patronizing. Talking down to anyone under the guise of
being nice will only escalate an already tense situation. Do not become
emotional. Regulate your breathing. Focus on maintaining a relaxed posture. Remember that body language gives you away; make every effort to
control yours.

Customer Service Skills

No matter what type of job you have, you most likely will have to deal with
customers or end-users of your company's products or services. Having
the knowledge to repair or use the equipment may not be enough – you
may be called on to walk someone else through use of the equipment, as
well. At other times, when you're working on equipment other people use,
you'll need to be able to listen to the user tell you exactly what the machine
is doing before you can assess the situation. The best service technicians
and customer support representatives know how to get the information
they need out of the people they need it from.

Consider your audience. Are you dealing with high-level business-
people or professionals such as engineers or doctors? You may possess
knowledge they don't, but make sure you do not speak in a condescending
way. Respect the position and title of the people you work with. Alternatively, don't be intimidated by the customer's position or credentials. You
are a professional called on to do a professional job.

Don't use technical jargon. Even though you must come across as
professional, make sure you don't slip into jargon. In other words, avoid
using job-specific or equipment-specific terminology that would mean
something only to you or others in your field. If you must use a technical
term, give a simple but not patronizing explanation of the term.

Use good listening skills. Actively focus on what the customer is
saying. Make sure that you hear the whole problem before you ask your
own questions. Then, respond to the customer's statements. Help the customer know that you understand by rephrasing their words. Say things
such as "So what you're saying is the machine doesn't operate when …" or
"I think you're telling me that …"

jargon

Technical language or dialect
specific to a particular field that
people outside of the field may
not understand

Remember common courtesy. You, as well as your customer, are busy and pressed for time, but don't let that cause you to seem intense, impatient, or frustrated. Chances are, you'll go on service calls for problems that you'll find ridiculous. Remember that your customers are your company's lifeblood. Without them, you don't have a job. Courtesy and helpfulness are soft skills that all people, customers and supervisors included, appreciate.

Developing Dynamic Presentation Skills

Sometimes the communicating you do in the workplace has nothing to do with conversation skills and everything to do with presentation skills. The majority of people are not comfortable in public-speaking situations, yet many jobs require employees to give some type of presentation. When every eye in the room is focused on you, it can be pretty intimidating. However, if you have a few tricks up your sleeve, you can overcome your nerves and give a dynamic presentation.

Take a minute to regulate your breathing just before you have to take the floor. If you've spent the last five minutes working yourself into a nervous frenzy, you'll be breathless and dizzy by the time you begin to speak. While you're being introduced, purposely take deep, regulated breaths. Then, begin by greeting your crowd. "How's everyone doing today?" and "I want to thank you all for your time" are general ice breakers that let the crowd know that you feel relaxed. If you relax, they'll relax.

Stay in motion. Don't shift back and forth from foot to foot, but don't stand rooted to the spot. Move around as you speak. Stand in the center for a while, then make your way to the left side of the audience. After a few minutes, move toward the center again, and eventually to the right side. Movement keeps you from locking your knees and keeps the audience from feeling hypnotized by staring in one position. Don't go to extremes with movement, however, or your audience will feel as though they're at a tennis match, constantly needing to turn their heads back and forth.

Make eye contact. As you speak, let your eyes lock briefly with the eyes of various audience members. Don't hold the gaze so long that it becomes a stare, but let your eyes tell that person, "Yes, I'm talking to you." This makes your audience feel engaged and keeps them interested.

Quick TIP

Practice in the clothes you'll be wearing for the presentation. This way, you'll know if you're comfortable in what you're wearing and can become confident in the way you present yourself as well as your presentation.

> ▶ **EXERCISE 9.3**

Class presentation: Prepare a three-minute speech on the importance of strong interpersonal skills and other soft skills in your particular field. Present your speech to the class, using the presentation methods recommended in this chapter.

Avoid fillers. As you speak, avoid saying things such as "um," "you know," or "okay." Overuse of any expression can become distracting to your audience. It also can make you sound as if you're making your presentation up as you go along.

Vary your voice inflection. Be careful that you aren't falling into a monotone speaking style. You'll find your audience yawning and letting their attention wander. Instead, use a conversational tone, letting your voice go up on questions and down on statements. Try recording yourself a few times before you actually give your presentation to make sure you find a good balance. Too much inflection and you'll sound as if you're trying to sing.

Modulate your speed. When people are nervous, they have a tendency to speak quickly. Your audience needs to hear what you have to say, so give them time to absorb your words by pausing where appropriate and by using a moderate speaking speed.

Most importantly, have fun with it. Public speaking can be a positive experience, even fun, if you interact with your audience. Smile, look friendly, and speak directly to audience members. Be careful not to embarrass anyone, but if someone seems receptive to you, ask that person's name. Have that person join you on stage for a demonstration or ask him or her a question. The audience will stay more alert if they know you might call on them, and you'll feel less like the spotlight is on you alone.

PRESENTATION PRACTICE CHECKLIST

While you're practicing your presentation, review this checklist:

- ☐ My notes are in the correct order.
- ☐ I have a timer on hand to keep track of time.
- ☐ My recording device is on to review speaking speed as well as to catch fillers.
- ☐ I have on the clothes I will be wearing on presentation day.
- ☐ I have planned how I will move during the presentation.
- ☐ The timing of the slides is not too fast or too slow.
- ☐ I have planned my eye contact.

Conclusion

In "8 Simple Ways to Effective Interpersonal Communications," performance expert Peter Murphy writes, "Effective interpersonal communication creates a feeling of community and intimacy where everyone's contributions are valued. It leads to proper understanding, sometimes on a deep level, depending on the circumstances of the communication. To have really effective communication, you need to make use of a set of skills and knowledge and to evaluate these and update your communication skills from time to time." Communication is a two-way street, a give-and-take, where you send and receive information. The stronger your skill set in doing both of these actions, the greater your success will be in your relationships – in your personal life, your education life, and your business life.

Further Reading

(7L) The Seven Levels of Communication: Go From Relationships to Referrals by Michael J. Maher. Authorhouse: 2010.

Everyone Communicates, Few Connect: What the Most Effective People Do Differently by John C. Maxwell. Thomas Nelson: 2010.

1. What is a sign that you might be talking too quickly? What is a sign you might be talking too slowly?

2. How can a voice recorder help you adjust your speaking speed?

3. What are the two types of listening?

4. What is SOLER? How is it applied?

5. How can you avoid conflict with "I" messages?

6. How should you approach a teacher about your grades?

7. What are some techniques to get along with your coworkers at work according to Susan M. Heathfield?

8. How should you handle a conflict at work?

9. Why shouldn't you use technical jargon?

10. What are some techniques to help you overcome your nerves and give a dynamic presentation?

▶▶ Are you puzzled?

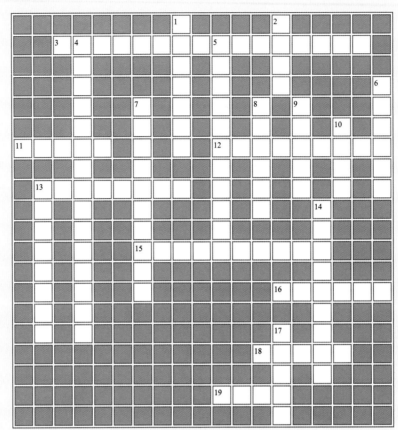

Scan this code to access the puzzle online or visit: *http://bit.ly/TC9Crword*

Across

3. Listening without interrupting, paying full attention to just the speaker (2 words)

11. What app has the ability to be used as a walkie-talkie, texting device, and much more?

12. University environments foster more of a listening and ____ environment.

13. Save ____ for after class.

15. Your face should have an appropriate ____ when speaking with others.

16. How many seconds does Susan Fee say you have to make a first impression?

18. The audience will stay more ____ if they know you might call on them during your presentation.

19. Who said, "The single biggest problem with communication is the illusion that it has taken place"?

Down

1. What do your instructors and faculty members deserve because of their position?

2. Who invented the telephone?

4. Listening but also interacting in the conversation (2 words)

5. At a two-year technical college, much of the learning activity is ____.

6. Technical language or dialect specific to a particular field that people outside of the field may not understand

7. Who said, "If you can't play well with others, you will never accomplish your work mission"?

8. Who said, "To be able to ask a question clearly is two-thirds of the way to getting it answered"?

9. Who invented the telegraph?

10. What word has taken on a life of its own in casual conversations?

13. ____ is an inevitable part of any relationship dynamic.

14. What is the earliest known form of writing?

17. Teachers don't appreciate a class ____.

JAMES MCKEOWN
English Instructor

Scan this code for additional info
or visit: *http://bit.ly/TC9Mckeown*

Read to Write Well

"The only way for students to learn to write is to read," says English instructor James McKeown. "Reading and writing are so closely intertwined." Whether they read car magazines or Shakespeare, McKeown believes reading gives students a feel for how authors put thoughts to paper.

McKeown has taught English since 1996. He went to Rowan University in Glassboro, Maryland, earning a bachelor's degree in English. He then came to Baylor University in Waco, Texas, to pursue his master's degrees and begin teaching college-level English.

College graduates must be able to communicate clearly and concisely on paper, says McKeown. They need to be able to write emails, memos, letters, and reports with ease. Every job deals with reading and writing on some level. "Reading and writing are the keys to everything in life."

McKeown encourages students to "just write." Even if a student doesn't particularly enjoy reading, he believes anything a student reads or writes is good. Only an individual can discover his or her own "voice" when writing. He advises students to keep personal journals and read anything of interest to them, even if it's simply a cookbook.

McKeown believes the most important thing students can do when learning to write is discover a process that works. He encourages student to find their own individual writing process. The important part of any writing process a student chooses is getting started. Students need to have a regular time and place to work. Getting into a routine when writing is important, he says. "If five o'clock in the morning works for you, you have to do it."

McKeown believes it's important for individuals to recognize when something they write is not good. He says 75 percent of what he writes "never [makes it] beyond the drafting stage. For this reason, students should not try to write an entire paper the night before it's due. He never gives less than two weeks for students to finish a paper and always suggests they start immediately. "Get it done in one week, then edit it the next," he advises.

When writing, McKeown also says it's important for students to follow instructions and meet requirements set by professors. "Life is full of rules." For the thesis he recently completed for his MFA from National University, McKeown had to reformat his table of contents five to six times before it met the instructor's guidelines. "If I wanted to graduate, I had to do what they wanted," he says.

CHAPTER 10 Writing

STUDENT DISORIENTATION

Carlos had finally gotten to see his final grades, and he was horrified that his reading teacher had given him a C in his class. He had read all of the books and gotten all of the facts right. He had even done pretty well on the essay section of the test he thought. He had lost all of his papers, and never checked the grades on them anyway, but he thought it would be fine since his tests were going well. He was fuming after he had opened up his grade book for the semester. He quickly sent an email to the teacher:

"hey why do i got a C in your class? all my tests were grate and i read all the books thats totally worth an a dude. you really need to stop being such a jerk just because im older then every body else."

He got a reply within a few minutes.

"Dear Carlos Rogers, Thank you for your concern about your grades. It warms my heart to see students taking an interest in their performance in class. The thing that didn't warm my heart was your cold tone. I think if you look back through your email you will see the many errors in grammar and spelling that I marked on each of your papers that you turned in. I kept hoping you would get better grades on your papers so that it would match your wonderful tests, but you never seemed to take any of my suggestions. Best wishes for the future."

Carlos stopped for a minute. He went back and reread his email. Now that he wasn't in such a hurry, even he could see there were a lot of mistakes. He had always been terrible at writing. How was he going to be able to get a job if everything he wrote made him sound like an uneducated and unqualified person?

CHAPTER OBJECTIVES:

- Giving the best impression through writing

- Writing in an academic environment

- Applying writing skills to your career

Although most people prefer face-to-face communication, many times it's just not possible. In certain situations, it's not even advisable. Written communication endures. Verbal communication, on the other hand, can be easily forgotten, misinterpreted, or misrepresented.

Through the years of the Information and Communication Ages, the art of letter writing has all but disappeared and been replaced with email, text messaging, and instant messaging. Granted, instantaneous delivery has tremendous benefits over "snail mail," as traditional mail is often called, but we've also given up something in exchange – well-crafted writing. In fact, the thought of having to write anything longer than a basic email often intimidates people. However, whether at school, at work, or in other areas of life, strong written communication skills will get you far.

Using Written Communication for Personal Purposes

❝Good writers are those who keep the language efficient. That is to say, keep it accurate, keep it clear. ❞

—Ezra Pound

You probably don't give much thought to it, but you use written communication every day. Emails, thank-you notes, and personal business letters require basic written communication skills. With the popularity of email, a conversational tone has become prominent in much of our writing, but this is not always appropriate. It's important to discern the voice, or tone, needed for your particular writing.

Email

Email has launched a completely new style and method of keeping in touch. Answers to your email can return to you in minutes rather than days or weeks, as was common before the Internet. While convenient and gratifying, email is not without challenges.

The idea that certain rules of etiquette apply online is called netiquette. When you communicate face-to-face, you and your conversation partner have the benefit of not only hearing the conversation but also seeing it through body language. Up to 93 percent of our conversation is nonverbal. When you use email, you may say something you think is funny or sarcastic, but the person reading your note may miss your tone entirely, not seeing the glint of humor in your eyes.

The following email netiquette tips by Aaron Turpen of Aaronz Web-Workz and by David Friedman, vice president and general manager of Telephone Doctor, can make your emails more effective and interesting. **To start with, do not to use all caps.** WRITING IN ALL CAPS IS THE EQUIVALENT OF SHOUTING!!!! (As is using more than one exclamation point!!!) If you absolutely must emphasize a point or a word, use the bold function or italicize.

Don't believe everything people forward to you. You undoubtedly receive plenty of emails with promises of a major corporation giving away money or dignitaries who need help transferring thousands if not millions of dollars out of their native countries. You may even receive warning emails or final notices from companies you may have never signed up with or from those you do frequently use. About 95 percent of these emails are bogus.

Check the veracity of an email by pasting a few keywords along with the word *hoax* into Google or another search engine. If the returns come back showing articles that claim the email is a fake, delete it. Additionally, many of these emails are specifically for the purpose of spamming and phishing. Government petitions can never be signed by email; they must always have ink signatures. All those emails asking you to digitally sign and send it on are really just spammers using you to collect email addresses from your friends. Also, bank and credit card companies will never ask you to simply email your social security number or other personal information.

netiquette

Internet etiquette or a set of social conventions intended to govern Internet usage and interaction

Having trouble determining if an email is a scam? Before you click on any links, right click on the link and select "Copy Link Address" from the menu. Paste the address into an Excel sheet or Word document. If it's a scam, it's likely the URL will have random letters or symbols.

APT APPS!

Grammar Girl App

Scan the code for additional information or visit: *http://bit.ly/TC10ggirl*

Whether writing an email or any other type of correspondence, it is important to follow grammar rules and proper spelling. The Grammar Girl App from The Grammar Girl's Quick and Dirty Tips for Better Writing podcast and website helps you keep up with different, confusing, and odd rules regarding writing.

Practice the twenty-four-hour rule when you're upset. Firing off a rude email when you're angry is never a good idea. Once you've hit send, those words can't be retrieved. Whether you're upset with a friend, family member, or business acquaintance, applying the twenty-four-hour wait rule can keep you from doing something you'll later regret. Give yourself time to cool off and consider your words before you send them.

ETHICAL DILEMMA

You have just received an angry email from a coworker addressed to the entire corporation. It accuses you and your team of being lazy, unprofessional, and impossible to work with based on a project your team and the coworker had been working on. You are infuriated that the matter was taken publicly first without private discussion and that the email was so rude. What do you do?

Scan the code for additional information or visit: *http://bit.ly/TC10email*

a.) Take an hour or two to calm down and then send an email to the whole corporation explaining the situation in a calm manner.

b.) Fire off an email to everyone explaining in a similar fashion the shortcomings of the coworker.

c.) Go to the coworker and yell at him for what he's written.

d.) Privately confront the coworker in a calm fashion once you've had time to cool down. Show you're the better person by acting professionally despite his behavior.

Business Letters

While most of your personal written communication will be casual, at times you will need to send a formal business letter. If you pay for services you never receive, you need to contact the IRS in writing. If you have a dispute with your credit card company over a fraudulent charge on your account, you will need to be able to craft a business letter that conveys a formal, professional tone. Using the appropriate letter format will let your recipient know you mean business from the very beginning and give you a much greater chance of being taken seriously.

Purdue University's online writing laboratory, OWL, offers an extensive tutorial on business letter formats, but here are a few basics from the site. Use the dateline to indicate when the letter was written. (However, if you write your letter over several days, use the date you finished it rather than when you started it.) Place the date flush left and two inches from the top of the page.

Including your address is optional. Place your address one line below the date. Do not write your name or title at this point, as you will write it in the letter's closing. Write out your street address, city, and ZIP code. Alternatively, you could write your address after your signature.

▶ **EXERCISE 10.1**

Business letter scenario: Assume you paid $300 to a home-improvement company for some repair work on your home. Not only did the contractor sent out by the company do a poor job, but he also damaged an area of your home and left a few details unfinished. Write a business letter to the home-improvement company detailing your situation and demanding restitution. Follow the business letter format.

The inside address is the recipient's address, and it is placed one line below the sender's address (if you have included it) or an inch below the date. It gives the best impression if you address your letter to a specific individual at the firm to which you are writing. If you do not know the person's name, call the company or speak with its employees. Include a personal or professional title such as Ms., Mrs., Mr., or Dr. If you are addressing a woman and are unsure of her preference, use Ms. as her personal title.

In the opening of your letter, or **salutation**, address the letter to the same name you used in the inside address, including the personal title. If you know the person personally on a first-name basis, it is acceptable to use only the first name. However, in professional cases, use the person's title and full name. If you don't know the person's gender, either write out the full name without a personal title or write "To Whom It May Concern."

salutation

Greeting used in written communication

USPS Mobile

Scan the code for additional information or visit: *http://bit.ly/TC10usps*

Ready to send that business letter? With the USPS Mobile app, find collection boxes, look up ZIP codes, and track the status of the letter from wherever you are.

USING CERTIFIED MAIL

Sometimes you may need proof that you actually sent a certain letter when you're writing to a person or company regarding serious financial matters or a dispute. In this case, use certified mail. This U.S. Postal Service tool costs very little and can save you from a financial loss down the road.

A CNNmoney.com article describes the plight of a person whose American Express card was used to fraudulently buy tickets and merchandise at Disney World. The charges totaled over $3,000. Although the customer followed American Express rules and sent his dispute in writing, he did not use certified mail, which would have given him a tracking number for the letter and proof that American Express actually received it. Eventually, American Express turned this person's account over to collections, saying they never received a letter and that there was no proof the

Single space and left justify each paragraph within the body of the letter. When writing a business letter, keep your content brief and to the point. In the first paragraph, address the main point of the letter. The next paragraph should explain the importance of the main point. Follow this with however many additional paragraphs you need to give background and supporting information. Remember, though, to stay concise; do not ramble on needlessly. The last paragraph should restate or summarize the main point and, if appropriate to the letter, request some sort of action.

Your closing greeting should be one line after the last paragraph and in line with the date at the top of the page. Use a greeting that is appropriate to the tone of the letter. In most cases, "Sincerely" is the best option, though you can also use "Best wishes." Note, if the greeting is longer than one word, only the first word is capitalized. Leave four blank lines between the greeting and type out your full name and title. The blank lines will be used for your signature after you print the letter.

When writing the body of your letter, pay attention to the tone you use. You may be irritated, but try not to let your emotion bleed through your writing. Also, make sure you aren't trying to impress your recipient with your ability to use big words and flattering terms. Your letter is likely to get much more attention if you write concisely and stick to a direct style that does not resort to overwriting to get your point across.

Words can be softened by a smile or a gentle look, but written words are simply what they are. The very fact that they are written down makes them a permanent record. Consider your writing carefully to be sure you aren't saying anything you may regret later.

charges had been disputed within the allotted timeframe. Fortunately, in this case, CNNmoney.com was able to mediate the situation, but their statement to this credit card customer was, "Having an advocate like us step in was lucky for you. But if you had used certified mail in the first place, the whole problem would have been avoided."

Anytime you send a business letter, your best practice is to use certified mail.

Store your receipt in a place where you'll be able to find it easily if needed. You can track the letter's progress over the Internet, and you can see when the letter is signed for. This practice can be effective in personal disputes as well, where, for instance, you have a disagreement with a neighbor over a property line and need to have a written record of the situation. No one can protect your financial interests like you can.

Writing Your Way to Success in College

Your college experience will undoubtedly give you many more opportunities to flex your writing skills than you will appreciate. Essays, research papers, and technical writing exercises may be regularly assigned to you. Knowing the basics of concise writing, along with simple grammar skills, will help your GPA and keep you from feeling overwhelmed every time you're faced with a blank computer screen and a looming due date.

The Essay

Teachers use essays to evaluate your understanding of the material you have learned. To write an effective essay, you must think critically, delving below the obvious surface applications or implications to the deeper meaning. Some students make the mistake of not doing this and simply write a review of the topic. In cases such as this, where the essay is shallow and shows no critical-thinking skills, instructors typically give a low grade.

Conversely, students may understand they need to write on a deeper level yet may not really be sure how to go about this. As a result, teachers often see essays filled with jargon, misused words,

> "However great a man's natural talent may be, the act of writing cannot be learned all at once."
>
> —Jean Jacques Rousseau

To participate in the online poll, scan the QR code or visit: *http://bit.ly/TC10Paper*

What part about writing a paper do you struggle most with?

○ The initial research

○ The outline and organization

○ The editing process

○ The thesis statement

and unorganized thought processes. Just because a word is long, that doesn't mean it needs to be in your essay. A well-crafted essay is thought out, organized, and uses words as if they were coins – sparingly. Although there are many models for writing essays, one of the best for writers who are just developing their composition skills is the five-paragraph essay. This style keeps your thoughts organized and has a clear beginning, middle, and end.

Choose a topic. Sometimes your instructor will assign you a topic, and other times you'll be able to choose you own. If you have the opportunity to choose for yourself, be sure you make a choice that has enough information available. You don't want to run out of ideas or information halfway through your composition.

Determine your purpose. Are you writing to persuade, instruct, explore, or inform? It's important to determine your purpose ahead of time because this will determine the tone of your paper and the way you present your information.

Develop a thesis statement. Once you've determined your topic and purpose, it's time to develop your thesis statement. This statement tells your reader what your paper is about. Since this is a five-paragraph essay, your thesis statement should make your point and offer three supporting details. For example, let's say your topic is "Why should someone choose graphic design as a career?" The first part of your thesis statement makes your point: "Graphic design is an excellent career choice because. ..." The second half of your statement supports this point and shows the reader what your body paragraphs will be about. So maybe your whole thesis statement would be this: "Graphic design is an excellent career choice because it offers creative students a job that complements their natural abilities, the general public makes buying decisions based on visual stimuli, and job availability is expected to increase at a faster than average rate over the next ten to fifteen years." Now you have a clear statement with three supporting details, which you will develop in the body paragraphs.

Organize your thoughts. Now it's time to get organized. A good way to do this is to draw a circle in the center of a blank sheet of paper. In that circle, write your topic and your thesis statement. Draw three straight lines out from your circle, randomly spaced, and draw a circle at the end of each line. In each of these circles, write the topic of each body paragraph. (These topics will come directly from the three parts of your thesis.) Underneath the topic heading, jot your supporting ideas for each topic inside the circle.

▶ **EXERCISE 10.2**

Write a five-paragraph essay on why you have chosen the major you have. Use the suggestions in this section and be sure to edit your writing according to the best practices listed.

As you sit down to write the rough draft of your paper, use this document to organize your thoughts. Be informal. This is an exercise to help get the process going.

For the sample template, scan the QR code or visit: *http://bit.ly/TC10Draft*

The main point/subject/objective of my paper is:	
My thesis statement is:	
My position on the point/subject/objective is:	
I believe that position because (two to three points):	
Sources that agree with me include:	
Another side to the point/subject/objective is:	
The other side believes that position because (two to three points):	
Sources that agree with that position include:	

Write your introductory paragraph. Think of your introduction as an upside-down triangle. It should start broad and move to a specific point, which is your thesis statement. Begin with something general, such as: "What do billboards, video games, and animated movies have in common? Graphic designers create them." Move through your paragraph logically, narrowing your focus until you end with your thesis statement.

Write your body paragraphs. Just as a train doesn't suddenly jump from one track to the next but instead uses a transitional piece to make the connection, so must each thought in your paper connect smoothly. The topic sentence of the first body paragraph will correspond to the first point in your thesis statement. Your second body paragraph will relate to the second point, but also transition smoothly out of the last sentence of your previous paragraph, and so on. As you write the body, refer to the information you put in your circle map. Make sure you elaborate on each of your points, developing it fully without becoming repetitive. Use transitional words such as *additionally*, *furthermore*, and *however* to link your sentences as well as your paragraphs. Read your sentences aloud. If a new thought feels abrupt, use a transition word.

Write your conclusion. Your conclusion is a triangle that is right side up. Begin by restating your thesis in different words. As you move through your conclusion, begin using broader concepts – for example, what will graphic design be like in twenty years? Be careful not to open a whole new topic, however. End by staying on your point, but in a broader, more general sense.

Edit your rough draft. Sleep on it and then reread your draft the next day. Look for grammar and punctuation errors. If you aren't sure about basic grammar, ask your English teacher for help. Also, you can check online sources for help. Again, Purdue's OWL is an excellent resource for all things pertaining to writing. Make sure your points are well-developed and supported. If you quoted someone or paraphrased a source, be sure you cited the source correctly. Plagiarism is a serious matter that can result in failure or even expulsion.

Research Papers

A research paper assignment strikes fear in the hearts of many students. If you dread this requisite project, you're not alone. However, using the principles you just learned for essay writing should make research papers much easier to handle. In Chapter 6, you learned how to organize research. You can apply that same knowledge to research papers so you can keep your writing focused as it progresses logically from point to point.

PROOFREADING CHECKLIST

Use the following checklist when you are ready to proofread your writing:

- ☐ All of my sentences are complete.
- ☐ I have cited my sources according to the recommended style guide.
- ☐ I have double-checked my subject-verb agreement.
- ☐ I have double-checked my punctuation.
- ☐ I have run the spell check.
- ☐ I have verified the spellings of names and places.
- ☐ I have read the paper out loud, word for word.

Keep in mind the most important thing to avoid when writing a research paper is plagiarism. Plagiarism is probably not an unfamiliar term to you, but you may not be aware of everything it encompasses. Anytime you use information that is not originally yours, you must credit the source. You will notice that in this book, as well as in most other textbooks you read, the sources are cited for all information that is quoted or paraphrased from another book, website, or magazine or newspaper article. Many students believe only direct quotations need to be cited, and this is where you could get into trouble. Even with paraphrased material, the source must be cited. Unless an idea or thought originated with you, you must give attribution to your source. Indiana University Writing Tutorial Services offers this advice:

plagiarism

Using another person's content, ideas, or writing without giving credit or permission; trying to pass someone else's work off as your own

- Use quotation marks around anything that you copy directly from a source.

- When you paraphrase, you must do more than just leave out a few words or put them in a different order. Make sure that you only use your own words. You still must cite your source because you are paraphrasing someone else's idea or writing.

- Check paraphrases against your source to make sure that you used your own words and stuck to the original idea without directly copying anything.

Many colleges use software that checks student essays against a database of already used essays, so avoid temptations such as copying from friends' essays or buying an essay. If you still have questions about plagiarism, ask your dean or adviser for advice.

Writing Laboratory Reports

In your technical classes, you may be required to write laboratory reports to record your observations. Laboratory reports differ from essays in that they are technical reports and stick to only observable facts. Don't include your feelings or narrative descriptions when writing this type of report, and remember to use past tense for describing what happened in a given experiment and present tense for describing chemical or mechanical laws and properties or statements of fact. Your various instructors may have specific guidelines for laboratory report writing, but the following sample laboratory report guidelines, modified from "Writing Lab Reports and Scientific Papers" by Warren D. Dolphin of Iowa State University, will give you a good feel for what a laboratory report includes.

According to Dolphin, the title of the report should be concise and to the point. "Scientific titles are not designed to catch the reader's fancy. A good title is straightforward and uses keywords that researchers in a particular field will recognize." After that, you should include an abstract, which is a very brief (100-200 words) summary of the report's content.

ON THE WEB

For more information about writing laboratory reports, visit:

http://bit.ly/TC10Lab

In the introduction, discuss any background directly relevant to the project, such as "Why was this study performed? What knowledge already exists about this subject? What is the specific purpose of the study?" Then, discuss the different materials and methods you used during your experiment. Dolphin writes, "The difficulty in writing this section is to provide enough detail for the reader to understand the experiment without overwhelming him or her."

In the results section, present your findings, often via charts and diagrams, but do not yet discuss the implications of the results. Interpret the information in the next section of your report, the discussion. At the end of your report, as with all reports, you must cite your sources.

Technical Writing

Technical writing bridges the gap between a research paper and a laboratory report. While a research paper might be about any topic, from controversial political issues to historical events to literary evaluations, a laboratory report is short, succinct, and focused on scientific method. A technical report uses a similar reporting style as the laboratory report but often incorporates the sources and discovery methods of a typical research paper. Technical writing seeks to inform or instruct, rather than persuade, and is usually focused on a scientific or engineering topic. Narration, emotion, and opinion do not belong in technical writing, but facts, data, and observations do. Technical writing may include graphs and illustrations, as well.

Anytime you buy a product that has a technical data sheet with it, you are looking at technical writing. You'll also see technical writing in professional journals and abstracts, as well as in many of your technical textbooks. Wordsworthwriting.net, a site that offers professional writing, editing, and formatting services, also offers some helpful writing tips. The following suggestions are adapted from their article "Technical Writing Tips."

Use active voice. *Active voice* and *passive voice* refer to the type of verbs you use. Active voice always makes writing clearer and easier to understand. Active: The IT manager evaluated the accounting software. Passive: The accounting software was evaluated by the IT manager.

Be specific. Technical writers must avoid vague language. For example, if there are three connecting wires, write "three connecting wires," not "a few connecting wires." Your readers need to know the specifics of the product or information you are sharing. Make sure they could walk away from your paper with all the knowledge necessary to make the same repair or achieve the same results that you did.

Eliminate jargon when possible. Sometimes you will not be able to avoid using technical jargon. Overusing jargon to prove how intelligent you are, though, actually backfires and makes your reader frustrated. Every field has slang, idioms, acronyms, and jargon that are specific to that field. If you can eliminate them in your writing, your meaning will be clearer and your writing easier to read.

If you are writing a technical research paper, you will still use references and sources, so be sure you cite your sources carefully to avoid plagiarism. Additionally, have someone else read your finished paper to see if it is well organized and follows a logical progression without any gaps in logic. Do you transition smoothly from one point to the next? Did your paper make and support a point?

No matter what type of writing you are assigned, remember the purpose of written communication is to convey your ideas clearly to your readers so they don't have to ask you for clarification. Before you turn in any paper, read it out loud. If you stumble over certain areas, it's a good sign you need to reword those areas. The skills you learn now will follow you into the work world, where you may be called on to use written communication regularly. Take advantage of the tips and suggestions in this chapter and the knowledge of your instructors while you have the opportunity. It could mean the difference between finding your dream job and staying in a rut because you don't have the needed skills to move ahead.

> " Writing is an exploration. You start from nothing and learn as you go. "
>
> —E. L. Doctorow

Writing on the Job

Many students leave college believing they'll never have to write anything again. They couldn't be more wrong. Take a quick look at the jobs available on any Internet job board, such as Monster.com, and you'll see that the majority of positions require "excellent written and verbal communication skills." The days of the VCR/television repairman sitting alone at his workbench have given way to team environments where creative thinking skills, a variety of writing skills (including technical writing), and people skills merge into a multitalented employee who brings diversity to his or her work situation. Moreover, being able to get your ideas on paper in a way that makes other people want to read them can help you get a better job, score a promotion, enjoy publication (and credibility) in your field, or even write a business plan that secures a bank loan for you.

Writing Your Way to Your Dream Job

When you first contact a company about a posted job, the potential employer has only one way to decide if you might fit their qualifications – by what you tell them in your cover letter and resume. For this reason alone, cover letters and resumes may be the most important things you'll ever write in your career. Resumes tell your potential employer what you experience you have. Your cover letter tells them who you are.

A recent survey by Accountemps found that 60 percent of executives believe that the cover letter is either as important as or more important than the resume. In his article "Covering Your Bases: Make Your Cover Letter Count," Max Messmer, Chairman and CEO of Robert Half International, Inc., says, "A cover letter allows you to direct the reader's attention to aspects of your resume that are most relevant, demonstrate your knowledge of the company you're writing to, and explain any part of your work history that needs clarification." Messmer's suggestions, explained in the following paragraphs, will help you craft interesting and effective cover letters that will draw the positive attention to you that you desire.

Follow the standard business format. Try to address the letter to a specific individual, even if it means making several calls to determine whom that should be. Be sure to ask for correct spelling, as a potential employer who sees his or her name misspelled may assume you are not detail oriented. For more suggestions on business letter writing, see the "Using Written Communication for Personal Purposes" section of this chapter.

The opening sentence of your cover letter should give the reader a compelling reason to continue reading. Let the employer know how you found out about the job opening. For example, "I am writing in response to the turbine technician job you described on the website Careerbuilder.com."

Demonstrate your knowledge of the company. Work a fact or observation that isn't commonly known into your opening statement. "I've been following with interest your company's success in the field of nano-technology." Then, explain your current situation. Are you finishing school or in a full-time job? When can you begin? Clarify these points in your cover letter.

Explain why this job interests you. Let your potential employer know what you have to offer. Do you have any special skills or abilities you could build on if hired? If you don't have much work experience, but you do have considerable education in this field, let them know. Emphasize your education.

Briefly elaborate on one or two key points in your resume. If you've held a job that would be specifically interesting to this employer, let them know. If you have attained impressive measurable goals, bring attention to that. For example: "The safety guidelines that I implemented in my last position saved the company more than $20,000 dollars the first year I worked there." Be specific and to the point. However, don't rehash your resume. Let it speak for itself.

Many times you may be replying by email to a posted job opening. You still need to send a cover letter. An online letter does not need to be as lengthy as a traditional letter, but remember your business letter format and courtesies.

After you've grabbed your potential employer's attention with a hard-hitting cover letter, you must follow up by showing that you can do the job. Your resume should highlight your experience and abilities. There are several resume formats to choose from, including chronological, functional, and combination. A **chronological resume** details the timeline of your experience, while a **functional resume** focuses on your skills. A **combination resume** blends these two styles, highlighting your skills before detailing your job experience.

If you are coming out of college and have little or no on-the-job experience, a functional resume may be more appropriate for you. In this instance, you would highlight the skills you learned from your studies. While experienced job seekers often begin resumes with a career objective, as a student just getting into your chosen career, you may still be formulating an objective. Robyn Feldberg, a certified career-management coach and owner of Abundant Success Career Services, says, "I don't recommend writing a vague objective, because it will typically focus on what the job seeker wants, which is usually of no consequence to the person making the hiring decision. Instead of an objective, I recommend that students format a profile section that clearly gives the reader a picture of the value they offer a potential employer."

Louise Fletcher, in "What to Include on Your First Resume," offers some great advice to students who as yet have little or no experience in their target career field. "Many students and recent graduates worry that they don't have enough experience to create a compelling resume. Don't be concerned. Once you start to really think about your background, you'll be surprised at what you have to boast about. The content of your resume will be determined by your own unique experiences, skills, and background." She suggests these general guidelines for what to include in an effective resume:

- Positive personal characteristics

- Technical and computer skills

- Education accomplishments (include your GPA if it's over 3.0)

- Skills and experience gained during internships or summer jobs

- Other related accomplishments (design awards, recognition, winning competitions, etc.)

- Work history (include unpaid work if it relates to your target positions)

chronological resume

Focuses on the timeline of your experience

functional resume

Focuses on your skills; good especially if you're just coming out of college and have little or no on-the-job experience

combination resume

Blends the styles of the functional resume and the combination resume, highlighting your skills before detailing your job experience

COACH'S CORNER

Why do you need writing in college? In Coach's Corner, Coach has the answer for you.

http://bit.ly/TC10CC

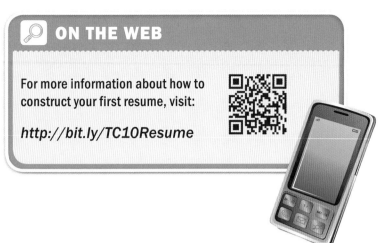

ON THE WEB

For more information about how to construct your first resume, visit:

http://bit.ly/TC10Resume

Fletcher goes on to say that it's important to accentuate the aspects of your experience, education, or personality that fit the profile for the job you are seeking and to leave the other qualities out. "For example, if you are looking to work in Information Systems, your ability to program in C++ will be important, but the fact that you have won awards for water skiing won't. Don't include hobbies unless they directly relate to your goal," she says.

Because so many high schools teach technology and vocational classes, many students do come to college with some solid work experience. Only use work experience or volunteer experience from high school if it is directly relatable to the job you are applying for; in general, it's not advisable to include high school information once you're in or about to leave college. You will need to decide which resume format suits your specific situation. For various formats and more advice, visit your graduate services department.

If you don't have any experience at all in the field you are seeking to enter, move your education information to the top so your potential employer immediately sees you are studying for that specific field. In the "Skills and Qualifications" section, highlight the skills you have learned in college that will benefit your employer. Remember your resume is the second part of your personal introduction to the prospective employer. It should show that you are capable of filling the open position. Because it is how you will get your foot in the door for an interview, you should have someone else, such as an instructor or advisor from your graduate services department, look at your first resume. Once you've been in your career for a while, you'll have a much longer resume with more experience to detail. Your first resume, however, should be no longer than a page; your potential employer wants to be able to scan the information.

Constructing a Business Plan

At some point in your career, you may decide to go out on your own in business, either in consulting or by opening your own business. The first step to starting a successful venture is to write a business plan. Think back to Chapter 1, where we discussed goals and charting your future. You could consider your business plan as another chart to keep you focused on your plans, only this chart applies directly to your professional life.

If you are going to be seeking third-party financing for your business, such as through a local bank or investment partners, you will need a formal business plan. In that case, it is advisable to pay a consultant to help formulate your plan. Adriana Copaceanu states in "Tips on Writing a Business Plan" that "often a small business will create their first business plan in the form of brainstorming notes or outlines. And this is fine to get started. The important part, though, is actually writing down some kind of plan."

The Franklin Covey Leadership Institute says each year nearly as many businesses fail as open. If you plan to start your own business, you need every possible advantage on your side. Having a focus and a strategy to make your goals a reality are the most important aspects of your business because everything else follows your focus. Copaceanu offers five things to think about when writing an informal business plan:

- What kind of company are you starting?

- What is the purpose of your new business?

- How will your business make money?

- Who will be your customers?

- How will you get your customers?

Writing your ideas down will help you galvanize your purpose and goals so that you are able to keep them SMART.

Employee Evaluation

If your career takes you to a management position, you may find that you will need to write annual or biannual employee evaluations. Using clear, concise writing will help your employees, as well as any upper management who may read the reports, understand your perspective.

Be specific. Give concrete examples whenever possible. Too many employee evaluations are filled with subjective information that can be argued. Concrete examples prevent this from happening.

Make your criticism constructive. Remember that your words can be very hurtful, even in professional situations, and unhappy employees move on to other jobs. If you need to correct an employee, use positive statements along with your criticism. For example, "Joe does not yet meet expectations in phone sales but is showing great improvement over last year's numbers." Use positive feedback wherever possible. Highlight your employees' strengths before you criticize their weaker areas.

Focus on the job description. Keep your comments relevant to the job the employee is to perform. Avoid letting personal conflicts color your comments. Also, keep your comments succinct. Avoid long, rambling sentences. While your evaluation should be thorough, using bullet points makes it easy to skim the highlights when reviewing it with your employee.

Conclusion

Regardless of whether you're writing an email, resume, business plan, or employee evaluation, having the skill set to make your writing strong and effective will help you take charge of your personal, academic, and career success. People who have strong written communication are typically seen as critical thinkers and perceived to be better communicators in general. It takes time and practice to develop these skills, but it doesn't require you to be an Ernest Hemingway. Anyone can improve their written communication by implementing the tips and tricks found in this chapter.

Further Reading

Job Hunting for Dummies, 2nd edition. For Dummies: 1999.

Grammar Girl's Quick and Dirty Tips for Better Writing (Quick & Dirty Tips) by Mignon Fogarty. Holt Paperbacks: 2008.

1. What are some netiquette tips for emails?

2. In the salutation of your business letter, what should you write if you don't know the gender of the person you are writing to?

3. How can using the certified mail be beneficial?

4. What is plagiarism? How can you avoid it?

5. How do laboratory reports differ from essays?

6. What are some tips to improve your technical writing?

7. Why are cover letters important?

8. What are three different kinds of resumes?

9. If you are coming out of college and have little or no on-the-job experience, which type of resume is most appropriate for you?

10. What questions should you answer while writing your business plan?

►► Are you puzzled?

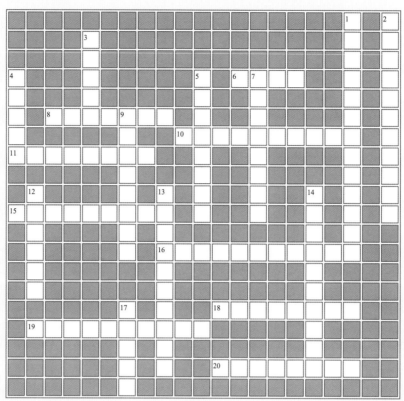

Scan this code to access the puzzle online or visit:
http://bit.ly/TC10Crword

Across

6. What app helps you find collection boxes, look up ZIP codes, and track the status of a letter?

8. Written communication ____ longer than verbal communication.

10. This type of resume focuses on your skills and is good if you're just graduating college.

11. Your conclusion when writing an essay is a ____ that is right side up.

15. What is traditional mail sometimes called? (2 words)

16. What app helps you with grammar rules and proper spelling? (2 words)

18. When writing a resume, give ____ examples whenever possible.

19. Greeting used in written communication

20. Who said, "However great a man's natural talent may be, the act of writing cannot be learned all at once"?

Down

1. This type of resume focuses on the timeline of your experience.

2. What percentage of our conversations are nonverbal?

3. Who said, "Good writers are those who keep the language efficient. That is to say keep it accurate, keep it clear"?

4. Practice the twenty-four-hour rule when you're ____.

5. Writing in all caps is the equivalent to what?

7. Words can be ____ by a smile or a gentle look.

9. In an employee evaluation, keep your comments ____ to the job the employee is to perform.

12. The ____ address is the recipient's address.

13. Using another person's content, ideas, or writing without giving credit or permission

14. Internet etiquette or a set of social conventions intended to govern Internet usage and interaction

17. Scientific titles are not meant to catch the reader's ____.

MARGARITA SANCHEZ
English Instructor

Scan this code for additional info
or visit: *http://bit.ly/TC10Sanchez*

Employers Look for Strong Communication Skills

"Being able to understand someone else's ideas and being able to express your ideas are at the core of every college course a student is required to take," says Margarita Sanchez, a college reading instructor.

For the past thirty-five years, Sanchez has dedicated her time to teaching students how to better understand, synthesize, and respond to what they read. Whether she's instructing traditional reading classes or hybrid and online courses, Sanchez spends each day teaching reading, helping solve technology problems, and advising students, all while encouraging their success. She is available seven days a week in her office or via email to assist and interact with her students.

After earning her bachelor's degree in elementary education with an emphasis in Spanish, Sanchez taught fifth grade for a year. She then returned to school and pursued her master's degree in education and curriculum instruction with an emphasis in reading from the University of Texas at Austin.

While working on her master's, Sanchez says a fellow graduate student and friend allowed her to teach his reading class at Temple College several times. Because of this experience, along with the mentorship of her UT professors, Sanchez discovered she wanted to teach adults and help "enhance their educational experiences."

Sanchez believes it's imperative for individuals to comprehend, analyze, and be able to communicate what they read. For example, to get the most from article, book, and chapter readings, Sanchez also suggests students familiarize themselves with how writers typically express their ideas on paper. When students become aware of contextual "clues," it's easier for them to understand an author's message, Sanchez says.

Creating summaries and outlines also help students remember and retain information from their assignments and readings. Outlining makes students aware of what points and parts of a reading are the most important, says Sanchez. The more practice students get outlining and summarizing what they read, the faster they will become at recognizing main points of an article or book.

Employers are always on the lookout for individuals who have strong written and verbal communication skills. "Every employer can teach their employees skills inherent in the jobs pertinent to the business," Sanchez says. "However, in order to learn those on-the-job skills, all job candidates must possess the ability to comprehend ideas in print and apply them when appropriate."

Students must know who they are and be able to evaluate what natural abilities, talents, and interests they possess. By communicating with her professors, Sanchez was able to express her interests with them. She was then able to choose a course of study and a career that complemented both her talents and passions. Sanchez says she got her current job because she was "in the right place at the right time, and more importantly had made [her] interests known and prepared for the position during [her] degree program."

She advocates students communicate their strengths, weaknesses, and interests to their professors as well. Through effective communication on the students' part, professors and counselors can better help students strengthen skills, overcome weaknesses, and prepare for the career of their dreams.

Notes

STUDENT DISORIENTATION

"What is that?" Misha nearly screamed as Kristen showed off her new tattoo.

"It's a tattoo," Kristen replied.

"Why would you get a tattoo? I mean, you're not a druggie."

"Tattoos don't make someone a druggie, Misha." Kristen defended. "You realize I have four, right?"

Kristen showed Misha her other tattoos. Misha looked more and more disgusted with each one. "It's one thing to have hidden ones, I guess, but your new one is on your arm where everyone can see it! Aren't you worried about the way people are going to perceive you?"

"My tattoos are personal. They're not about anyone else." Kristen folded her arms across her chest.

"I don't get it. You're a smart person, but with this … I mean, no respectable company is going to hire you. They're just all going to think you're trash with all those tattoos!"

"Just because I have these doesn't make me any less intelligent or skilled a worker than anyone without them!"

"That's not the way you look."

"Just don't talk to me, Misha." Kristen stormed out of the room.

CHAPTER OBJECTIVES:

- Practicing tolerance in your personal life

- Learning in a diverse educational setting

- Handling discrimination and harassment at work

Look around at the people you go to school with. Every individual has specific qualities, beliefs, ethnicities, and values, which they contribute to society. When we embrace those differences, a rich, multicultural, multi-dimensional fabric is woven that allows each person to find his or her unique place. President Franklin D. Roosevelt demonstrated his full understanding of this concept when he said, "If civilization is to survive, we must cultivate the science of human relationships – the ability of all peoples, of all kinds, to live together, in the same world at peace."

We live in a much smaller world than the people of even two generations ago. Not that the world has shrunk in size, and certainly not in population, but in boundaries. Perhaps you are from a small town where you see mostly the same people every day, many of whom have a belief system similar to yours and have the same traditions as you. Maybe you're already accustomed to the diversity found when we open our eyes and senses to the world beyond our front door. It's likely that as you go through college and then move into your career field, you will increasingly come into contact with people who are different from you. As global boundaries continue to shrink, so must personal biases based on religion, gender, politics, life choices, sexual orientation, and ethnicity.

Appreciating Diversity and Practicing Tolerance in Your Personal Life

Diversity has been a political and social buzz-word since the early 1980s, but diversity has always existed in the United States. Our country was founded on the concept – differences in political and religious ideologies, various ethnic groups – and our founding fathers wrote the Constitution to protect diversity. Nonetheless, some people have difficulty accepting people of other ethnic groups or beliefs. Some consider certain careers to be "men's work" and other careers to be better for women. Some hold stronger biases against various ethnic groups and differing religious beliefs. As our world has evolved toward a greater social consciousness, intolerance of diversity has become less and less acceptable. To truly enjoy success in today's world, it is imperative to learn tolerance toward other people.

> We have become not a melting pot but a beautiful mosaic. Different people, different beliefs, different yearnings, different hopes, different dreams.
>
> —Former President Jimmy Carter

Stereotypes, Prejudice, and Discrimination

To understand why tolerance is vital, it is necessary to first know what stereotypes, prejudice, and discrimination are and the profound effects they can have on individuals, groups, and entire nations. When we assign characteristics to entire groups of people solely on the basis of their membership in a particular group without seeking facts about each person, we are creating stereotypes. We may believe in "positive" stereotypes, such as "She's a woman, so she must be a nurturer," or "negative" stereotypes, such as "He's a boy, so he's boisterous."

When we take stereotypes further and form attitudes about members of a group just because they are part of a group that we have stereotyped, we have developed a prejudice. As with stereotypes, there are both positive and negative prejudices. If we have a "positive" prejudice toward women as nurturers, we may assume that every woman can be a great parent or teacher and will be better at those tasks than a man. If we have a negative prejudice against boys as being boisterous, we may not want to be around boys for fear they will disrupt everything or may not give them opportunities to engage in quieter activities.

If we act on our prejudices, we are engaging in discrimination. In holding our prejudice that all women are nurturers, we might refuse to consider hiring men as elementary-school teachers. Also, in holding our prejudice that all boys are boisterous, we might not allow our daughter, a second-grader, to invite any boys to her birthday party – even though her best friend is a boy – for fear the party will get out of control.

Stereotypes can lead to prejudices, and prejudice can lead to discrimination. You might not think refusing to hire men as elementary-school teachers or refusing to invite boys to a girl's birthday party would have far-reaching repercussions, but they can. When talented men aren't considered for teaching jobs in elementary schools, children miss out on the chance to have nurturing male role models. When boys are denied the chance to associate with girls, both groups miss out on chances for good friendships and for learning about interacting with the other gender. Those who are discriminated against may not develop a healthy self-esteem and may end up not living up to their full potential.

stereotype

A widely held but oversimplified concept or belief of a particular type of person often based on religion, heritage, socioeconomic status, or sexual orientation

prejudice

A preconceived notion or belief not based on experience but on stereotypes

discrimination

An act against certain people based on stereotypes and prejudices, such as segregation, refusal to hire, or name-calling

How Do I Practice Tolerance in My Personal Life?

Consider your social group. Does everyone look the same, act the same, vote the same, or practice the same religious beliefs? Of course not. We don't expect our immediate social group to all be just like us, even though we share similarities and common bonds, so why do we expect our society at

COACH'S CORNER

As the saying goes, diversity is the spice of life, but it can also be challenging to deal with. In Coach's Corner, Coach has some advice on how to get passed stereotypes and prejudices.

http://bit.ly/TC11CC

tolerance

Fair and respectful treatment of all people, regardless of differing heritages, religions, sexual orientations, and genders

large to be made up of people who are exactly alike? We tolerate differences among those we love, respect, or hold deep affection for. We understand that accepting differences in the people within our social groups doesn't mean we have to incorporate those differences into our own lives. Tolerance, then – speaking in societal terms – is extending that same respect to everyone else.

▶ EXERCISE 11.1

In your journal, describe a situation in which you practiced tolerance. How did you feel about this situation? Who were the people involved, and what did you do? How did they react?

Before you create a stereotype, step back and think about all the ways you could be stereotyped based on your heritage, gender, orientation, religion, or lifestyle.

The U.S. Department of Education says "one of the most effective means of teaching respect for diversity is eliminating ignorance. When we come to an understanding, we begin to gain a sense of perspective that allows us to see things more clearly and with less bias." The best way to develop tolerance in your own life is to take time to understand the people around you. If you have neighbors from another culture, get to know them. Ask them about their festivals and beliefs. If they invite you to a celebration, go. You might like their traditional foods or music. If you approach the situation with open-mindedness, you may even discover you have much more in common than you ever believed possible.

World Customs & Cultures

Scan the code for additional information or visit: *http://bit.ly/TC11ccapp*

As the world becomes a smaller place, it's becoming more and more important to understand how best to interact with all the different cultures in a respectful manner. The World Customs & Cultures App will help you understand the greetings, communication style, and gestures of different cultures around the world.

If you don't have the opportunity to get to know someone of another culture or belief system, you can still develop tolerance by employing the Golden Rule: "Do unto others as you would have them do unto you." It's such a simple concept. If you want to be accepted, tolerated, and treated with respect, do the same for everyone else. Extend the freedom to be themselves to those around you, even if who they are isn't who you want to be or goes against what you believe. They still have the right to their own beliefs, and you wouldn't want them to restrict your beliefs or practices.

One way to learn how to fight prejudices and intolerance is to understand how unique each person is and how no one can fit perfectly into generalizations. Use this worksheet to explore what makes you unique, and then talk to a friend or classmate and ask them these same questions.

For the sample template, scan the QR code or visit:
http://bit.ly/TC11WS

	My answer	My friend/classmate's answer
Where were you born?		
What do your parents/ guardians do for a living?		
What would you describe your heritage as?		
What music do you like to listen to?		
How would you describe the way you like to dress?		
What do you want to be doing in five to ten years?		
What religion (if any) do you practice? Why?		
How would you describe your political views?		
How would you describe your work ethic?		
What one word do you think best describes you?		
What is your outlook on life?		

Practicing tolerance in your personal life can open you to new friendships and cultural experiences, but it can also help you lessen tensions and defuse or avoid conflict. Among your immediate social group, even though you all have differences, you also have many things in common. That's normally what draws people to the friendships they have. Your friends and you may discuss controversial issues and air your differences of opinion freely; you have a socially safe environment for you to do so. Even if you end up in a heated debate, friendship usually wins out.

In a group setting, however, where not everyone is your close friend, or maybe most are even strangers to you, tolerance and tact are partners. You may find yourself in a meeting or party where you don't have the safety zone of your personal social group. There are a few things you can do to avoid tensions or conflict. Be polite and courteous to everyone. Treat everyone you meet with equal courtesy, regardless of color, sexual orientation, gender, or religion.

Do not bring up any controversial topics, and don't allow yourself to be drawn into any heated conversations. This is not the forum for you to share your political leanings and social gripes. Keep the conversation general. Avoid politics, religion, and biased remarks.

Avoid telling ethnic, sexist, political, or otherwise biased jokes. Jokes that target any specific group will inevitably insult someone. You'd do better to keep your humor broad, staying away from anything that could be construed as derogatory or offensive.

Follow your mother's advice. "If you can't say something nice, don't say anything at all." Mom was right. If the conversation or social situation distresses you to the point that you're ready to let fly with your own diatribe, step away. Pretend it's the television and you can turn off what you don't like. Offending your host and his or her guests isn't worth having the chance to put in your two cents' worth.

> " We all should know that diversity makes for a rich tapestry, and we must understand that all the threads of the tapestry are equal in value no matter what their color. "
>
> —Maya Angelou

Diversity on Campus

People who learn to practice tolerance and respect for others in their personal life will naturally do the same in their education. Everyone deserves to have a non-hostile environment in which to learn. Unfortunately, in recent years schools have often proven to be one of the least tolerant areas of society, sometimes leading to tragic and violent results. Teachers and administrators at all levels of education are working to instill a balance of tolerance and respect, but colleges and universities bear the final responsibility of training students to be sensitive to and accepting of other people before they're launched into the workplace.

College, therefore, should be a place where ideas can be freely exchanged without the fear of reprisal, judgment, or bias. Our nation's college campuses have students from a multitude of nationalities and who have many different traditions, belief systems, and abilities, yet often students congregate only with those who are "just like" themselves. Fear, whether of change or of rejection, is a powerful force that keeps students divided. Students must consciously work

to overcome biases in the classroom so that their professional growth isn't inhibited by intolerance and misguided judgments. Moreover, prejudices don't extend only to people of other nationalities and personal beliefs. Gender bias is just as real and detrimental as any other intolerance.

I Can't Understand What You're Saying!

Tolerance in education means accepting the accent differences of U.S. regions other than yours and language differences of other nationalities. College campuses have become quite a mosaic of cultures, and you are likely to hear any number of languages and accents that are unfamiliar to your ears throughout the day. Be respectful of the fact that many of these students may be learning concepts, abstract ideas, and difficult technical material in a language that is foreign to them. It is possible in some cases that their challenges are greater than those for native English speakers, simply because they have a cultural gap and a language barrier to overcome.

If you can't understand what someone with another accent is saying, ask them to repeat themselves more slowly. Don't be rude, though. Put yourself in their shoes. What if you were studying graphic design in China? Or Italy? Or any other non-English-speaking country, for that matter? People who practice intolerance are fond of saying, "This is America. Learn the language." Do you remember taking a foreign language in high school? How much did you learn from that experience? Were you able to speak fluently after two years of instruction? Undoubtedly, the answer is no.

Sometimes, students encounter instructors who speak something other than English as their first language. This can be difficult in a class setting where you need to take notes and understand everything your instructor says. If you find yourself in such a situation, make sure to write down everything that the instructor puts on the board or overhead. If you aren't sure about some of the key concepts after the instructor lectures, ask for a private appointment to go over your notes.

Watch Your Own Words

Words are a powerful weapon. Simply by using a few words, you can wound someone's spirit to the point that a relationship is destroyed forever. Even if you consider yourself highly evolved in the area of tolerance, you must be careful about what you say. Something as innocent-sounding as "women are good in nurturing careers" could be taken as a sign of disapproval or an insult by a woman entering the technical field.

Avoid racial, gender, and sexual-orientation stereotyping. Stereotyping is one of the most common forms of intolerance. Broad, sweeping generalizations are seldom true and can be very hurtful. Be aware of the difference between a statement of fact and a statement of stereotyping. Think about what you are going to say before you say it.

To participate in the online poll, scan the QR code or visit: *http://bit.ly/TC11DPoll*

What types of differences make you most uncomfortable (be honest)?

- Other religions

- Different sexual orientations

- Alternative political views (liberal, conservative, moderate, other)

- Other heritages

IS THAT A WOMAN IN MY LABORATORY?

Yes, it probably is! In technical programs, where many of the courses have been considered primarily a man's domain in the past, women have an especially hard time gaining acceptance and respect. A study by M. Thom, M. Pickering, and R. Thompson, discussed in the 2002 article "Understanding the Barriers to Recruiting Women in Engineering and Technology Programs," found that when asked about the social factors of concern in entering a technical career, young women's top responses included discrimination, prejudice/hostility, male domination, and schedule. Both the establishment of work schedules to accommodate women's other responsibilities and male dominance in the profession were seen as detriments to attracting women to technical professions in both this study and the EDUCAUSE Center for Applied Research (ECAR) study on leadership in the information technology (IT) profession.

Tolerance toward women in the technical workplace is an issue that must be addressed at the college level if it is to be conquered at the professional level. Instructors and administrators can and do provide gender-sensitivity information in the classroom, but it's up to the individual to make a decision for tolerance.

If you're feeling uncomfortable with someone's presence in your class, ask yourself a few questions. **Why do I feel threatened or uncomfortable?** Sometimes, our biases are based on fear of fail-

Quick TIP

If your school has an international students program, get involved. You'll make more friends and get to experience their cultures, as well as share your own.

Avoid sexist language. Be careful that what you say cannot be construed as sexist or sexually inappropriate. Remember: Men are by no means the only offenders in this category. Women can be just as guilty of making sexist statements as men. Also, even a simple compliment can become sexually offensive when accompanied by certain body language, so be aware of that too.

Avoid racial slurs and epithets. Familiarize yourself with the socially accepted terminology when referring to other ethnic groups. Avoid insulting racial terms at all times. These words not only hurt other people but they make the user sound ignorant as well.

Creating an environment that nurtures learning and acceptance isn't solely the responsibility of our educators. Individuals must take responsibility for their own actions and work together to create a safe zone in our colleges, where people of all backgrounds can prepare for a future that will benefit everyone.

ure on our own part or fear that we may be overlooked. Do you feel that your own achievements will be lessened in light of the other person's? You may need to consider how to strengthen your skills, rather than worrying about someone else.

Am I acting fairly toward that person? Be careful not to instigate prejudice toward a person in your class. People tend to act with a herd mentality, and if one or two students align themselves against another student, more may join in. Don't be the class bully.

Use the sunlight test. In Chapter 8, you learned about the sunlight test, in which you should ask yourself, "Would I want this action to be on the nightly news?" If you can't be proud of an action

you're about to make, don't make it.

What do I gain from acting out intolerance? Take a hard look at yourself and be honest. Does making someone else feel bad make you feel better? Are you boosting your ego by putting someone else down? These are hard questions to ask yourself, but if you're willing to look at the root cause behind your unwillingness to accept other people, you may be able to uncover a hidden stumbling block in your own life.

What if it were me? Apply the Golden Rule. Treat others as you want to be treated. You want respect; give respect. You want acceptance; grant acceptance. It's not so hard to get along if you just remember your manners and everyone else remembers theirs.

The Diverse, Non-Hostile Workplace

Merriam-Webster's Third New International Dictionary, Unabridged (2002) defines *diversity* as "the condition of being different or having differences." Although everyone in your company and on your team will have common professional goals, you will all have your own qualities that make each of you uniquely the person you are. Protecting the rights of workers to be themselves is partly the job of the Equal Employment Opportunity Commission (EEOC).

“ Diversity is not about how we differ. Diversity is about embracing one another's uniqueness. ”

—Ola Joseph

APT APPS!

diversityDNA
Scan the code for additional information or visit: *http://bit.ly/TC11DNA*

The workplace is becoming an ever-increasingly diverse place. The diversityDNA app is a mini diversity training program designed to help people understand cultural differences and how they affect communication at work.

▶ EXERCISE 11.2

How do you think your specific career field could be improved to make a more level field for all employees, regardless of gender or national origin? Be prepared to discuss in class.

The EEOC was established in 1964 with the Title VII Civil Rights Act. It is a government entity established to prohibit discrimination for any reason in the workplace, whether based on ethnic group, national origin, gender, sexual orientation, religion, or physical disabilities. Under the Title VII Civil Rights Act of 1964, along with the Americans with Disabilities Act and the Age Discrimination in Employment Act, it is illegal to discriminate in any aspect of employment, including:

- Hiring and firing

- Compensation, assignment, or classification of employees

- Transfer, promotion, layoff, or recall

- Job advertisements

- Recruitment and testing

- Use of company facilities

- Training and apprenticeship programs

- Fringe benefits

- Pay, retirement plans, and disability leave

- Other terms and conditions of employment

Discriminatory practices under these laws also include:

- Harassment on the basis of ethnic group, skin color, religion, sex, national origin, disability, or age

- Retaliation against an individual for filing a charge of discrimination, participating in an investigation, or opposing discriminatory practices

- Employment decisions based on stereotypes or assumptions about the abilities, traits, or performance of individuals of a certain sex, national origin, age, religion, or ethnic group, or individuals with disabilities

- Denial of employment opportunities to a person because of marriage to, or association with, an individual of a particular ethnic group, religion, or national origin, or an individual with a disability

🔍 ON THE WEB

For more information about the EEOC, visit:

http://bit.ly/TC11EEOC

Title VII also prohibits discrimination because of participation in schools or places of worship associated with a particular racial, ethnic, or religious group.

Do these laws mean that discrimination never occurs in the workplace? Unfortunately, no they do not. Creating a non-hostile work environment is the responsibility of each individual. These laws do mean that if any discrimination occurs, there is a legal recourse available to the victim.

▶ EXERCISE 11.3

Visit the EEOC website and read some of the news stories. Choose one story to summarize in your journal. After you write your summary, answer the following questions:

a.) What decision was made?

b.) What are the important implications of this news?

c.) Do you agree or disagree with the findings? Why?

d.) What could have been done to prevent this situation?

ETHICAL DILEMMA

You witness a coworker being discriminated against by your boss and other coworkers because she is Muslim and wears a hijab, or traditional headscarf, to work. While you don't share her religion, you are very concerned with her treatment. However, with your boss participating in the discrimination, you fear you could lose your job if you speak up. What do you do?

Scan the code for additional information or visit:
http://bit.ly/TC11ED

a.) Comfort her and stick up for her whenever someone says anything discriminatory or harasses her.

b.) Ignore it but refuse to participate. You can't afford to lose your job.

c.) Consult her and suggest she take the issue to her boss's superior, the HR department, or the EEOC.

d.) File a formal complaint about the issue with the HR department and EEOC yourself.

What Should I Do If I Am Harassed or Discriminated Against?

The EEOC also deals with harassment in the workplace, stating:

> "Harassment is a form of employment discrimination that violates Title VII of the Civil Rights Act of 1964, the Age Discrimination in Employment Act of 1967 (ADEA), and the Americans with Disabilities Act of 1990 (ADA)."

Harassment is unwelcome conduct that is based on ethnic group, skin color, sex, religion, national origin, disability, and/or age. Harassment becomes unlawful where (1) enduring the offensive conduct becomes a condition of continued employment or (2) the conduct is severe or pervasive enough to create a work environment that a reasonable person would consider intimidating, hostile, or abusive. Antidiscrimination laws also prohibit harassment against individuals in retaliation for filing a discrimination charge; testifying or participating in any way in an investigation, proceeding, or lawsuit under these laws; or opposing employment practices that they reasonably believe discriminate against individuals.

Petty slights, annoyances, and isolated incidents (unless extremely serious) will not rise to the level of illegality. To be unlawful, the conduct must create a work environment that would be intimidating, hostile, or offensive to reasonable people. Offensive conduct includes offensive jokes, slurs, epithets or name-calling, physical assaults or threats, intimidation, ridicule or mockery, insults or put-downs, offensive objects or pictures, and interference with work performance.

Harassment can occur in a variety of circumstances. The harasser can be the victim's supervisor, an agent of the employer, a coworker, or a non-employee. The victim does not have to be the person harassed but can be anyone affected by the offensive conduct. Unlawful harassment may occur without economic injury to or discharge of the victim.

Stress Doctor

Scan the code for additional information or visit: *http://bit.ly/TC11Stress*

Harassment in the workplace can create a stressful, hostile work environment. The Stress Doctor app helps you lower your stress by guiding you through some breathing techniques. It will help you calm down, relax, and become more focused.

Of course, the best deterrence to harassment is prevention, and most companies and employers have strict guidelines and policies regarding harassment because the financial consequence of harassment litigation can be devastating. Money alone can't always make reparations for the damage done in a hostile work environment. Sometimes victims suffer ongoing mental and physical illness or strains when discrimination or harassment has been severe and long-lasting.

If you believe you are a victim of harassment, then you should keep a log of the inappropriate behavior that happens to you at work. Document every conversation or action. If you have proof of harassment through email, print out copies and place them in a binder.

You probably remember the phrase "ladder of escalation" from our discussion of workplace ethics in Chapter 8. Begin your "ladder of escalation" with your immediate supervisor, unless he or she is the source of discrimination. In that case you'll want to go above your supervisor to middle managers. Give them an adequate and fair amount of time to investigate and solve the problem. If you don't get results within a couple of weeks, take it to the next step.

Speak up. If you see someone at work being discriminated against or harassed, approach the person and encourage them to speak up. If they feel supported, they may garner the courage to confront the issue. If you are the one being harassed, confront your persecutor. Bullies will bully as long as no one calls them out.

If the inappropriate behavior continues, take the issue to the next person in authority. This would normally be the immediate supervisor, unless that person is the one causing the problem, in which case, speak with his or her supervisor.

Make a formal complaint. If the issue cannot be resolved at the management level, consider filing a formal complaint with your human resources department. However, different companies have varying views of whistle blowers. You must decide whether you are willing to risk your job, or possibly future promotions, to help someone else who is being harassed.

Seek independent counsel. Many companies have ethics committees for reporting abuse or breeches of company principles. Additionally, in some states you can contact a special state workforce organization, which acts as a mediator between employers and employees with ethical conflicts. The Equal Employment Opportunity Commission (EEOC) also handles such cases.

How Can I Avoid Harassing Others?

Employers are not the only people in the workplace who get sued. Fellow employees can be sued for discrimination or harassment. The non-hostile workplace is a serious matter, and a wise employee will make sure that he or she does nothing that could be misconstrued as discriminating.

Respect other people's personal space. Keep an invisible personal boundary between you and your coworkers. Standing too close to someone can be seen as intimidating or harassing. Also, don't be overly friendly with your hands. A firm handshake is always acceptable. A sympathetic but quick pat on the shoulder may be fine. Be aware that lingering touches are usually construed as inappropriate and could leave you open to a sexual harassment lawsuit.

Censor your emails and keep private mail off your company computer. The IT manager at your company has access to everything you send and receive across company servers. Moreover, the files on your company-supplied computer are actually the property of your employer, so it is a good practice not to keep personal mail, files, pictures, or software on that computer. You could be required to turn your computer over to IT at any time, and if inappropriate material is found on your hard drive, it could mean the end of your job.

As society moves toward even more diverse workplaces, we must be increasingly aware of the consequences of a hostile workplace. Elizabeth Mitchell writes in her article "Working in a Diverse Society" that U.S. census data indicates that by the year 2050, nearly half of all people living in the United States will be from a nonwhite, non-Anglo culture. "Those who have the knowledge and ability to work within an increasingly diverse society will be in the best position to gain employment. Cultural knowledge and awareness, multilingual ability, and a true skill in working with people from other cultures will be sought after," she writes.

Conclusion

The concepts of diversity and tolerance may seem complicated at first glance, especially when you consider the EEOC regulations and the number of harassment suits brought to court each year. However, the concept is really not complicated at all. Tolerance simply creates an environment of mutual respect, in which everyone is allowed the freedom to be themselves, within the confines of the law, of course. When you stop feeling threatened by another person's beliefs or traditions and look for the similarities you share, the feelings you can empathize with, and the common goals the two of you work toward, you'll be able to see the differences for what they really are – the variety that keeps life interesting.

Further Reading

The Hard Truth About Soft Skills: Workplace Lessons Smart People Wish They'd Learned Sooner by Peggy Klaus. HarperBusiness: 2008

35 Dumb Things Well-Intended People Say: Surprising Things We Say That Widen the Diversity Gap by Maura Cullen. Morgan James Publishing: 2008.

1. What is a stereotype?

2. How can you practice tolerance in your personal life?

3. According to the U.S. Department of Education, what is one of the most effective means of teaching respect for diversity?

4. What did M. Thom, M. Pickering, and R. Thompson find to be the top social factors of concern among young women?

5. Why should you avoid racial, gender, and sexual-orientation stereotyping in conversation?

6. According to *Merriam-Webster's Third New International Dictionary, Unabridged* (2002), what is diversity?

7. What is the EEOC?

8. What are examples of discriminatory practices?

9. What should you do if harassed or discriminated against?

10. When does harassment become unlawful?

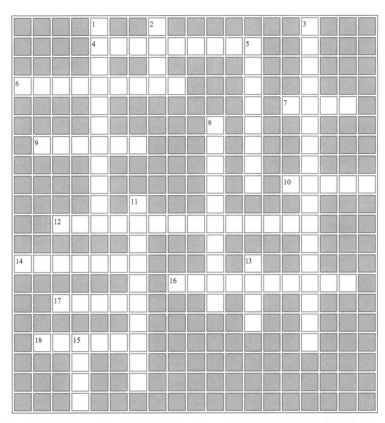

Scan this code for to access the puzzle online or visit:
http://bit.ly/TC11Crword

Across

4. The fair and respectful treatment of all people

6. One of the most effective means of teaching respect for diversity is elimination what?

7. In a group, tolerance and what else are partners?

9. Who said, "We have become not a melting pot, but a beautiful mosaic. Different people, different beliefs, different yearnings, different hopes, different dreams"?

10. We understand that accepting differences in our social groups doesn't mean that we have to incorporate those differences into our own _____.

12. An act against certain people based on stereotypes and prejudices

14. Extend the freedom to be themselves to those around you, even if who they are isn't who you want to be and even if who they are goes against what you _____.

16. Those who are discriminated against may not develop healthy _____.

17. When talking in groups, you'd do better to keep your humor _____.

18. Who said, "Diversity is not about how we differ Diversity is about embracing one another's uniqueness"?

Down

1. Widely held but oversimplified concepts or beliefs of a particular type of person

2. Protecting the rights of workers to be themselves is partly the job of whom?

3. As global boundaries continue to shrink, so must personal biases based on religion, gender, politics, life choices, _____, and ethnicity. (2 words)

5. The files on your company-supplied computer are actually the property of your _____.

8. What is the phrase "Do unto others as you would have them do unto you" called? (2 words)

11. Even if you end up in a heated debate, _____ usually wins out.

13. The best way to develop tolerance in your own life is to take time to _____ the people around you.

15. _____, whether of change or of rejection, is a powerful force that keeps students divided.

GILBERT MONTEMAYOR
Social & Behavioral Sciences Department Chair

Scan this code for additional info
or visit: *http://bit.ly/TC11GM*

Rising above Intolerance
and Discrimination

"If we cannot end our differences, at least we can make the world safe for diversity." John F. Kennedy made this statement nearly fifty years ago, yet the issue of diversity still remains a point of contention in schools and in the workplace today. Learning tolerance and respect for people from different cultures, backgrounds, and beliefs is the key to cultivating a productive, harmonious environment. Meeting people from different backgrounds will broaden world views and acquaint you with intriguing people along the way.

Gilbert Montemayor, chair of social and behavioral sciences at a community college, says every student should be aware of diversity and how to handle situations with sensitivity and dignity. Respect, especially, is a topic he has found very important throughout his life.

Known as "Coach" by many of his former students, Montemayor used to play semiprofessional baseball. Montemayor's passion for baseball and education led him to a career in coaching and teaching. He says his experiences playing baseball and coaching taught him about the value of conducting oneself with dignity and respect toward others.

As a Mexican-American, Montemayor had to overcome many obstacles. What many people would consider major setbacks in regards to their education and employment, Montemayor simply viewed as challenges to overcome.

Receiving a quality education was very important to Montemayor. He began his education at Hill College in Hillsboro, Texas. After transferring to Baylor University in Waco, Texas, and earning undergraduate degrees in journalism and history in 1969, Montemayor returned to Baylor and received a master's degree in history in 1974.

Montemayor's success is exemplified not only by the degrees he holds or through his position, but by the profound impact he's had on his former students. Before being promoted to department chair, Montemayor taught history and government full-time. He developed the first Mexican-American history course at the college where he currently works. He says it helps for all students to learn the historical significance of minority and diversity issues.

Montemayor believes students in minority situations must learn to exemplify dignity and respect in all situations. It's important to remember the old adage "actions will speak louder than words," he says. Students in the minority must conduct themselves in this manner because when they fail or stumble, they will most likely be met with unfounded cultural criticism. "When you fail, you [individually] didn't fail. You failed because you are black, or you failed because you are Hispanic, because that's the way society judges you," Montemayor says. "It's a luxury to be able to fail individually."

When faced with an issue, Montemayor says it's important for students not to "lose their cool," but to step back from the situation and respond wisely. It's also essential for minority and diversity-related issues to be dealt with honestly. In his advice to minority students facing these issues Montemayor says, "Be as professional as you possibly can be and don't waver on your goals and objectives."

STUDENT DISORIENTATION

Everyone gathered together around Misha's table for one last meal to share stories of the semester that had passed by so quickly. They reminisced about the lessons they had learned, many of which learned the hard way.

"I never thought I'd even be able to make friends going back to school this late," said Carlos.

"You're lucky you did. Otherwise you never would have been able to pay off your rent that one time," added Aaron.

"I was just so unorganized. I barely got through because I never kept track of anything, especially my money. Next year I'll be way better about that and writing. I read through my old stuff. It's embarrassing."

"I know what you mean. Once I got organized after the first project, I was much better off."

"Except you still got horrible grades on your projects after that," said Misha.

"That is because I didn't really think before I spoke, but I'm trying to get better about that. Even if I disagree with someone, I need to think more about when, where, and how to discuss it a little better."

"I'm just glad I started taking my papers more seriously and learned why I should properly cite my sources. No wonder my teacher gave me a D."

The rest of the meal was filled with stories and laughter. They made plans for the next semester and chatted about what they were going to do over the winter holidays. Each had learned so much over the course of the year and each still had quite a bit more to learn, but they all felt confident and prepared to take charge of their futures.

CHAPTER OBJECTIVES:

- Applying what you've learned to your personal life

- Succeeding in an educational setting

- Moving forward along your career path

Congratulations! By this time, you are well into the semester at college. You have a journal filled with goals, time-management strategies, conflict resolution ideas, and photos or other representations of the life you want to live when you graduate. You have tangible reminders of why you want to major in the field you've chosen, so that when you lose sight of your goal, you can easily refocus yourself. All of the strategies, lessons, and philosophies you have learned in this book are presented with one common goal: to help you take charge of not only your education, but also your life.

Personal Skills

The first four chapters of this book focused on helping you build a solid foundation of personal discipline that could be used in your life. In Chapter 1, you learned how to make your goals more effective by using the acronym SMART. Although you learned this while you were studying about how to set personal goals, it can be used in every area of your life.

Specific: If you make specific goals you can visualize, you're more likely to achieve them. An example of a specific goal is "I want to use my degree to become an IT manager." A nonspecific goal would be "I want a good job someday."

Measurable: A goal that is measurable has steps associated with it. As you achieve each step, you know you have passed a milestone in your life plan. For example, "I want to start out as a customer support specialist for ABC company and work my way to IT manager" is a measurable goal. Each step you pass along the way lets you know you're getting close to reaching your goal.

Attainable and Realistic: You probably remember that attainable and realistic goals are partners. For example, let's say you are really great at basketball. In fact, you are fantastic, but you are very short as far as the NBA standard is concerned. A realistic goal might be to become a professional basketball player, but due to your height limitation, that may not be attainable for you. Your goals must be suited to your life. Is it attainable for you and is it realistic, or likely to happen?

Timed: Putting a time limit on attaining your goals will help you stay focused and prevent disillusionment. If you say, "I want to be an IT manager someday," there is no time

> " The person who gets the farthest is generally the one who is willing to do and dare. The sure-thing boat never gets far from shore. "
>
> —Dale Carnegie

framework to keep you on track. If you say, "I want to become an IT manager within five years of graduating," you have a focus.

Chapter 2 taught you organizational skills by using to-do lists and master schedules to keep you on track to meet your goals and responsibilities. Through the POSEC method you learned to **prioritize** your time according to your life's goals, **organize** the things in your life that you must take care of regularly like financial obligations, **streamline** your tasks by doing everything you need to in one area so you aren't wasting time going back and forth between different areas, **economize** your free time so you have enough time for your priorities, and **contribute** personal time to worthy causes.

In Chapter 3, you learned how to stretch your dollar through careful budgeting and planned saving. We also talked about the importance of handling your credit well and protecting your financial identity. Here is a brief review of the key highlights for controlling your credit, rather than letting it control you:

- A credit card is not free money.

- Pay in full every month to avoid costly interest charges.

- Pay attention to interest rates and annual fees.

- Limit the number of cards you have.

Chapter 4 focused on your personal health and safety with tips and reminders about quick and healthy eating and the importance of personal hygiene not only to your own health, but also to the health of those around you. You learned that college students are twice as likely to suffer from depression as the general population, and we discussed the importance of sleep in staving off this condition.

ON THE WEB

For more information on staying healthy, visit Choose My Plate:

http://bit.ly/TC12CMP

There are some simple things you can do to help you stay healthy during your semester. Wash your hands with antibacterial soap well and often. Especially practice this after shaking hands with others, being in public places, or using shared items, such as phones or computers. Use a paper towel to turn off faucets in public bathrooms or to open the door as you leave. Never eat or drink after anyone. Get plenty of sleep, drink water, and make healthy food choices. Keep your vaccinations up-to-date.

Chapter 5 took an in-depth look at the importance of thinking logically. From logical fallacies to the Socratic Method, we discussed problem solving and making rational judgments. You learned that the best way to make decisions is to have a strategy in place so you are not taken by surprise when decision time sneaks up on you, think before you act, fully evaluate every decision, and conduct due diligence by taking advantage of every means of research available before you make your decision.

Chapter 6 delved further into critical thinking by examining the uses and methods of research. You learned how to research a decision effectively by breaking your topic into manageable pieces. You also learned how to research a purchase decision in ever-widening circles, using the following method:

- **Begin in the center.** Go directly to the website of the manufacturer of the product you are considering.

- **Look for product reviews.** Widen your circle by checking for reviews on the product and the manufacturer.

- **Find someone with personal knowledge.** If you can find a person who has bought the same product, you can ask his or her opinion, and you will have the opportunity to examine the product out of the retail store environment.

You learned in Chapter 7 that it is important to keep up with your vital documents and records, including tax information, vaccination records, and passports. You learned organizational methods to help you stay on top of this task, and you learned that organizing your thoughts into a personal journal can be just as important as organizing your life. If you choose to blog or use social networking for journaling, you learned there are some safety precautions that should always be followed.

 **Dragon Dictation**

Scan the code for additional information or visit: *http://bit.ly/TC12dragon*

Sometimes you don't have the time or energy to type. Dragon Dictation is a voice-recognition app that will take what you say and write it down. You can record meetings, brainstorm sessions, and even lectures with this handy app.

Protect your privacy. Screen people who want to be your friends and utilize privacy settings. Anything posted on the Web is open to everyone's eyes unless you take this precaution. Don't say anything you wouldn't want a potential employer to see. Corporate recruiters use social networking sites to check up on potential employees. Don't limit your opportunities by badmouthing your former employers.

Don't write anything online you wouldn't want repeated. Remember that the world is a smaller place with the Internet. Don't ruin friendships or other relationships by gossip, malicious words, or other hurtful attitudes.

In Chapter 8, we looked at ethical and moral dilemmas, decisions, and judgments. We discussed the difference between values and ethics. Everyone has values, some negative and some positive, but not everyone has ethics, or high moral standards they adhere to. Additionally, we established that integrity must go along with ethics and values to create an individual who consistently makes decisions that take the well-being of others into account.

▶ EXERCISE 12.1

In your journal, write a five-paragraph essay, using the technique taught in this book, to analyze your journey through *Taking Charge: Your Education, Your Career, Your Life.* **Here are some things to consider:**

a.) Where were you in your time-management and goal-setting skills at the beginning of the semester compared to now? How has this discipline helped you?

b.) What were your feelings about diversity and tolerance before reading this book, compared with how you feel now? What changes, if any, have you made?

c.) What stage of Lawrence Kohlberg's moral development scale fits you best when you began this book? What about now? What has caused you to change?

d.) How has your financial decision making changed during the process of reading the book?

e.) How will you apply critical-thinking skills in your career? Has your ability to think critically changed over the course of this book? If so, how?

Chapter 9 focused on interpersonal communication. You learned some effective conversation techniques, and we discussed how body language often says more than our words. You also learned how to be a good listener by using the acronym SOLER:

- **Sit** squarely facing the other person.

- **Open** your posture toward the speaker. Don't cross your arms or hunch your shoulders. Be in a receptive position.

- **Lean** forward.

- **Eye** contact is important. Don't stare intently, but maintain good eye contact.

- **Relax.**

Chapter 10 continued the communication theme with a discussion of written communication. You learned how business letters should be formatted, and we also discussed the purposes of certified mail. We looked at ways to make email more effective and how to protect your friends from spammers and phishers. The following is a review of netiquette (online etiquette, especially relevant to email):

- Don't use all caps when you type.

- Don't fall for urban legends or scams.

- Practice the twenty-four-hour rule before sending an angry/emotional email.

In Chapter 11, you learned that tolerance is a term "used in social, cultural, and religious contexts to describe attitudes and practices that prohibit discrimination against those practices or group memberships that may be disapproved of by those in the majority."

There are certain things you can do that will help you develop and practice tolerance. Avoid controversial conversations. In social situations where you are part of a diverse group, it's better to avoid topics such as religion and politics. Be polite to everyone. Treat everyone with equal respect. Avoid telling biased jokes. Stay away from humor that denigrates a segment of the population, such as women or minorities.

> " Success means having the courage, the determination, and the will to become the person you believe you were meant to be. "
>
> —George Sheehan

Education Skills

The foundations you began building regarding your personal skills carry over to your educational life. From goal setting and time management to critical thinking and communication skills, you will tap into all of your strengths, sometimes in combinations and on a daily basis, to make the most of your academic experience.

Chapter 1 demonstrated how a statement of purpose could help keep you focused on your goals when college becomes stressful and difficult and you start questioning your decisions.

The time-management skills in Chapter 2 built on the ideas of master schedules and to-do lists with some suggestions for staying motivated so that you do not fall into the procrastination trap. Reward yourself. Take a ten-minute break for every fifty-minute stretch of studying. Schedule free time and fun activities to fall in between projects or homework assignments so you enjoy longer breaks.

David Burns, author of *Feeling Good: The New Mood Therapy*, says that giving yourself permission to cross some things off your list, even if not accomplished, will make you feel less overwhelmed and more excited about completing other tasks. Also, shut yourself away from distractions. Put your email alert on mute, your cellphone on silent, and don't answer the door.

Chapter 3 explained the basics of financial aid, which is a crucial part of your entire financial picture. You learned that there are five primary types of financial aid. The Pell Grant is the primary government grant available to students, but other grants do exist, so check with your financial aid officer. Most students finish college with some amount of debt. Loans are available from the government or from private sources, such as banks and credit unions. When you fill out the FAFSA form, you are applying for all assistance available to you from the government, including grants and loans. Your college will have funds available from the government to pay the wages of students who qualify for a work-study program. To find out if you qualify, set an appointment with your counselor.

APT APPS!

iTunes University

Scan the code for additional information or visit: *http://bit.ly/TC12ituniv*

Through this app, which you can also access on your computer, you can subscribe to courses from top universities like Oxford University and Stanford for free. Learn more about literature, writing, engineering, and science.

Chapter 4 dealt with ways to stay safe around campus. You may not hear about every crime committed on your campus, but you can bet campus crime exists. Review Chapter 4 carefully for safety precautions and advice. Parties and other campus-related events often present the opportunity for excessive drinking, sexual encounters, and potentially violent situations, so be sure to check out the reminders about proper conduct and safeguards.

At a two-year technical college, where the majority of your class time is laboratory-based, laboratory safety is especially important. The following suggestions can prevent disaster in the laboratory:

- Don't wear loose, floppy clothing in the laboratory.

- Wear close-toed shoes.

- When handling chemicals, remember your personal protective equipment (PPE), safety glasses, and vinyl or nitrile gloves.

- If required for safety in the lab, wear PPE such as a hardhat, ear protection, and steel-toed boots, in addition to safety glasses.

- Don't eat or drink in a chemical laboratory.

- Familiarize yourself with the location and use of fire extinguishers, eyewash stations, and first-aid kits.

- When using electrical equipment, follow proper safety procedures, including keeping live current away from water, wearing electrically insulated lineman gloves, and using electrically insulated tools.

In the next four chapters you turned your focus toward critical thinking. In Chapter 5 you learned that education is a two-part process. When you learn a fact, you internalize it. When you reflect on that fact, question it, and use it, you've applied what you learned. The discovery of new purposes for proven ideas or correction of wrong ideas comes through investigation – asking the questions "Why?" and "What if ...?" To help strengthen your critical-thinking skills, you learned how to apply the Socratic Method to all areas of your educational experience so that you can find further applications for the information you learn.

Chapter 6 built on your critical-thinking skills in education by teaching you how to use research effectively. You learned how to use your library and how to choose and research a topic. This section concluded with some tips on how to organize your research so that you get the most from your efforts.

Number all of your sources sequentially. Use note cards to take notes from each source. Number each of your note cards with the number from the corresponding source, then subhead the card with an alphabetic character. Remember, the note-card system can be approximated on a computer by using a table with columns for each source, notes from each source, full publication information from each source, and notes on when and where you use each note. On each note card, be sure to include the page number where the information was located in its corresponding source. If you create an outline before beginning your paper, which is advised, write the associated note card numbers next to each point of your outline. Finally, as you write your paper, place a big check mark on each card as you use the information from it. This way, you will know you have incorporated all of your information in the appropriate places.

Chapter 7 provided tips and tricks for improving your study habits through better note taking. You learned how to use an outline method for your notes so that you can easily review them later and pull out the most pertinent information. You also learned what you should write down:

- Dates of events

- Names of people

- Theories

- Definitions

- Arguments and debates

- Images and exercises

- Anything your teacher writes on the board

- Questions to ask later

Chapter 8 presented ideas on how to improve your test scores through better study habits and reducing test anxiety. We also looked at the effects of cheating or plagiarism on your education, which can be devastating.

We considered several techniques for learning new material that are based on your particular learning style, including the following:

- Multisensory learning

- Overlearning

- SQ3R

We followed up by discussing strategies for helping you relax as you take the exam. Read all directions first! Preview the test to get the big picture. Complete the parts that are easiest for you first. Find out if you are penalized for incorrect responses but not for ignored questions. When answering essays, make sure your answers are legible, well organized, and supported from material you have learned. Leave time to check over the test for any questions you neglected to answer.

Chapter 9 looked at how to use more effective communication techniques to improve relationships with teachers and fellow students. You learned how to be a better classroom contributor and how to participate in a group project setting.

Another key concept you learned was how to approach a teacher when you have a discrepancy about your grades. Set an appointment and be on

To participate in the online poll, scan the QR code or visit:
http://bit.ly/TC12Poll

What area do you think you've most improved in after reading this book?

○ Communication

○ Organization

○ Health and safety

○ Study skills

time. Break the ice with polite conversation, and use your best manners throughout the meeting. Use "I" messages to get your point across. Don't argue with your teacher. Show gratitude for your teacher's time and consideration. Move through the administrative hierarchy if you can't resolve the situation.

In Chapter 10 you learned how vital effective written communication is to your educational success. You learned the steps of a five-paragraph essay, along with some suggestions to better your writing skills. You also learned how to compile your research from Chapter 6 to actually write the research paper, paying special attention to plagiarism and the citing of sources. You also learned the basics of technical writing and the steps to writing an excellent laboratory report.

Finally, Chapter 11 examined on-campus tolerance and diversity. While many technical jobs were once considered a man's domain, now more than ever, women are entering these fields. Although we discussed tolerance of all groups and ways to avoid appearing intolerant, we focused especially on eliminating sexism in technical education.

Professional Skills

After a thorough review of the personal and educational portions of each chapter, we're ready to look at the final section: how these skills apply to your professional life. Everything you're learning and putting into practice now has one focus, helping you find a fulfilling, satisfying career.

Chapter 1 offered you opportunities to research your chosen career field through www.salary.com and other resources so you could have accurate information for setting your professional goals. We also reviewed the SMART acronym for goal setting and showed you how to use it in designing goals for your career. One key concept to remember in keeping your goals measurable is that great careers often begin with baby steps.

“Nothing can stop the man with the right mental attitude from achieving his goal; nothing on Earth can help the man with the wrong mental attitude.”

—Former President Thomas Jefferson

Let's review: Set your goals in measurable units, such as "I want to enter a management training program by my third year in the automotive field." Being able to measure the incremental successes in your career builds job satisfaction and self-confidence. Remember that you may have to adjust your goals as you move through life. If you find yourself in a job that does not advance employees the way you had first believed, it doesn't mean you have failed. Some things will be out of your control. Focus on the factors you can control and evaluate the other aspects to see whether you are willing to live with the situation or if you need to change directions.

 WORKSHEET

Use this worksheet as a way to explore the lessons you've learned from reading this book.

For the sample template, scan the QR code or visit: *http://bit.ly/TC12WS*

The main thing I've taken from this book is:	
I'm more successful now at:	
I wish I knew more about:	
I need to improve in:	
My original goals were:	
My goals have evolved to:	

Chapter 2 provided tips on how to take control of the time clock at work by minimizing distractions and by using schedules and lists to stay organized. We also looked at some coping strategies to help you stay focused as you climb the corporate ladder:

- Don't be a jack of all trades.

- Spend an hour each morning taking care of your most pressing issue(s) before you check voicemails or emails.

- Staring at a blank computer screen for an hour won't help you get started on a difficult project. Make yourself begin.

- Don't confuse activity with results.

- Optimize your time so you spend as much of your energy as possible on the high-payoff tasks.

- Just because someone leaves you a voicemail or sends an email, it doesn't mean you have to respond immediately.

Chapter 3's focus was on helping you make the most of your salary and benefits through wise budgeting and saving. From insurance to company-sponsored retirement plans, we looked at the avenues available to help you strengthen your bottom line.

In particular, most companies offer a corporate-sponsored retirement account – a 401k in most instances or a 403b if your employer is a civil government, nonprofit organization, or public school. These retirement accounts allow you to contribute pretax dollars out of each paycheck. The company will then match a portion of that money. This essentially gives you a raise. If you contribute $300 per month, and your company matches 25 percent of that amount, you are earning an extra $75 per month, or an extra $900 per year. Because this money comes to your retirement fund tax-deferred (meaning you do not pay taxes on it until you use it), it is actually the equivalent of earning $1,125, if you are in the 20 percent tax bracket. Additionally, the money you contributed to your account is also tax-deferred, and that is the equivalent of keeping an extra $720 per year, assuming you are in the 20 percent tax bracket. You are earning an extra $1,845 per year just by contributing to a tax-advantaged savings plan.

Monster.com Jobs
Scan the code for additional information or visit: *http://bit.ly/TC12Monster*

Keep an eye on the jobs out there and apply anytime, anywhere with the Monster.com Jobs app. The app syncs with your online account so you can send out your résumé and cover letter on the go. You can also do job searches and browse your saved searches.

Chapter 4 discussed the importance of on-the-job safety. We learned that 6,000 employees in America die every year from workplace-related injuries, and another 50,000 die from illnesses caused by exposure to workplace hazards, according to a 2002 survey. We also looked at the role the U.S. Occupational Safety and Health Administration (OSHA) plays in your workplace safety and well-being, and you learned how to bring up safety issues to company management.

In Chapter 5, we discussed how critical analysis and evaluative thinking will play an important part in your work. We also talked about the difference between intuition, which experienced employees tend to rely on, and critical thinking.

In Chapter 6, you learned about how you can use research and networking to advance your career. We considered professional journals, email discussion lists, Internet forums, and RSS feeds, as well as professional blogs. We also discussed the importance of joining a professional organization, even while you're still a student. Here are some of the benefits associated with being in a professional organization:

- Meeting people working in your field of interest

- Learning about job or internship openings

- Understanding trends in the field

- Polishing your communication and presentation skills

- Proving your future career really matters to you

ON THE WEB

For more information on your chosen career, visit the U.S. Bureau of Labor Statistics:

http://bit.ly/TC12Bureau

In Chapter 7 you learned about a few of the ways you'll use documentation in your professional life. From social networking at sites such as LinkedIn to blogging on your own site, careful documentation will be an important resource in your career. You may use note taking and documentation in the work world in business and management meetings, project documentation, career recognition through publication, and professional blogging.

Our discussions in Chapter 8 centered on the ways you will experience "exams" once you are employed in your career. From continuing education to on-the-job training and employee reviews, you are likely to see exams often. We also discussed the importance of ethics on the job and looked at some ways to use a ladder of escalation if you experience unethical situations at work. Let's review those steps now:

- Speak up.

- Escalate the issue by taking it to the next person in authority.

- Make a formal complaint with your human resources (HR) department.

- Seek independent counsel.

The next three chapters of the book examined how your communication skills will affect your job. Chapter 9 discussed the fluid dynamics of work relationships and examined such issues as being a contributing member of a group, dealing with difficult coworkers, and developing awesome presentation skills.

You also learned the importance of strong customer service skills. Consider your audience. Respect the position and title of the people you work with. Alternatively, don't be intimidated by the customer's position or credentials. You are a professional called on to do a professional job. At the same time, though, don't use technical jargon.

Use good listening skills. Actively focus on what the customer is saying. Make sure you hear the whole problem before you ask your own questions. Respond to the customer's statements. Help the customer know that you understand by rephrasing their words. Remember common courtesy. You, as well as your customer, are busy and pressed for time, but don't let that cause you to seem intense, impatient, or frustrated.

▶ EXERCISE 12.2

Group project: Each group will create a visual presentation of one section, either personal, educational, or professional, of any one chapter. Your project must give everyone a chance to participate, but no more than two people should present. Use the presentation and group-project skills taught in Chapters 9 and 10. Your project should be a visual illustration of the key concepts in the section and chapter you have chosen.

Written communication, as you saw in Chapter 10, is vital to your success on the job. You'll need to be able to craft convincing cover letters and strong resumes. If you go into a management position, you may be called on to write employee reviews. Many technology graduates eventually choose to go into business for themselves. In this case, you would need a business plan. Here is a quick reminder of business plan basics:

- What kind of company are you starting?

- What is the purpose of your new business?

- How will your business make money?

- Who will be your customers?

- How will you get your customers?

Finally, Chapter 11 presented a thorough look at workplace diversity, tolerance, and discrimination. We established that every worker has the right to function in a non-hostile environment, a right the Equal Employment Opportunity Commission (EEOC) upholds. For a thorough review of what constitutes harassment or discrimination, refer to the chapter, but here is a second look at what you should do if you are the victim of discrimination:

- Keep a log of the inappropriate behavior that happens to you at work.

- Begin your ladder of escalation with your immediate supervisor, unless he or she is the source of discrimination.

- File a formal complaint with your human resources department, providing copies (not originals) of your documentation.

- Contact your state's workforce agency. Such agencies investigate and mediate employee harassment and discrimination cases.

- If you still don't get satisfaction from your company, or you feel you truly have a litigation case, consult a lawyer who specializes in employment-related disputes.

- File a claim with the EEOC if you feel you have a strong enough case to go to court against your employer.

COACH'S CORNER

You've gained so many skills along the way. In Coach's Corner, Coach highlights some of the most important ones to remember as you go forward in life.

http://bit.ly/TC12CC

Additionally, we looked at ways to avoid being the instigator of discrimination or intolerance. Watch your words. Make sure you understand the difference between appropriate and inappropriate conversations. Respect other people's personal space. Keep an invisible personal boundary between you and your coworkers. You may think your emails are private, but they definitely are not. The information technology manager at your company has access to everything you send and receive across company servers.

Conclusion

As our exploration of self-discipline, critical thinking, and communications comes to a close, spend some time reflecting on how this book has affected you. We hope you have matured and grown as you've learned new techniques to strengthen your relationships, make better use of your time, and prepare for the career you soon will have.

1. How can SMART be applied to your professional goals?

2. What does POSEC stand for? How is it applied?

3. What are the three general kinds of expenses you should include in your budget?

4. What are the effects caused by getting less than six and a half hours of sleep a night?

5. What are the questions you should ask in the Socratic Method?

6. What are some benefits of joining professional associations as a student?

7. What are some key types of information to pay special attention to when taking your notes?

8. Identify and explain Lawrence Kohlberg's six stages of moral development.

9. What is SOLER, and how is it applied?

10. What questions should you answer while writing your business plan?

11. What did M. Thom, M. Pickering, and R. Thompson find to be the top social factors of concern among young women?

▶ ▶ Are you puzzled?

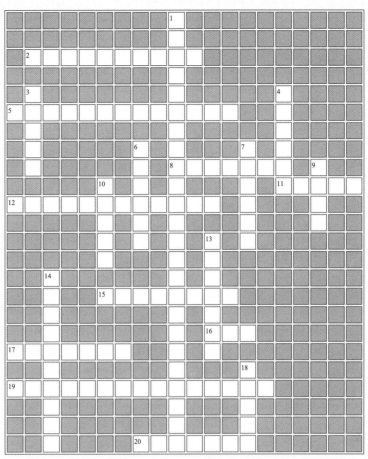

Scan this code to access the puzzle online or visit: *http://bit.ly/TC12Crword*

Across

2. The first four chapters of this book focused on helping you build a solid ____.

5. To prevent interpersonal conflict, avoid ____ conversations.

8. You learned how to use an ____ method to organize your notes for class.

11. You learned how to make your goals more effective by using the acronym ____.

12. ____ often says more than our words. (2 words)

15. Don't write anything online you wouldn't want ____.

16. When taking a test, read ____ of the directions first.

17. Censor your emails and keep ____ files off your company computer.

19. What app is a voice-recognition app that will take what you say and write it down? (2 words)

20. What app helps you keep an eye on the jobs out there and apply any time?

Down

1. We discussed the importance of joining a ____ prove your credibility in Chapter 6. (2 words)

3. A credit card is not free ____.

4. Everyone has ____, some negative and some positive.

6. Don't use technical ____ when speaking to customers.

7. To avoid being accused of being discriminatory, avoid telling ____ jokes.

9. Don't be a ____ of all trades.

10. When you fill out the ____ form, you are applying for all assistance available to you from the government.

13. Who said, "Success means having the courage, the determination, and the will to become the person you believe you were meant to be"?

14. Chapter 5 took an in-depth look at the importance of thinking ____.

18. You learned how to be a good listener by using the acronym ____.

DR. ELTON E. STUCKLY, JR.
College President

Scan this code for additional info
or visit: *http://bit.ly/TC12Stuckly*

Just Go for It!

"You can do just about anything you want to if you set your mind to it," says Dr. Elton E. Stuckly, Jr., college president. He encourages students to take risks, take chances, and "just go for it" in regards to their dreams.

Stuckly describes himself as a "true people person." He is deeply committed to education and his college's employees and students. He says his role as president is "not a stagnant job." He works some nights and weekends and is always met with different responsibilities.

When he was a student, Stuckly says he was given so many opportunities to succeed. Because of what his college did for him, he now wants to give back. "You just reach a point in life where you can help others," Stuckly says. "Even though I'm not a teacher anymore, I still can help others, just at a different level."

Stuckly, who has two sisters, was the only member of his family to go to college. His parents were successful farmers near Penelope, Texas, and Stuckly was working and riding a tractor by the time he was five years old. Although his mother completed high school, his father only finished the eighth grade. For this reason, Stuckly's parents couldn't give him much guidance in his educational pursuits. However, his father did tell him, "Son, you don't want to farm."

After earning his associate degree in electrical power technology, Stuckly worked in the industry for twelve years. He worked for five years with an engineering company in Houston as a senior electrical designer before moving to the General Tire and Rubber Company in Waco, Texas, working for five years as an electrical/electronic technician. In 1987, Stuckly applied and was asked to return to his alma mater to teach electrical power technology by the same department chair who was there when he was a student. Since then, he has served as an instructor, department chair, technology cluster director over the engineering programs, and vice president of instruction. He is now the college's president.

In 1989, Stuckly started working on his bachelor's degree from the University of Texas at Tyler. He finished the degree and went on to earn his master's degree, as well. He recently completed his doctor of education degree from the University of Mary Hardin-Baylor after three years in the program. Out of the twenty-two students who began the program, only sixteen continued, and a mere six graduated on time. Stuckly was one of them. He was also one of the older students in the program and believes "you're never too old to continue learning."

Stuckly believes successful students have to plan, stay focused, be committed, and not procrastinate. Students also don't need to be afraid to make mistakes. If people do not make mistakes, they usually won't do or experience much in life, he says.

"Take every opportunity to learn as much as you can while you're here," he advises students. "Anything you gain will add to your skill set and your résumé."

Stuckly also encourages students to look at his background to see where he came from and where he is today. Above all, Stuckly wants all students to be successful. "I want [students] to go out there, take advantage of their opportunities, and just be a success," he says.

Glossary

active listening: Listening but also interacting in the conversation

advertorial: An advertisement in a magazine or newspaper that resembles an editorial article

adviser: School official, usually assigned by your college or university, who can help you choose your classes and make sure you are taking the right courses to graduate

associate degree: A type of degree awarded to students at a U.S. community college, usually after two years of a full-time load of classes

chronological resume: Focuses on the timeline of your experience

circular argument: An existing belief is true and therefore anything that does not align with the belief must be wrong

combination resume: Blends the styles of the functional resume and the combination resume, highlighting your skills before detailing your job experience

continuing education: Classes that you take once you have earned your degree or certain certifications associated with your career, to ensure that your knowledge of your profession remains current

Cornell Method: Two-part method: information that you take down during a lecture and cues to help you remember the information

discrimination: An act against certain people based on stereotypes and prejudices, such as segregation, refusal to hire, or name-calling

externship: Supervised work done with a company outside of the classroom as a part of a course or class

fallacious: Incorrect or logically unsound

formal outlining: Highly structured method of note taking

functional resume: Focuses on your skills; good especially if you're just coming out of college and have little or no on-the-job experience

grant: A form of financial aid from a nonprofit organization (such as the government) that you do not have to repay

hierarchy of needs: A categorization of the levels of human need

informal outlining: Unstructured note taking and a form of brainstorming

jargon: Technical language or dialect specific to a particular field that people outside of the field may not understand

job shadowing: A technique for learning more about the job you would like to have after you graduate one or more days following a person as he or she works

learning disability: Neurologically based processing difficulty that can interfere with learning basic skills, such as reading, writing, and math, and/or with higher-level skills, such as organization, time planning, and abstract reasoning

leptin: The hormone that tells your body either that you're full or that you need to eat more

multisensory teaching and learning: Techniques that use several senses to teach and to learn new materials

netiquette: Internet etiquette or a set of social conventions intended to govern Internet usage and interaction

Occupational Safety and Health Administration (OSHA): The main federal agency charged with the enforcement of safety and health legislation

overlearning: A learning technique that involves continuing to study or practice material that you've already mastered

passive listening: Listening without interrupting; paying full attention to just the speaker

plagiarism: Using another person's content, ideas, or writing without giving credit or permission; trying to pass someone else's work off as your own

POSEC method: A time-management method that helps control your personal time in order to better handle outside responsibilities; stands for prioritize, organize, streamline, economize, and contribute

prejudice: A preconceived notion or belief not based on experience but on stereotypes

professional journal: A periodical or magazine published by a professional organization, society, or group

salutation: Greeting used in written communication

secondary source: An evaluation, discussion, and/or interpretation of a primary source, such as biographies, history books, and journal articles

SMART technique: A technique that helps you increase the chances of reaching your goals; stands for specific, measurable, attainable, realistic, and timed

SQ3R: A reading strategy that helps you learn new reading material; stands for survey, question, read, recite, and review

stereotype: A widely held but oversimplified concept or belief of a particular type of person often based on religion, heritage, socioeconomic status, or sexual orientation

student loan: A form of financial aid that you must repay

syllabus: A description of a course that also lists the dates of major exams, assignments, and projects

tertiary source: A collection of primary and secondary sources, such as in encyclopedias, almanacs, and directories

tolerance: The fair and respectful treatment of all people, regardless of differing heritages, religions, sexual orientations, and genders

transcript: An official academic record from a specific school that lists the courses you have completed, your grades, and information such as when you attended

Index

A

accidents at workplace, 64–65
active listening, 159
advertorials, 79
adviser, 7
affective domain, 139
alcohol abuse, 60
Allen, David, 16, 17
American Opportunity Credit, 44
associate degrees, 6
auditory learning, 139
aural learning, 139

B

Bankrate (website), 37
bank statements, 111
benefits at work, 46–47, 232
Bennis, Warren, 74
blogging, 115, 122–23, 224
Bloom, Benjamin S., 139
Bloom's Taxonomy of Learning, 139
Bowles, Roger, 82–83
brain foods, 54–55
budgets, 34–37, 223
Burns, David, 25, 227
business letters, 180–82
business plans, 192–93, 234

C

campus safety, 62, 227–228
Carr, Judy, 87
Cassidy, Daniel J., 43
certified mail, 182–83
Chavez, Guadalupe, 30–31

chronological resumes, 191
circular argument, 75
citations for sources, 96, 187
classroom safety, 61
CNN, 47
CNNmoney.com, 182–83
cognitive biases, 83–84
cognitive domain, 139
college life realities, 6
college transcripts, 112
combination resumes, 191
communication tips, 157–62, 207–8
conflict resolution, 161, 168–69
continuing education, 145
Copaceanu, Adriana, 192–93
Cornell Method, 118, 119
Cornell University, 54
cover letters, 190–91
credit, 38, 223
critical-thinking skills
    education and, 82, 228
        problem solving and, 72–74
        professional application of, 82–84
customer service skills, 169–70, 234

D

databases, 94
Dave, R. H., 139
decision-making skills, 76–79, 223
depression, 54, 56
diarists, 114
difficult people, dealing with, 168
digital recordkeeping, 112–13
discrimination, 203
distractions at work, 25–27, 231–32
diversity, 206–09, 231
Dolphin, Warren D., 187–88

E

Ebbinghaus, Hermann, 141
educational journaling, 122–23
education goals, 5–8, 226
education research, 94–98
education time management, 22–25
email lists, 101, 233
email scams, 179, 226
email tips, 178–79
emergency savings fund, 45-46
employee evaluations, 193
Equal Employment Opportunity
    Commission (EEOC), 147, 209–12,
    214, 235
essay construction, 183–86, 230
ethical principles, 137
ethical tests, 136
ethics, 133, 147, 225
externships, 23

F

FAFSA (Free Application for Federal Student
    Aid), 42, 227
fallacious thinking, 75
Family Educational Rights and Privacy Act
    (FERPA), 112
family records, 111–12
Fee, Susan, 156
Feldberg, Robyn, 191
FERPA (Family Educational Rights and
    Privacy Act), 112
financial aid, 40–44, 227
financial aid officers, 41
first resumes, 190–92
Fletcher, Louise, 191–92
formal outlining, 118
43 Folders, 20–21, 111
forums, 101, 233
401k (retirement account), 46–47, 232
Franklin Covey Leadership Institute, 193
Free Application for Federal Student Aid
    (FAFSA), 41, 42, 227

Friedman, David, 179
functional resumes, 191

G

germs, 58–59
Getting Things Done (personal management
    model), 17
goals
    education, 5–8, 226
    personal, 2–4, 222
    professional, 8–10, 45
    SMART technique and, 45
    See also SMART technique
Golden Rule, 204, 209
grants, 41–43
group projects, 164–65
Grulick, Aprilsue, 151–52

H

Hansen, Katharine, 164
Hansen, Randall S., 164
harassment, 147, 211–15, 235
health foods, 54–55
healthy habits, 54–60, 144, 223
Heathfield, Susan M., 168
Hess, Jonathan A., 168
Hiemstra, Roger, 122
hierarchy of needs, 19, 20–21
Hills, Fred, 129
Hope Scholarship Credit, 44

I

identity theft, 38–40
"I" messages, 161, 166
income-based repayment (IBR), 42
Indiana University Writing Tutorial
    Services, 187
informal outlining, 117-18
insurance, 47
integrity, 133

Internet Duct Tape, 124
interpersonal learning, 140
intrapersonal learning, 140
intuition, 83, 233

J-K

jargon, 169, 189, 234
Jeanne Clery Act of 1990, 62
job shadowing, 8-9
journals (personal), 2, 114–15
journals (professional), 100, 122, 233
kinesthetic learning, 140
Kohlberg, Lawrence, 134
KXAN (NBC news affiliate), 38

L

laboratory reports, 187–88, 230
laboratory safety, 61, 227–28
ladder of escalation, 147, 213–14, 233
Lagan, Attracta, 133
learning disabilities, 140
Learning Disabilities Association of
    America, 140
learning styles, 139–40
learning techniques and styles, 139–44
leptin, 56
Levine, Stuart, 72
libraries, 94
Lifehacker (blog), 25, 78, 116–17
Lifetime Learning Tax Credit, 44
linguistic learning, 139
listening skills, 159–61, 169, 234
lists, to-do, 17, 24–25
logical fallacies, 75–76
logical learning, 140

M

Mann, Merlin, 20
Mary Guy model, 136
Maslow, Abraham, 19, 20–21

Maslow's hierarchy of needs, 20–21
master schedules, 19
mathematical learning, 140
McKeown, James, 175
Messmer, Max, 190
Michigan Daily, 61
Mitchell, Elizabeth, 215
money-management counselors, 41
Montemayor, Gilbert, 218–19
Moran, Brian, 133
Moss, Steven, 105–06
MSNBC (financial news network), 38
multisensory teaching and learning, 140, 229
Murphy, Peter, 172

N

National Mental Health Association, 54
negative prejudices, 203
negative stereotypes, 203
negative values, 133
netiquette, 178–79, 226
newspaper test, 136
Nielsen, Arthur, 90
nonverbal communication, 157, 170
note-taking skills, 116–21

O

Occupational Outlook Handbook, 8
Occupational Safety and Health
    Administration (OSHA), 62–64, 66, 232
O'Keefe, Steve, 122
on-the-job safety, 62–66, 232
on-the-job training, 145–46
organization of research, 96–98
overlearning, 140–41, 229
OWL (Purdue), 180–82

P

Pareto, Vilfredo, 26
Pareto Principle, 26
passive listening, 159

student depression, 54, 56

student-teacher communication, 164–67, 229–30

study strategies, 140–43

sunlight test, 136

Sutton, Stephanie, 50

Swayze, Ed, 159

syllabi, 23

symptoms of test anxiety, 137–38

T

technical writing, 188–89, 230

tertiary sources, 94

test anxiety, 137–38

test of time, 136

Texas B-On-Time Loan, 42

thesis statements, 184

Thom, M., 208

Thompson, R., 208

time management
    distractions and, 25–27, 231–32
    personal, 7
    techniques for, 16–27, 227

Title VII Civil Rights Act, 210–12

to-do lists, 17, 24–25

tolerance, 203–08, 226
    See also diversity; ladder of escalation; workplace harassment

transcripts, 112

Trapani, Gina, 25

tuition reimbursement, 44

Turpen, Aaron, 179

twenty-four-hour rule, 179, 226

U

University of California at Los Angeles, 157

University of Michigan Health Service, 56, 57–58

University of Reading, 164–65

U.S. Bureau of Labor Statistics, 8

U.S. Department of Education, 204

U.S. Department of Health and Human Services, 59

V

vaccinations, 58–59

values, 132–33, 225

verbal learning, 139

visual learning, 139

Vital Information File, 112–13

Volney, Cindy, 69

W-Y

Washington State University, 119

Wibisono, Ria Angelia, 161

Wolaver, Rob, 13

women in workplace, 208–09, 230

work benefits, 46–47, 232

work distractions, 25–27

workplace accidents, 64–65

workplace harassment, 147, 211–15, 235

work-study programs, 43, 227

Young Money (website), 34

About the Authors

Karen Mitchell Smith, a graduate of Texas Tech University, has been an English and Spanish teacher, a motivational speaker on the importance of post-secondary education, and a technical college recruiter. An award-winning writer and editor for more than twenty years, she has an abiding concern for students and a wish to see them succeed and writes on many education-related topics. Her website is www.topshelfediting.com. She can be reached for questions or comments at karen@topshelfediting.com.

Katharine O'Moore-Klopf, a graduate of the University of Houston, began her career as a journalist in Texas, and then moved into production editing and copyediting for publishers in Colorado and then in New York City. She has been a self-employed copyeditor of books and peer-reviewed journal articles since 1995. She enjoys working with authors who are non-native speakers of English and has helped researchers from more than twenty nations achieve their dream of having their articles published in U.S. medical journals. She enjoys helping others succeed, so she developed and serves as curator for the Copyeditors' Knowledge Base, which is housed within her website at www.kokedit.com.

Texas State
Technical College™

In 2004 Texas State Technical College started offering
instructors the opportunity to initiate and participate in
a variety of textbook development projects. Of course, in
the twenty-first century, a book is no longer "just" a book,
so Texas State Technical College Publications projects
now include such ancillary products as instructor guides,
student workbooks, and CD-ROMs. In addition to offering editorial help and guidance to authors, assistance also
is available in the areas of materials production, layout and
design, and technical illustrations.

More information about the products and services
offered please visit our website:

https://www.waco.tstc.edu/ideas